THE RISE OF THE IMAGE

The Rise of the Image:
Essays on the History of the Illustrated Art Book
is published in the series
Reinterpreting Classicism: Culture, Reaction and Appropriation
edited by Caroline van Eck, Vrije Universiteit, Amsterdam

IN THE SAME SERIES

The Rise of the Image

Essays on the History of the Illustrated Art Book

Edited by Rodney Palmer and Thomas Frangenberg

ASHGATE

Published by
Ashgate Publishing Limited   Ashgate Publishing Limited
Gower House   Suite 420
Croft Road   101 Cherry Street
Aldershot   Burlington, VT 05401–4405
Hants GU11 3HR   USA
England

Ashgate website: http://www.ashgate.com

British Library Cataloguing-in-Publication Data
The Rise of the Image : Essays on the History of the Illustrated Art Book. —
(Reinterpreting Classicism)
    1. Illustrated books—History. 2. Illustration of
    books—History. I. Palmer, Rodney. II. Frangenberg,
    Thomas.
    096.1′09

Library of Congress Cataloguing-in-Publication Data
The Rise of the Image : Essays on the History of the Illustrated Art Book/edited by
Rodney Palmer, Thomas Frangenberg.
    p.   cm. – (Reinterpreting Classicism)
    Includes bibliographical references and index.
    1. Illustration of books. 2. Art – Reproduction.
    3. Visual communication in art. 4. Illustrated books
    – History.   I. Palmer, Rodney. II. Frangenberg, Thomas. III. Series.
    NC960.R57 2002
    741.6′4′09 – dc21

                                                    2002038340

ISBN 0 7546 0559 0

Typeset in Palatino by Manton Typesetters, Louth, Lincolnshire, UK and printed in Great Britain by Biddles Ltd, Guildford and King's Lynn.

Contents

Figures

1 Seventeenth-century illustrations for the chapters on motion in Leonardo's *Trattato*

1.1 René Lochon after Nicolas Poussin, *A man throwing a stone*, engraving, in Leonardo's *Trattato della pittura*, ed. Raphaël Trichet Du Fresne, Paris 1651, p. 51 (detail) (Photo: Bodleian Library, University of Oxford; shelfmark Vet. E3 b.19)

1.2 Nicolas Poussin, *Demonstration of violent motion: a man throwing a spear and another throwing a stone*, drawing, Milan, Biblioteca Ambrosiana, MS H 228 inf., fol. 74v (after Leonardo da Vinci) (Photo: Biblioteca Ambrosiana; property of the Ambrosian Library. All rights reserved. Reproduction is forbidden)

1.3 Giuseppe Fabbrini after Stefano della Bella, *A man in the act of throwing*, engraving, in Leonardo da Vinci, *Trattato della pittura*, ed. Francesco Fontani, Florence 1792, p. 40 (detail) (Photo: Bodleian Library, University of Oxford; shelfmark Vet. F5 d.129)

1.4 Stefano della Bella, *Two men in the act of throwing*, drawing, after Leonardo da Vinci, Florence, Biblioteca Riccardiana, MS Riccardianus 2275, fol. 22v (Photo: Biblioteca Riccardiana; no unauthorized reproduction)

1.5 Leonardo da Vinci, the sheet *Notes on the geometry of optics, illustrated with diagrams*, detail incorporating 'the hammering man', Windsor, Royal Library (Photo: The Royal Collection of Her Majesty Queen Elizabeth II)

1.6 After Leonardo da Vinci, *Demonstrating violent movement: two stages of a man throwing a spear*, drawing (from a lost original), in Biblioteca Apostolica Vaticana, Codex Urbinas Latinus 1270, fol. 105v (Photo: Biblioteca Apostolica Vaticana)

1.7 Leonardo da Vinci, *Study for The Battle of Anghiari*, drawing, Venice, Gallerie dell'Accademia (Photo: Gallerie dell'Accademia, with the permission of the Ministero per i Beni e le Attività Culturali)

1.8 After Leonardo da Vinci, *Demonstration of two kinds of movement: a man throwing a spear and another throwing a stone*, drawing (from a lost original), in Biblioteca Apostolica Vaticana, Codex Urbinas Latinus 1270, fol. 106r (Photo: Biblioteca Apostolica Vaticana)

1.9 Nicolas Poussin, *Illustration of the equilibrium of stationary figures: a man standing*, drawing, Milan, Biblioteca Ambrosiana MS H 228 inf., fol. 79v (Photo: Biblioteca Ambrosiana; property of the Ambrosian Library. All rights reserved. Reproduction is forbidden)

1.10   Nicolas Poussin (or his circle), *Castor and Pollux*, drawing, Chantilly, Musée Condé (Photo: Giraudon)

1.11   Stefano della Bella, *Boy with a lamb*, drawing, Rome, Istituto Nazionale per la Grafica (Photo: Istituto Nazionale per la Grafica; reproduced by kind permission of the Ministero per i Beni e le Attività Culturali)

1.12   Stefano della Bella, *Galloping horseman*, drawing, Paris, Musée du Louvre, Département des Arts Graphiques (Photo: Reunion des Musées Nationaux)

2   'The outer man tends to be a guide to the inner': the woodcut portraits in Vasari's *Lives* as parallel texts

2.1   Giorgio Vasari, *Le Vite de' più eccellenti pittori scultori e architettori*, Florence 1568, III, p. 805: portrait of Titian, woodcut

2.2   Titian, *Self-portrait*, c. 1562, oil on canvas, Berlin, Gemäldegalerie (Photo: Jörg P. Anders)

2.3   Giorgio Vasari, *Le Vite de' più eccellenti pittori scultori e architettori*, Florence 1568, I, p. 385: portrait of Fra Filippo Lippi, woodcut

2.4   Fra Filippo Lippi, *Coronation of the Virgin* (detail), 1439–47, tempera on panel, Florence, Galleria degli Uffizi (Photo: Art Resource, New York)

2.5   Giorgio Vasari, *Le Vite de' più eccellenti pittori scultori e architettori*, Florence 1568, II, p. 20: portrait of Piero di Cosimo, woodcut

2.6   Giorgio Vasari, *Le Vite de' più eccellenti pittori scultori e architettori*, Florence 1568, II, p. 1: portrait of Leonardo da Vinci, woodcut

2.7   Cristofano dell'Altissimo, *Portrait of Leonardo da Vinci*, c. 1552–58, oil on panel, Florence, Vasari Corridor, Galleria degli Uffizi (Photo: Art Resource, New York)

2.8   Andrea Mantegna, *Self-portrait*, before 1506, bronze relief, Mantua, Sant'Andrea (Photo: author)

2.9   Giorgio Vasari, *Le Vite de' più eccellenti pittori scultori e architettori*, Florence 1568, I, p. 487: portrait of Andrea Mantegna, woodcut

2.10   Giorgio Vasari, *Le Vite de' più eccellenti pittori scultori e architettori*, Florence 1568, III, p. 625: portrait of Francesco Salviati, woodcut

2.11   Francesco Salviati, *Triumph of Furius Camillus* (detail), 1543–45, fresco, Florence, Palazzo Vecchio: Sala dell'Udienza (Photo: Art Resource, New York)

2.12   Giorgio Vasari, *Le Vite de' più eccellenti pittori scultori e architettori*, Florence 1568, III, p. 474: portrait of Jacopo Pontormo, woodcut

2.13   Agnolo Bronzino, *Martyrdom of St Lawrence* (detail), 1567–69, fresco, Florence, San Lorenzo (Photo: Art Resource, New York)

2.14   Giorgio Vasari, *Le Vite de' più eccellenti pittori scultori e architettori*, Florence 1568, II, p. 204: portrait of Rosso Fiorentino, woodcut

2.15   Andrea del Sarto, *Head of a man*, c. 1520–26, black chalk on white paper, Florence, Gabinetto Disegni e Stampe degli Uffizi (Photo: Art Resource, New York)

3   'Of little or even no importance to the architect': on absent ideals in Serlio's drawings in the Sixth Book, on domestic architecture

3.1   Sebastiano Serlio, 'Architettura civile: libro sesto', Bayerische Staatsbibliothek Munich, Codex Icon.

cartoon in the Victoria and Albert Museum (Photo: author's collection)

7.9   R. H. Smith, *Expositions of Raphael's Bible*, London: A. Miall 1868, frontispiece: albumen print of Raphael (then attrib.; now ascribed to Gianfrancesco Penni), *The Dream of Jacob*, drawing in the British Museum (Photo: author's collection)

7.10   J. P. Walker, *The Madonnas of Raphael*, New York: Leavitt & Allen 1860, title-page after Raphael: albumen print by E. Hufnagel (Photo: author's collection)

7.11   J. P. Walker, *The Madonnas of Raphael*, New York: Leavitt & Allen 1860, plate accompanying p. 23: engraving after [Auguste Gaspard Louis] Desnoyers, after Raphael, *Vierge au berceau*, albumen print by E. Hufnagel (Photo: author's collection)

8   'Still a makeshift'? Changing representations of the Renaissance in twentieth-century art books

8.1a   Paul Schubring, *Donatello: des Meisters Werke*, Stuttgart and Berlin: Deutsche Verlags-Anstalt 1922, p. 64: photograph of Donatello, *The Ascension with Christ giving the Keys to Saint Peter*, marble, c. 1438, Victoria and Albert Museum (Photo: Warburg Institute)

8.1b   Paul Williamson, ed., *European Sculpture at the Victoria and Albert Museum*, London: Victoria and Albert Museum 1996, p. 76: photograph of Donatello, *The Ascension with Christ giving the Keys to Saint Peter*, marble, c. 1438, Victoria and Albert Museum (Photo: Warburg Institute with the permission of the National Art Library)

8.2   Ludwig Goldscheider, *Donatello*, Phaidon edition, London: George Allen and Unwin Ltd 1941, p. 121: photograph of the head of the rider in Donatello, *Equestrian Monument to Gattamelata*, 1445–50, bronze, Padua (detail) (Photo: Warburg Institute)

8.3a   Kenneth Clark, *A Catalogue of the Drawings of Leonardo da Vinci in the collection of H. M. the King at Windsor Castle*, 2 vols, Cambridge: Cambridge University Press 1935, II, no. 12502, n.p.: photograph of Leonardo da Vinci, *Head of a man with sketch of a lion's head*, red chalk, c. 1505, The Royal Collection (Photo: Warburg Institute)

8.3b   Kenneth Clark, *The Drawings of Leonardo da Vinci in the Collection of Her Majesty the Queen at Windsor Castle*, 3 vols, London: Phaidon 1969, II, no. 12502, n.p.: photograph of Leonardo da Vinci, *Head of a man with sketch of a lion's head*, red chalk, c. 1505, The Royal Collection (Photo: Warburg Institute)

8.4   André Malraux, *The Psychology of Art*, transl. Stuart Gilbert, 3 vols, New York: Pantheon Books 1949–50, vol. II: *The Creative Act*, p. 93: photograph (inverted) of Giotto, *The Raising of Lazarus*, c. 1305–06, fresco, Padua, Arena Chapel (Photo: Warburg Institute)

Contributors

JULIANA BARONE, *Trinity College, University of Oxford*

THOMAS FRANGENBERG, *Department of History of Art, University of Leicester*

SHARON GREGORY, *Department of Art and Art History, The University of the South, Sewanee, Tennessee*

ANTHONY HAMBER, *Heritage Images, London*

VAUGHAN HART, *Department of Architecture and Civil Engineering, University of Bath*

VALERIE HOLMAN, *Birkbeck College, University of London*

RODNEY PALMER, *School of World Art Studies and Museology, University of East Anglia, Norwich*

ROBERT TAVENOR, *Department of Architecture and Civil Engineering, University of Bath*

Acknowledgements

The editors are indebted to Francis Ames-Lewis, David Armstrong, David Cohen, Vanessa Corrick, Mercedes Davies, J. V. Field, Lauren Golden, Philip Harley, Eileen and John Harris, Vaughan Hart, Valerie Holman, Charles Hope, Martin Kemp, Nigel Llewellyn, Stefan Muthesius, John Onians, Patricia Rubin, Nicolas Savage, Margit Thøfner and Elizabeth Witchell.

We also warmly thank the Getty Grant Program, the Leonardo da Vinci Society, the Warburg Institute and the World Art Research Programme.

Thanks for permissions to reproduce to Art Resource, New York; the Bayerische Staatsbibliothek, Munich; the Biblioteca Ambrosiana, Milan; the Biblioteca Apostolica Vaticana, Rome; the Biblioteca Casanatense, Rome; the Biblioteca Riccardiana, Florence; the Bodleian Library, University of Oxford; the British Library; the Gabinetto Disegni e Stampe degli Uffizi; the Gallerie dell'Accademia, Venice; the Galleria degli Uffizi, Florence; the Gemäldegalerie, Berlin; Anthony Hamber; the Istituto Nazionale per la Grafica, Rome; the Ministero per i Beni e le Attività Culturali, Italy; the Musée Condé, Chantilly; the Musée du Louvre, Paris; Oxford University Press; Photo Giraudon, Paris; the University of Reading; the Royal Library, Windsor; Salvat Editores, Barcelona; the National Art Library at the Victoria and Albert Museum, London; and the Photographic Collection of the Warburg Institute, London.

Introduction

Rodney Palmer

This volume addresses book illustration as a vehicle for ideas rather than as dependent on its accompanying text. The anthology can be read as an attempt to point out some directions for an agenda of image-and-word, as distinct from existing word-and-image, studies. While it remains appropriate to talk of the 'illustrated book' since books are normally typographical documents sometimes containing images, these images might be better described as 'images' rather than as 'illustrations' since they often create their own discourse rather than merely exemplifying the text's. The essays which follow offer a number of examples and analyses of the variety of roles that images play in art books. They tackle issues that have hardly ever been addressed but are important since illustrated books are a major factor in the dissemination of artistic ideas.

The Rise of the Image describes how over the last 500 years book imagery – even though existing in a reciprocal relation to text, and therefore not always entirely independent of it – has increasingly played a primary rather than a secondary role in manuscript and printed sources on art and architecture. With the exception of architectural treatises, from the sixteenth to the eighteenth century few books on art were illustrated. A shift occurred in the nineteenth and twentieth centuries, to meet a general expectation of copious illustrations in all genres of art books. As moments in this rise are analysed, a tension will emerge. Despite their growing abundance, images in books, especially those reproducing 'original' works of art, have continued to be recognized as fallible, as is signposted by the title of the final essay here: 'Still a makeshift?'. Although this volume will take technical considerations into account, the underlying aim is to see beyond them to the cognitive premises of any given illustrated book.

Italian art of the early modern period has been chosen as the focus, but not with a view to reinforcing the perceived hegemony of Italian visual arts in the west. Although not itself the subject of this book, and thus absent from the title, Italian art was among the most widely illustrated subjects of early modern book culture and therefore provides an optimal, because multifaceted, case study for the history of illustration.

Before introducing the present volume, it will be helpful to review the studies on illustration written in the second half of the twentieth century. Erwin Panofsky in his lecture of 1952 on the Renaissance *Dämmerung* remarked that the rise of observational science was 'directly predicated upon the rise of representational techniques' – and historians of science have contributed much to the general understanding of the illustrated book, as will emerge shortly.[1] William M. Ivins's *Prints and Visual Communication* of 1953 was a didactic account of graphic illustration from the fifteenth to the nineteenth century. Ivins's interim conclusion on fifteenth- and sixteenth-century illustration was that the

webs spun by these busy spiders of the exactly repeatable visual statement were in some respects much like what the geometers call the 'net of rationality', a geometrical construction catching rational points but missing irrational ones. The effect of these rationalized webs on both vision and visual statement was a tyranny, that, before it was broken up, had subjected large parts of the world to the rule of a binding and methodically blighting visual common sense.[2]

For Ivins, this 'tyranny' survived the course of the seventeenth and eighteenth centuries, and Abraham Bosse's *Traité des manières de graver en taille douce* of 1645 typified the ideal of the 'tidy, regular, systematized … net of rationality'.[3] Both the implicit primacy of imagery and the disjunction between imagery and text are issues that will be pursued in the present volume, while Bosse's 'interest in theoretic matters', mentioned in passing by Ivins,[4] has been revisited by William MacGregor in his recent article on the 'authority' of prints, of which more below. Ivins's point of arrival was the nineteenth century, when in his view 'the printed picture came of age'.[5]

Twenty years on, Estelle Jussim's *Visual Communication and the Graphic Arts* began from the premise of the 'alteration of visual perception and habits through the impact of photography on the graphic arts'.[6] Ivins's and Jussim's view that photography marked an irreversible watershed in the history of graphic art is, as Jussim made explicit, inherited from André Malraux's opinion in his *Musée imaginaire*, that 'from the sixteenth to the nineteenth century the masterpiece existed in its own right. There was little or no question of comparing a work with other paintings by the same artist.'[7]

However, prior to the advent of photography, works by the same artist were of course compared by writers on art, relying on a combination of memory and engraved evidence; that is, photography immeasurably improved the possibilities of, rather than creating the desire for, connoisseurial enquiry. Moreover, as the last two chapters in the present volume show, the art book with photographic imagery was hardly less beset by problems of veracity than its woodcut- and engraving-bearing precursors. It is worth making our position painstakingly clear in counterpoint to Jussim's. Jussim worked inwards by asking:

In what ways did the introduction of photographic technologies alter the artistic and informational capabilities of the graphic arts? In what ways did the capabilities of the photographic technologies for artistic expression and information transfer differ not only from nonphotographic processes but from each other?[8]

Here we will ask: what cognitive approaches to the graphic representation of early modern art and theory have persisted in spite of technological change?

Despite such fundamental differences, Jussim's book warrants further attention here, not least on account of its critique of Ivins. While praising Ivins for being, unlike most connoisseurs, 'more interested in the visual communication aspects of his charges than in their rarity or preciousness', Jussim also suggested that some of Ivins's assumptions needed to be examined with extreme care; in particular she questioned Ivins's view, held prior to *Prints and Visual Communication* and underpinning the 'tyranny' hyperbole therein, that 'engravers were taught and disciplined in conventional artificial, linear styles'.[9] Following Jussim's signpost back to Ivins's *How Prints Look*, one reads of 'not only a rather high average level of technical skill among the professional print makers but also rather a dead level of impersonal, undifferentiated skill. Engraving and etching became mechanical crafts.'[10]

As we shall see, engravers did personalize and differentiate their cuts – and not only by signing them – no less than did artists working in any other graphic medium.

One premise both of Ivins's *Prints and Visual Communication* and of Jussim's book which the present one largely shares is that of choosing 'Art history, as the one major subject field for study … because the development of the graphic arts has been bound up with the reproduction of art from the very beginning.'[11] This premise, for all its validity and apparent obviousness, was generally ignored in the later decades of the twentieth century, which goes some way towards explaining why surveys of the illustrated book in general, and of the imagery in particular types of text, appeared intermittently, but without constituting a field of enquiry characterized by any thematic fluency. The surveys are here addressed chronologically, starting from David Bland's *History of Book Illustration* of 1969. Showing an interdisciplinary instinct, Bland was keen to draw analogies with other media, especially the frequently invoked relationship, corroborated by early modern bibliographical nomenclature (especially in Italian), of architecture to the typography as well as the images in seventeenth-century books.[12] The following year, John

Lewis published his *Anatomy of Printing: The Influences of Art and History on its Design*, the well-conceived project of which was to analyse the part of visual art in typography from the Renaissance until the 1960s; Lewis's enquiry was, as its title suggests, about the aesthetics of textual rather than visual information. It should be pointed out how outmoded the word 'influence' in Lewis's title has become for the analysis of printed imagery and of the models and ideas disseminated by it.[13] The term 'influence' precludes any impartial consideration of the reciprocal, elastic relation between image and text, and admits the cognitive agency only of the initial propagator of any given image.

The common ground of the literature around 1970 was the readiness to apply analogical models, whether architectural or anatomical, to the aesthetics of the book. While one can well understand why analogical approaches were – and indeed still are[14] – adopted as a way of understanding book illustrations, they can be limiting when allowed to preclude full consideration of the illustrated book's complexities.

Partly in reaction to architectural and other analogical models, the core of the argument of Sergio Samek Ludovici's history of the illustrated book from the fifteenth to the seventeenth century was that the history of the book must consider the history of engraving.[15] This is true as far as it goes, but recent studies have shown that the engraving techniques available for any given book were only a part of the equation.

Published in 1975, Christopher Lloyd and Tanya Ledger's catalogue accompanying the exhibition *Art and its Images: An Exhibition of Printed Books Containing Engraved Illustrations after Italian Painting* relates less to the literature of its time on illustrated books than to its initial stimulus, Ivins's *Prints and Visual Communication*.[16] The discursive introduction to *Art and its Images* opened with the subject of photography, and by so doing intuitively called into question the medium's objectivity. By drawing attention to John Ruskin's view that woodcut is the medium best suited to the reproduction of Giotto's work,[17] *Art and its Images* also signposted the relativity of every reproductive image to its prototype and thus hinted at the argument against any over-simplistic interpretation of technical advance. *Art and its Images* revealed some of the chronological and geographical range of books on Italian art as a field of enquiry, considering as it did books printed in Italy, England, France and Germany over the course of 400 years.[18]

A project of still broader scope, Michel Melot's *L'Illustration* of 1984, amply demonstrated the fallibility of concentrating any analysis of book illustration on engraving techniques alone.[19] By surveying illumination and engraved imagery together, Melot compared attitudes to imagery-in-text before and then during the age of the printed book. Strategies of manuscript decoration can tell us much about attitudes to imagery within the printed book. The chapters on illumination in Michael Camille's *Image on the Edge* reveal imagery's often maverick roles around text.[20]

The present enquiry is located within what can usefully be understood as 'the age of the printed book', from around 1500 when the printed book became the principal means of the dissemination of knowledge, to around 2000 when the book's dominance is being challenged by other information media. The technical history of the printed book is a major but not a dominating concern of this anthology. Every book printed at any given time has of course been illustrated subject to the materials and techniques then available. However, graphic style does not depend solely on technological developments but also on the intellectual context of any given discourse. This has been demonstrated very clearly by Martin Kemp in his analysis of the imagery in the editions of Copernicus on the solar system and of Vesalius on anatomy, both printed in 1543 – the diagrammatic simplicity of the former as opposed to the artful specificity of the latter relating to the state of each of the two sciences.[21] Brian Baigrie, the editor of *Picturing Knowledge*, in which Kemp's essay appeared, glossed that Kemp thus undid assumptions of any 'unifying theme' in book illustration.[22] The problem of a 'unifying theme' is a central concern of this volume: its remit, to examine illustrated books on the visual arts, was conceived to supply a degree of unity, but there are differences between images in books on art, on architecture and on both.

David Topper's contribution to Baigrie's *Picturing Knowledge* synthesized observations of later twentieth-century historians of science, at least three of which go a long way to defining the theoretical role of imagery. These statements are here rearranged, for the sake of historiographical clarity, into the order in which they were made: first Martin Rudwick's of 1976 that in the hierarchy of educational institutions 'visual thinking is not valued as highly as verbal or mathematical dexterity';[23] secondly, Barbara Marie Stafford who distinguished between the 'descriptive word' and 'accurate image';[24] and thirdly, Stephen Jay Gould who wrote that 'scientific illustrations are not frills or summaries; they are foci for modes of thought',[25] thus bringing 'visual thinking' so much into the foreground that one does indeed question the adequacy of the term 'illustration'. Topper himself, writing on the images in scientific literature, noticed the 'extensive copying from other illustrators rather than from nature! Indeed, most illustrations were copies of other illustrations … '.[26] This was hardly less the case in literature on art. For instance, Piero della Francesca's designs of perspective construction in *De prospectiva pingendi* were largely taken up by Daniele Barbaro in his *La pratica della perspettiva* of 1569. The diagrams remained essentially unaltered, but Barbaro sometimes expanded and sometimes abbreviated Piero's explanations of them.[27] This is a clear instance of imagery providing a template for visual communication, secondary textual explanations of which varied. The essay in this volume on Andrea Pozzo's *Perspectiva* takes account of how a graphic model of fifteenth-century origins, first published in Viator's *De artificiali perspectiva*, remained sufficiently useful to appear, essentially unaltered, in a Qing edition of the eighteenth century. In short, the diagrammatic image has proved to be a culturally universal means of conveying visual information for design ideas – however culturally specific the latter tend to become.

Theoretical work of the 1980s and 1990s by scholars from a literary background addressed issues such as 'iconology', 'illustrations' and 'iconotexts'. Even those sceptical of usages of the word 'theory' over recent decades would admit the term's derivation from the Greek 'theoria' (θεωρία) for 'contemplation' or 'thing looked at', from 'theoros' (θεωρός) or 'spectactor', and ultimately 'thea' (θέα) or 'view'. The term thus refreshed, book imagery can be described as theoretical and not just illustrative.

Stemming from his *Blake's Composite Art* and *The Language of Images*, W. J. T. Mitchell's *Iconology: Image, Text, Ideology* anticipated our 'image-and-text' premise. Mitchell's section on 'The Idea of Imagery' created a genealogy of imagery, subdividing the 'image' into five main branches: graphic, optical, perceptual, mental and verbal. Describing each branch as 'central to the discourse of some intellectual discipline', Mitchell then tried to match types of image to disciplines: in the cases of specifically visual imagery, 'optical imagery to physics; graphic, sculptural and architectural imagery to the art historian'.[28] Such definitions are over-specific, optics being central also to illustrated discourses on art, and graphic imagery a prerequisite of scientific exposition; to understand how imagery works one should not so much relate aspects of it to any discipline as enquire how it works across disciplines. The limitation of the present book in this respect, that it is wholly by historians of art and architecture, is offset by the fact that all of the authors are well equipped to discuss imagery.

Where Mitchell's *Iconology* privileged 'verbal imagery', in his *Picture Theory* of 1994 he took a 'pictorial turn' and challenged art history 'to offer an account of its principal theoretical object – visual representation – that will be usable by other disciplines in the human sciences'.[29] The present collection of essays aims to do so by drawing attention to the importance of book imagery, illustrated books having been a principal means of communication on all manner of subjects for over 500 years.

Peter Wagner's *Reading Iconotexts* of 1995 discussed the relationship between printed image and text in eighteenth-century publications. The term 'iconotexts' is one of many post-structuralist neologisms in Wagner's book. Of these, alongside 'iconotext' itself the idea of 'visual pre-texts' is the most pertinent to the present collection of essays.[30]

In recent years, the graphic and photographic reproduction of imagery in texts on art has increasingly become an object of art historical enquiry. Two anthologies on the art historical applications of photography, *Art History through the Camera's Lens* and *Sculpture and Photography*, will be discussed in more detail towards the end of this introduction, in relation to Hamber's and Holman's chapters on photographic illustration.[31] A fitting point of arrival for this survey of the literature on printed imagery is William B. MacGregor's recent article on the 'authority' of early modern prints.[32] MacGregor scrutinizes examples of print-making in seventeenth- and eighteenth-century France, Holland and England in the light of didactic texts by, among others, Descartes, Gérard de Lairesse and Roger de Piles. MacGregor's argument for the cognitive authority of prints is successfully underpinned by his discussion of the double valence of words such as 'impression' and 'trace'.[33] His article will prove indispensable to future scholars investigating the intellectual background to the relationship between printed imagery and text in early modern Europe. However, MacGregor's study is not principally concerned with the question of how specific texts are illustrated since MacGregor discusses the engravings in one book in the light of a different book's text, for instance arguing that certain plates in Bosse's *Traité des manières de graver* 'make more explicit the technical procedure which Descartes' theory [in *La Dioptrique*] implicitly references'.[34] The present collection of essays addresses imagery and text within the same books. Imagery in books on the visual arts is understood as supplying an inner thematic coherence, related to that envisaged by Ivins and Jussim.

By its heterogeneous nature book illustration inevitably creates discourses as diverse as the ways in which printed image and illustrated text interact. The accentuated spirit of dialogue between – rather than any artificial monologue uniting – this introduction and the essays which follow is a response to the unusual complications presented by the illustrated book as a field of study. For instance, even while recognizing that the history of engraving techniques is by no means the whole story, the following pages consider certain minutiae of information about engravers, without which nuances of illustrated books as cultural statements would be lost. As a rule, while the authors of each essay have with good reason emphasized the *messages* of the objects of their enquiries, attention is here drawn to the various media (drawing, engraving, typography, bookbinding) involved in the fabrication of books, so as to link the essays with one another as markers in the bitty and uneven, but crucial, history of the illustrated book as artefact.

The essays

Juliana Barone addresses the use of visual imagery in art theory. She discusses the two sets of illustrations to the sections on movement in Leonardo's *Trattato della pittura*, those after drawings by Poussin engraved and published in the *editio princeps* of 1651 and those by Stefano della Bella, posthumously engraved and published in 1792. Barone argues that the balanced appearance of Poussin's designs is not principally due to the fact that they were made for publication; she explains her position by relating Poussin's drawings to the 'stable and decorous' classical qualities of Poussin's other works of the same time.

Barone's essay raises matters that, while extraneous to her argument, are relevant to the history with which this book is mainly concerned, that of illustrations in printed books. The 1651 Italian- and French-language editions of Leonardo's treatise illustrated with the same plates mark an early instance of a book being published simultaneously in different languages with the same engraved imagery.

The Poussin-derived series was considered sufficiently appropriate to be almost exactly replicated in the Naples 1733 edition of the *Trattato*.[35] The editor of the 1792 edition, Francesco Fontani, on the other hand, published della Bella's drawings, claiming that della Bella's 'figures made practice of the precepts he so admired'. The 'visual demonstrations of theoretical principles' which Barone's chapter discusses also reflect technical advances: Fontani's 1792 edition, illustrated with engravings that closely replicate della Bella's fluid drawings, would have been inconceivable without the eighteenth-century invention of the aquatint.[36]

Sharon Gregory's essay analyses the earliest imagery inserted into a volume devoted to artists' lives. Vasari had probably planned to include woodcut portraits in the first edition of his *Lives*, but they were executed only for the second edition of 1568. Gregory locates Vasari's *Lives* within a tradition of antique origins exemplary biography. She establishes that the portraits were drawn for publication by Vasari himself, and demonstrates that, at least in all cases for which Vasari's drawings survive, details of pose, physiognomy and clothing were meticulously followed by the woodcutters. These images were intended, in close conjunction with Vasari's text, to provide insight into the character and social standing of the depicted artists.

As much as Vasari's biographical method, his use of portraits set a precedent for subsequent historiographers of art, such as Giovanni Pietro Bellori. Whereas in artists' lives, as Charles Hope's and Sharon Gregory's enquiries have shown,[37] the apparently auxiliary portraits were in fact integrally related to the text, the possibilities of woodcuts and engravings for the detailed replication of works of art were only extremely rarely capitalized upon by sixteenth-century authors and printers of books on art.

The sixteenth-century history of books on architecture is in this respect quite distinct, partly because architecture is less easily open to verbal exposition and to the reader's imagination than painting and sculpture. Chapters 3 and 4, on imagery in sixteenth-century Italian books on architecture, address Serlio, Palladio and Daniele Barbaro. Vaughan Hart's essay analyses one of the few of Serlio's Books to have remained in manuscript during his lifetime: the Sixth, on domestic architecture. The trial woodcuts, important visual communications intended for publication, are here published for the first time (see Figs 3.1– 3.5). Hart points out that the layout of Serlio's manuscript, incorporating spreads composed of imagery on the right and text on the left, departs from the format of his published books and of earlier printed literature on architecture in general. However, this same layout – spreads with imagery on one page and relevant text on that facing it – is often found in subsequent literature on architecture, not least in Giacomo de' Franceschi's compendium of Serlio's works printed in 1619.[38] We are not here dealing with a technical advance: printing text and imagery separately is more straightforward than printing them together. Nor was the use, first in manuscript and then in printed books, of the image-opposite-text a theoretical choice, although cognitive experience certainly played a part in it: the increasing autonomy of imagery within books on architecture was the result of accumulative praxis.

Hart's chapter discusses the role of imagery in Serlio's 'pragmatic strategy towards the contemporary problems of social organization and the diversity of political systems which the artist might encounter'. He explains Serlio's adaptability to a variety of political systems – communal Bologna, oligarchic Venice and monarchic France; this adaptability to 'variables of context' manifested itself in adjustments to window-types and other significant details of his designs. As is shown by the 'licentious' design ideas he published in the *Libro extraordinario*, Serlio was more free to express his architectural imagination in his book illustrations than in his architecture for patrons. The 'link between biography and pragmatic architectural theory' he achieved through the 'earthly pragmatism of his drawings' and his role as 'selector' of any number of possible models, as described by Hart, contributed to making Serlio's books, with their balance of image and text, the most influential sixteenth-century architectural treatises, from Protestant England to colonial Spanish America.[39]

Far from being of merely marginal interest, early modern Iberian America, distant as it was from Europe and thus from actual European architecture, is the continent in which the influence of Italian (and other European) printed imagery emerges most clearly.[40] It has become something of a truism to say that the planar quality of much Spanish American architecture was rooted in its derivation from engravings, usually book illustrations. The veracity of this assertion will be tested both later in this introduction and in chapter six, in relation to the uses made in Spanish America of imagery in books by Serlio, Vignola and Pozzo. The premise of a connection between illustration and architecture of planar character raises as many issues as it settles about two-dimensional European representations of architecture, their cognitive assumptions and implications, as well as their effect on architectural practice.

Robert Tavernor's chapter traces illustrations of architecture back to their origins in the earliest editions of the treatises by Vitruvius and Alberti to which figures were added. Vitruvius had intended his *De architectura* to be illustrated, but Alberti did not envisage imagery in *De re aedificatoria*. Francesco di Giorgio Martini (1439–1501) was the first modern to argue systematically for the importance of imagery in literature on architecture;[41] by the early Cinquecento there was quite a vogue for illustrating Vitruvius, as is evidenced by Peruzzi's marginal illustrations to Vitruvius, mentioned by Gregory as well as by Tavernor. Tavernor identifies Serlio's vital role in the history of the illustrated architectural treatise, as the first author whose method was founded on (woodcut) imagery in close proximity with printed text. Linking Serlio with Palladio via their mutual patron Giangiorgio Trissino, Tavernor proceeds to discuss Palladio's method which, like Serlio's, combines text and imagery, but abbreviates the former and lavishes greater care on the latter. Even though Tavernor is mainly concerned with the intellectual and artistic roles of Barbaro and Palladio – which were 'complementary', just as Tavernor argues their books were intended to be – his essay does acknowledge the indispensable roles of Venetian typographers, 'the ingenious [Francesco] Marcolini' and Francesco and Domenico de' Franceschi, all of whom actively affected the appearance of the illustrations in their editions of Barbaro and of Palladio.

Three points made in the course of Tavernor's essay deserve to be emphasized since they contribute to our understanding of the inextricability of the histories of cognition and of vision: first, the discussion of Barbaro's *segni* as opposed to the text they illustrate; secondly, the observation of similarities between illustrations to Palladio and to Vesalius; and thirdly, Tavernor's comments on the 'architectural' relationship between words and images in Barbaro's books. All three of these matters have implications that are by no means limited to sixteenth-century northern Italy: the derivation of *segno* and thus *disegno* from the Latin *signum* takes us back towards the visual origins of cognition. Illustrated humanist editions of classical texts made palpable the visual origins of much ancient thought, particularly that on art and architecture.

While there are significant differences between Palladio's and Vesalius's approaches to design – whereas Palladio honed his representation of architecture down to elevational and sectional views, Vesalius inclined to artful three-dimensional poses and accompanying iconography – they are certainly connected as contemporary graphic products of the intellectual culture of the Veneto.[42] In terms of the binding of imagery into printed text, Vesalius's *Fabrica*, as the first book to deploy full-page engraved imagery,[43] was a precedent for long sections in Serlio.

That the notion of the 'architecture' of the illustrated book was an enduring one emerges clearly from Thomas Frangenberg's chapter analysing the engravings in Girolamo Teti's *Aedes Barberinae*, which Teti formulated as a 'second building' standing in for a visit to the Palazzo Barberini itself. The idea of the book itself as a second building, more recently echoed by the very title of Vaughan Hart and Peter Hicks's *Paper Palaces*,[44] alters the role of architecture in the discussion of illustrated books from one of mere analogy into one of extended metaphor.

Frangenberg's essay sheds light on the function of Teti's luxuriously illustrated volume (the importance of which was recognized by Francis Haskell[45]), both in contrast to Mattia Rosichino's unillustrated pamphlet and in its own right. Teti's *Aedes Barberinae* went into a second edition enlarged with verse plaudits, one of which maintains that the volume was disseminated in 'hundreds' around the 'world' (for which we should probably read 'Europe').

At the heart of Frangenberg's chapter lies an analysis of Teti's attitude to verbal–visual cognition. Teti's claims for his own description's efficacy in visualizing the Barberini decorations ultimately conceded the greater 'beauty and majesty' of the fold-out engravings. These engravings presuppose reading on a library table; they also imply contemplative scrutiny of the image, interrupting reading activity.[46] The 'beauty and majesty' of the fold-out engravings in the *Aedes Barberinae* were of course dependent on improvements in the techniques not only of engraving but also of the binding of imagery into books. The relatively underdeveloped state of the latter is evidenced by the fact that, as Frangenberg observes, fold-out engravings are found at differing places in different copies of the *Aedes Barberinae*; a further symptom of a complete interrelation between text and image not yet having been achieved is that only one type of engraved illustration, those replicating sculptures in the Barberini collection, are keyed into the text.

No less revealing of the plurality of responsibility in the fabrication of the illustrated book is a frequently overlooked stage in the fabrication of the *Aedes Barberinae*: the successive compositional decisions made first by those who drew and then by those who engraved the plates. Engravers, answerable (in varying degrees in different instances) to authors, designers and printers were socially the junior party in the production of any given book. However, their role was the definitive one for the realization of the illustrations. The engravings for the *Aedes Barberinae* were cut by Cornelis Bloemaert (Utrecht 1603 – Rome 1692), Michael Natalis (Lüttich 1606/10 – 1668/70), Johann Friedrich Greuter (Strasbourg c. 1590/93 – Rome 1660) and Camillo Cungi (Borgo Sansepolcro 1570/80 – Rome 1649). To use terminology that has recently gone out of fashion – the usefulness of which, if overrated 20 years ago, need not be altogether denied now – the names of Bloemaert, Natalis and Greuter, engravers for Teti, are themselves signifiers in the cultural field of the *Aedes Barberinae*, to which they bring a cosmopolitan dimension. Frangenberg documents Filippo Baldinucci's account, in his *Notizie dei professori del disegno* (1681), of Bloemaert's reservations about collaborating with Pietro da Cortona. Even though Bloemaert was answerable not to Pietro da Cortona but to Teti, Baldinucci's version, seconded by Pascoli, testifies to the growing status of reproductive engraving. Works by leading Italian artists were interpreted by largely the same northern European engravers in arguably the most important illustrated book printed at Rome in the 1640s: Giovanni Battista Ferrari's *Hesperides* of 1646, in which compositions by Albani, Sacchi, Romanelli, Reni, Domenichino and Lanfranco as well as Poussin were engraved by Bloemaert and Greuter, and by the Frenchman Claude Goyrand.[47] Baldinucci's life of Bloemaert discussed his contribution to the *Hesperides* as well as to the *Aedes Barberinae*.[48] Later seventeenth-century attention to engraving and its deployment in books is testified to by the fact that Baldinucci's *Notizie* on engravers including Bloemaert were published separately as *Cominciamento, e progresso dell'arte dell'intagliare in rame* of 1686; in his 'Proemio' Baldinucci asserted that 'of all the arts that have design as their father, aside from architecture, painting and sculpture … none is more delightful and useful than copper- or wood-engraving'.[49]

The identities of the engravers for Andrea Pozzo's *Perspectiva pictorum et architectorum* (Rome 1693–1700) relate to those in the above mid-Seicento Roman editions insofar as they included at least a couple of northern European engravers, the Dutchman Theodor Verkruys and Jean Charles Allet (Paris c. 1668 – Rome 1732), the latter moreover strongly indebted to Bloemaert.[50] The Italians Domenico Mariano Franceschini (Verona? – after 1725), Girolamo Frezza (Tivoli 1659 – 1741) and Vincenzo Mariotti (? – Rome 1738) were equally responsible for the signed imagery.[51] Most of these engravers were near the beginning of their careers when they worked for Pozzo (indeed, ignoring their work for Pozzo's *Perspectiva*, the repertories still date Franceschini's and Verkruys's careers from 1705 and 1707 respectively).[52] A principal characteristic of the *Perspectiva*, resulting from Pozzo's authority over his manual executants, is the homogoneity of their realization of his visual ideas.

The essay on Pozzo's illustrated books on perspective relates to the earlier ones by Hart, Tavernor and Frangenberg, engaged as Pozzo was both with sixteenth-century methods of representing architecture in books and with reproductions of seventeenth-century ceiling paintings. The essay was also conceived as a test case of practising artists' active reception of illustrated books. The *Perspectiva* had an impact on the development of art and architecture in Europe and further afield. Widespread aesthetic tendencies in building and decorating in Europe and beyond are connected to the illustrated books from which they were sourced. For instance, as much as the planar quality of early modern Spanish American architecture relates to its basis in two-dimensional engraved imagery, the very sculptural three-dimensional conception of the *retablos* in the Compañía at Quito depends upon the emphasis of their source illustrations, in Pozzo's *Perspectiva*, on three-dimensionality.

Pozzo's dual role as designer for the engravings and author of their accompanying texts ensured the coherence in the *Perspectiva* between image and text. Pozzo's dual authorship invites us to glance back at the varying relationship between imagery and authorship in the preceding chapters. The crucial importance of the visual image in Leonardo's *Trattato* was never fully respected by the editors of the printed editions. Gregory has plausibly argued for Vasari's agency, both iconographic and graphic (as artist-author turned author-artist), in the headers to the second edition of the *Lives*. Serlio's role as designer-author is most akin to Pozzo's, since both in Barbaro's and Palladio's illustrated publications and in Teti's *Aedes Barberinae* the social relationships of designers, writers and engravers were far more complex and disjointed.

Concerns stemming from the Italian fifteenth and sixteenth centuries still prevailed in the production of eighteenth-century European illustrated books, and not just of reprints but of original and controversial ventures such as Fontani's edition of Leonardo's *Trattato*. This is no less the case with books on architecture, as is here exemplified with reference to English architectural books.

Robert Morris inherited and extended Serlio's role as selector in *The Architectural Remembrancer: Being a Collection of New and Useful Designs, of Ornamental Buildings and Decorations* (London 1751); Eileen Harris's gloss on the pictures as 'a useful substitute (or "remembrancer") for the words which many patrons lacked to describe to their builders or architects precisely what they had in mind' explains the usefulness of architectural pattern books.[53] In the eighteenth century, the representation of architecture in illustrated books relied mainly on Alberti's and his successors' conceptions of the orthographic and ichnographic views. For instance, the first two volumes of Colen Campbell's *Vitruvius Britannicus* of 1715 depended wholly on plans and elevations.[54] However a shift occurred in the course of the publication of the *Vitruvius Britannicus*. The third volume, of 1725, incorporated three bird's-eye 'prospects in Perspective', the fourth volume, of 1739, thirty.[55]

By the mid-nineteenth century both the intellectual premises of and the media available for the printed dissemination of knowledge had diversified. The concluding two essays in this book examine mainly English-language photographically illustrated books on Italian 'Renaissance' art. Useful background to the epoch in which the narrative of this book resumes is provided by John Ruskin. Ruskin's 'paradoxical' attitude towards photography has been discussed by Anthony Hamber, in his contribution to *Art History through the Camera's Lens*. Hamber pointed out that little had been done 'to clarify a chronology' of Ruskin's attitude to photography, and contrasted Ruskin's admission of the 'truth' of the Daguerrotype in the 1840s with his expressions in the 1870s of the fallibility of the medium (and Ruskin was by no means alone among his contemporaries in thus revising his opinion on photography's potential).[56] In the present context of illustrated books on Italian visual culture, it is worth briefly reconsidering Ruskin's *The Stones of Venice*; in the successive volumes of the second edition Ruskin ruminated on graphic and photographic illustration. Notwithstanding his awareness of the Daguerrotype, as Ruskin wrote in the Preface to the second edition of 1858, to illustrate his text he had:

used any kind of engraving which seemed suited to the subjects – line and mezzotint, on steel, with mixed lithographs and woodcuts, at considerable loss of uniformity in the appearance of the volume, but, I hope, with advantage, in rendering the character of the architecture it describes.[57]

In volume III of the same edition, Ruskin would write: 'a power of obtaining veracity in the representation of material things, which, within certain limits and conditions, is unimpeachable, has now been placed in the hands of all men'; on the probable results of the Daguerrotype and calotype in the near future Ruskin commented, 'I have little doubt, that an infinite service will soon be done to a large body of our engravers; namely the making them draughtsmen (in black and white) on paper instead of steel.'[58]

Ruskin's rhetoric reiterated Fox Talbot's in *The Pencil of Nature*, published in fascicles in the 1840s, on photography as 'drawing';[59] the view that 'photography differs from drawing in degree but not in kind' is still tenable in our times.[60] The description of photography as drawing both admits the subjective agency of the photographer and reveals the extent to which the concerns surrounding reproductive media remained consistent notwithstanding technological changes.

Hamber's chapter in the present volume revises his previous article on the use of photography by nineteenth-century art historians by placing illustrated books on Italian and other early modern art in the broader context of nineteenth-century photographic publishing. Exemplifying the limited quantitative scope of the photographically illustrated art book up to the mid-nineteenth century, only 25 copies were issued of one of the earlier books that Hamber discusses, the fourth volume of William Stirling's *Annals of the Artists of Spain* of 1848.[61]

Twenty-odd years later, photography was sufficiently amenable to the illustration of books on art to be the main medium deployed in the publication of Prince Albert's collection of reproductions of the works of Raphael. Hamber quotes the cataloguer, Carl Ruland (who knowingly or otherwise echoed Ruskin's remark cited here) on the 'unimpeachable fidelity' of photography. Nonetheless, as Jennifer Montagu showed in her contribution to *Art History through the Camera's Lens*, the 'new and experimental' medium of photography in the 1870s was still of only limited usefulness in replicating Raphael's oeuvre, its principal (but by no means only) shortcoming being its technical inadequacy for reproducing yellow.[62] Thus the *Madonna and Child* at Kensington Palace (now attributed to Annibale Carracci) was initially replicated in watercolour rather than photographed for the 'Ruland/Raphael Collection'.[63] Montagu also pointed out that 'the formation of the "Ruland/Raphael Collection" was a stimulus both to the use of photography for the reproduction of works of art, and to the creation of those photographic departments of public museums on which we now rely'.[64] The most important such photographic collection in nineteenth-century Britain is that at the South Kensington (now Victoria and Albert) Museum, the instigator of which, J. Charles Robinson, is the test case for Hamber's chapter.

Hamber reveals that Robinson's illustrated books on aspects of the South Kensington Museum's collection were realized not in isolation but in reciprocal relation to the private market. The South Kensington Museum was enticed by Ottavio Gigli's catalogue of 1858, illustrated with 117 photographs of his collection of early Italian sculpture, to buy parts of the collection, a copy of the catalogue itself being given to the museum in 1860. It is more than coincidental that, while this transaction was in progress, in 1859, Robinson launched his serial publication *Museum of Art, South Kensington: Photographic Illustrations of Works in various Sections of the Collection*, illustrated with albumen prints. Robinson's catalogue of the museum's Italian sculpture collection was illustrated with line engravings based on photographs; as Hamber points out, contrary to Malraux's and Ivins's assumptions, engraving retained its popularity until the end of the nineteenth century. One of the images in Robinson's catalogue of 1862 appeared as a mounted carbon print in Charles Christopher Black's *Michael Angelo Buonarotti* of 1875, an instance of the museum's publishing activity feeding back into that of the private sphere to which it was responding. The replication of the same image in quite different books is reminiscent of pre-photographic illustrating practices. It also leads us to the opening remark of Valerie Holman's chapter, that the 'history of illustration … suggests the prior existence of text and the subordinate role of imagery': an expression of the assumption which all the papers in this volume, in their different ways, call into question. One well-known example of reproductions having persistently informed, or rather misinsformed, textual analysis is the historiography of Raphael's Stanza della Segnatura frescoes from Vasari to Wölfflin.[65]

In the early part of her chapter, Holman establishes that nineteenth-century connoisseurship 'paved the way' for photographic illustration in twentieth-century art books. However, Holman quotes Rosanna Pavoni to the effect that the nineteenth-century belief (which, as we have seen, was often doubted) in the objectivity of the photograph was 'a typically positivist error'. Holman's analysis of 'photographic reproductions as coded, proble-matic images' leads off from Wölfflin's critical comments on 'aesthetic' and 'picturesque' photography, and her discussion of Donatello's *Ascension* relief clinches the first part of her argument, that no single reproduction wholly recreates the original from which it derives. One mid-twentieth-century response to this problem, especially of course in the case of sculpture, was to illustrate a single object with numerous images. However, the quantity as well as the quality of reproductions in all art books are dictated by cost and other practical considerations. Holman's discussion of the correspondence surrounding Bernard Berenson's *Florentine Drawings* leads her to demonstrate that reproductions cannot be 'seen as disembodied images' any more than they can be 'identified with originals'. Holman mentions that Walter Benjamin's 'The Work of Art in the Age of Mechanical Reproduction' both reflected and informed early twentieth-century attitudes to multiply reproduced imagery. Benjamin was readier than many of the twentieth-century authors between him and us to recognize similarity in the effect of graphic and photographic prints. He observed that 'the invention of the woodcut may be said to have struck at the root of authenticity', and thus that 'to ask for the "authentic" [photographic] print makes no sense'.[66] Benjamin's central thesis – that in the process of replication imagery loses the 'aura' of the original – has latterly been questioned. Shedding light on a number of issues raised in this book, Norbert Lynton has perceptively remarked that rather than negating an image's aura, 'multiplication through mass reproduction creates a different kind of aura, associated … with world-wide possession'.[67] Lynton's affirmation can itself be juxtaposed with the following observation by J. Hillis Miller:

In a development not mentioned by Benjamin, a work intended for unique display in a museum or home, in an aestheticized corruption of aura, may be reproduced in an advertisement. Religious or aesthetic works may also be duplicated in forms increasingly far from the original, for example by scanner for digital storage and retrieval.[68]

Advertising, as well as digital and other IT media, supplies useful evidence for interpreting illustrations in art books. If it is questionable whether digital imagery is necessarily any further from the original than are preceding means of reproduction, it is certain that, even leaving aside the issue of aura, available techniques do not and never will entirely reproduce the physical (let alone spiritual) qualities of original objects. This is especially the case with regard to colour.

Holman's analysis of Albert Skira's and Bernard Berenson's comments on the variability of all original artefacts' colour, especially of those *in situ*, and thus the impossibility of adequately reproducing them, raises a problem that still applies, and continues to inhibit historians' analysis of colour: for instance, as Craig Hugh Smyth commented in 1962 and reiterated 29 years later, the analysis of colour in Italian sixteenth-century painting of the *Maniera*.[69] Due to the fact that, to borrow the title of Holman's chapter, colour reproduction is 'still a makeshift', colour reproductions have been eschewed in this book because they are inevitably subject to variabilities or, to put it another way, invariably flawed.

In her essay Holman suggests that the inclusion of copious reproductions has been 'the defining characteristic of the art book' from the 1960s on. Copious reproductions became a palpable objective of books on art in the seventeenth and eighteenth centuries. One of the reasons for examining the history of illustrated books from the sixteenth to the twentieth century is that by so doing continuities and discontinuities can be made apparent in the deployment of images, be they woodcuts, engravings or photographs. In the terminology of the anthropology of art, every engraved image is subject to at least double and usually multiple 'agency';[70] for example, as Gregory describes, Vasari selected imagery from the works of usually unwitting agents which were then manufactured by the almost anonymous 'Cristofano' or 'Cristoforo'; or, as Barone narrates, Leonardo's designs were redrawn by Poussin and again by Errard, and by Della Bella and then engraved by René Lochon and Giuseppe Antonio Fabbrini, respectively. As Hamber and Holman reveal, photography's relationship to the extant imagery from which it derives is no less mediated, problematic. It is therefore essential to consider all these media together.

In illustrated books these mediated images are further complicated by their reciprocal relationship to texts. Only by bearing in mind all of the agents involved can we start to grasp the richness of the art book as a cultural phenomenon.

To recapitulate the issues involved in book illustration raised in this volume, all of the first six essays reveal the active contribution of imagery to early modern books on art and architecture. They all describe what we might define as visual information, independent of verbal reasoning, as a conduit of discourse. All consider the crucial decision-making phases in the illustration of any book, of 'selection'. The last two essays discuss photographic illustrations as commodities.

To conclude by sketching an agenda for future research, the issue of 'visual information' that this volume addresses opens a huge field. The history of the image as a main conduit of discourse, to which text plays a secondary role, is by no means confined to (and can even be seen as having been temporarily interrupted by) the age of the printed book. Much work remains to be done on the issue of the role of print imagery from books in the development of other media. An exhibition of 1993 demonstrated 'that the figurative sources of majolica decorated with historic scenes may above all be found in the immense wealth of graphic and printed works, in particular the illustrations of incunabula and sixteenth-century printed books' and thus the 'close iconographic connections linking majolica decorated with historic scenes to illustrated books'.[71] Further research can show that Gianvittorio Dillon's affirmation of 'the circulation and the success enjoyed by certain editions in relation to production and stylistic development of majolica'[72] was matched by adaptations of imagery from books in *intarsie* and other media.

A volume on the role of book illustration in formulating northern European perceptions of art and architecture would complement the present one. To give one example: a series of engravings, mainly from Bernardino Passeri and Martin de Vos by Antwerpian engravers,[73] was published in Antwerp under the name of Jeronimo Nadal (1507–80), first in 1593 as *Evangelicae historiae imagines* with concise legends engraved on the images and then three years later embedded in the lengthy text *Adnotationes et meditationes in Evangelia.*[74] Such an order of publication suggests that imagery generating verbal thought was as much the norm in northern Europe as in Italy. Like Pozzo's for the *Perspectiva*, its designs were widely taken up in Europe, Iberian America and Asia. The complex publication history of the *Evangelicae historiae imagines*, involving writers and artists in Rome and Antwerp for several decades, distinguishes it from Serlio's and Pozzo's works, discussed in the third and sixth essays of this volume. Because Serlio and Pozzo created the images for their own works they provide the more amenable vehicle for the analysis of illustration.

Prints, including those made for illustrated books, were commodities very much as photographs are here shown to have been. For example, proofs of the engraved plates for the *Vitruvius Britannicus* were circulated as an inducement to subscribe.[75] In the course of discussing photographs for art books as commodities, Holman reveals the cognitive shifts that they can effect. She shows how photographs of the *Gattamelata* taken for H. W. Janson's

The Sculpture of Donatello of 1957 created a viewing experience of the statue that Donatello cannot have intended. Her example of Malraux reproducing a photograph of Giotto's *The Raising of Lazarus* upside-down so that the image would not distract from the point he wished to make about the painting's sculptural effect reveals Malraux's awareness of how images in books can supply more information than that solicited by the text. In short, the revelations of the image working as a conduit of discourse in the first six essays below, and existing as a commodity in the last two, are interchangeable in that the earliest engravings for books were also commodities and the most recent ones remain conduits of discourse.

The issues raised by this book matter because the illustrated book was a main means of communication, and not only of design ideas. Some of the strategies described here, for instance Vasari's use of portraits as parallel texts, were also germane to other books on other subjects. This book redresses an imbalance by asserting the autonomous role of imagery. Our collection of essays starts to shed light – as far as possible in terms that would make sense to authors, publishers, engravers and photographers – on the dialogue between visual information and verbal reasoning in illustrated books.

Notes

1.   E. Panofksy, 'Artist, Scientist, Genius: Notes on the Renaissance *Dämmerung'* (1952), in *The Renaissance: Six Essays*, ed. W. K. Ferguson, New York 1962, pp. 121–82, esp. p. 140.

2.   W. M. Ivins, *Prints and Visual Communication*, London 1953, ch. II: 'The Road Block Broken – The Fifteenth Century', pp. 21–50, and ch. III: 'Symbolism and Syntax – A Rule of the Road – The Sixteenth Century', pp. 51–70, esp. p. 70.

3.   Ibid., ch. IV: 'The Tyranny of the Rule – The Seventeenth and Eighteenth Centuries', pp. 71–92, esp. p. 75.

4.   Ibid., p. 75.

5.   Ibid., pp. 93–180, esp. p. 93.

6.   E. Jussim, *Visual Communication and the Graphic Arts*, New York 1974, p. 1.

7.   A. Malraux, *Museum without Walls*, transl. (French into English) S. Gilbert, London 1949, p. 18.

8.   Jussim (as in n. 6), pp. 16–17.

9.   Ibid., pp. 9, 31.

10. W. M. Ivins, *How Prints Look: Photographs with a Commentary*, New York 1943, p. 148.

11. Jussim (as in n. 6), p. 4.

12. See D. Bland, *A History of Book Illustration*, Berkeley 1969, p. 144, on architecture as 'never far from the seventeenth century book'; on 'typographic architecture', see E. Coen Pirani, *Il libro illustrato italiano: secoli XVII–XVIII*, Rome 1956, p. 7. Architectural vocabulary in Italian-language bibliographical description includes 'antiporta', 'frontispizio' and 'fregio'.

13. J. Lewis, *Anatomy of Printing: The Influences of Art and History on its Design*, London 1970.

14. J. Demarcq, 'La Relation texte–image', in A. Zali ed., *L'Aventure des écritures: la page*, exh. cat. Paris 1999, pp. 163–88, esp. p. 169: 'La page, la lettre, l'image: une architecture'.

15. S. Samek Ludovici, *Arte del libro: tre secoli di storia del libro illustrato, dal Quattrocento al Seicento*, Milan 1974, p. 154: 'una storia del libro illustrato non può prescindere dalla storia dell'incisione'.

16. *Art and its Images: An Exhibition of Printed Books Containing Engraved Illustrations after Italian Painting*, ed. C. H. Lloyd with T. Ledger, Oxford 1975, 'Preface', pp. 3–4, esp. p. 3.

17. Ibid., 'Introduction', pp. 5–21; pp. 5–6 on photography; pp. 11, 22 n. 11 on the reproduction of Giotto, citing J. Ruskin, *Giotto and his Works in Padua*, London 1854, pp. 32–3.

18. Ibid. The earliest imprint therein considered is Rome 1473 (cat. 1, pp. 26–7), the latest Paris 1868 (cat. 12, pp. 48–51).

19. M. Melot, *L'Illustration: histoire d'un art*, Geneva 1984.

20. M. Camille, *Image on the Edge: The Margins of Medieval Art*, London 1994, ch. 1: 'Making Margins', pp. 11–52, ch. 4: 'In the Margins of the Court', pp. 99–127, ch. 5: 'In the Margins of the City', pp. 129–52, are all mainly on illustration.

21. M. Kemp, 'Temples of the Body and Temples of the Cosmos: Vision and Visualization in the Vesalian and Copernican Revolutions', in *Picturing Knowledge: Historical and Philosophical Problems Concerning the Use of Art in Science*, ed. B. S. Baigrie, Toronto 1996, pp. 40–85.

22   Baigrie, 'Introduction', in Baigrie (as in n. 21), p. xxii.

23. M. Rudwick, 'The Emergence of a Visual Language for Geological Science 1760–1840', *History of Science*, 14, 1976, pp. 149–95, esp. p. 150, cit. in D. Topper, 'Towards an Epistemology of Scientific Illustration', in *Picturing Knowledge* (as in n. 21), pp. 215–49, esp. p. 216.

24. B. M. Stafford, *Voyage into Substance: Art, Science, Nature and the Illustrated Travel Account*, Cambridge MA 1984, p. xx, cit. in Topper (as in n. 23), p. 218.

25. S. J. Gould, *Bully for Brontosaurus: Reflections in Natural History*, New York 1991, p. 171, cit. in Topper (as in n. 23), p. 215.

26. Topper (as in n. 23), p. 226.

27. On the relation between Piero's and Barbaro's treatises, see T. Frangenberg, 'Piero della Francesca's *De prospectiva pingendi* in the sixteenth century', in *Piero della Francesca tra arte e scienza*, ed. M. D. Emiliani and V. Curzi, Venice 1996, pp. 423–36, esp. pp. 428–35.

28. W. J. T. Mitchell, *Iconology: Image, Text, Ideology*, Chicago 1986, 'The Family of Images', pp. 9–14, esp. p. 10.

29. W. J. T. Mitchell, *Picture Theory*, University of Chicago 1994, ch. 1: 'A Pictorial Turn', pp. 1–39, esp. p. 15.

30. P. Wagner, *Reading Iconotexts: From Swift to the French Revolution*, London 1995, esp. p. 28.

31. H. E. Roberts ed., *Art History through the Camera's Lens*, Amsterdam 1995; G. A. Johnson ed., *Sculpture and Photography: Envisioning the Third Dimension*, Cambridge 1998.

32. W. B. MacGregor, 'The Authority of Prints: an Early Modern Perspective', *Art History*, XXII, 3, 1999, pp. 389–420.

33. Ibid., p. 404.

34. Ibid., pp. 407–9, esp. p. 409.

35. Leonardo da Vinci, *Trattato della pittura*, Naples: F. Ricciardi (a spese di N. and V. Rispoli) 1733 (British Library 561*.e.18, Biblioteca Vinciana Milan E.V.38, Biblioteca Nazionale di Napoli XXXV.G.11).

36. On the aquatint, see L. C. Hults, *The Print in the Western World: An Introductory History*, Madison 1996, pp. 305–10.

37. C. Hope, 'Historical Portraits in the "Lives" and in the Frescoes of Giorgio Vasari', in *Giorgio Vasari: tra decorazione ambientale e storiografia artistica*, Florence 1985, pp. 321–38.

38. S. Serlio, *Tutte l'opere*, Venice 1619, 'Libro Secondo della Prospettiva', fols 23r, 24r, 26r, 28r–36r; 'Libro Settimo', every odd page from 3 to 243, bar only [p. 219; sic, for] p. 209, is entirely given over to imagery.

39. S. Sebastián, 'La influencia de los modelos ornamentales de Serlio en Hispanoamerica', *Boletín del Centro de Investigaciones Históricas y Esteticas* (Caracas), VII, 1967, pp. 30–67.

40. R. Palmer, 'Adaptations of European Print Imagery in two Andean *Sillerías* of circa 1600', in *Raising the Eyebrow: John Onians and World Art Studies*, ed. L. Golden, Oxford 2001, pp. 229–52.

41. J. Onians, *Bearers of Meaning: The Classical Orders in Antiquity, the Middle Ages, and the Renaissance*, Princeton 1988, pp. 172–5.

42. R. Leppert, *Art and the Committed Eye: The Cultural Functions of Imagery*, Boulder 1996, p. 124.

43. A. Vesalius, *De humani corporis fabrica*, Basle 1543; 2nd edn Basle 1555; Leppert (as in n. 42), p. 123.

44. V. Hart and P. Hicks eds, *Paper Palaces: The Rise of the Renaissance Architectural Treatise*, New Haven 1998.

45. F. Haskell, *The Painful Birth of the Art Book*, London 1987, pp. 8–9.

46. Leppert (as in n. 42), pp. 132–3.

47. On G. B. Ferrari, *Hesperides sive de malorum aureorum cultura et usu*, Rome 1646, see O. Bonfait, 'La galleria degli Esperidi', in *Roma 1630: il trionfo del pennello*, exh. cat. Milan 1994, pp. 248–53; some engravings by Bloemaert are erroneously given to Greuter there.

48. F. Baldinucci, *Notizie dei professori del disegno da Cimabue in qua* (1681), ed. F. Ranalli, vol. IV, Florence 1846, 'Cornelio Bloemaert', pp. 596–601, esp. p. 599 on the *Aedes Barberinae* and *Hesperides*.

49. F. Baldinucci, *Cominciamento, e progresso dell'arte dell'intagliare in rame*, Florence 1686, 'Proemio', pp. i–viii, esp. p. i: 'Fra le arti, che hanno per padre il Disegno, alcuna forse non ve ne ha toltane l'Architetura, Pittura, e Scultura … la quale maggior diletto, ed utilità soglia arrecare agli studiosi, e dilettanti di sì nobile facoltà, che quella del Intaglio o siasi in rame, o pure in legno per la stampa'; p. 61–4, 'Vita di Cornelio Bloemaert'.

50. *Allgemeines Künstler-Lexikon* (hereafter *AKL*), Leipzig and Munich 1992–, vol. II, 1992, p. 511: 'Sein Werk ist stark beeinflußt von C. Bloemaert.'

51. See L. Salviucci Insolera, 'Le prime edizioni del Trattato', in A. Battisti ed., *Andrea Pozzo*, (1st edn 1996) Milan and Trent 1998, p. 209, for minutiae of the various engravers' respective contributions to Pozzo's *Perspectiva*.

52. *AKL, Bio-bibliographischer Index*, 10 vols, Munich and Leipzig 1999–2000, III, p. 761, dates Franceschini's activity from 1705; ibid., X, p. 226, dates Verkruys's from 1707.

53. E. Harris, *British Architectural Books and Writers 1556–1785*, Cambridge 1990, p. 34.

54. C. Campbell, *Vitruvius Britannicus or The British Architect*, vols I–II, London 1715 (repr. *Vitruvius Britannicus*, 4 vols, New York 1967–72, vol. I).

55. C. Campbell, *The Third Volume of Vitruvius Britannicus*, London 1725 (repr. as in n. 54, vol. I), 'prospects in Perspective' of Castle Howard (pp. 5–6), the Royal Hospital Greenwich (p. 4) 'from the Geometrical Plan and Elevation' and Wilton House (pp. 57–60). *Vitruvius Brittanicus* [sic], *Volume the Fourth … design'd by J. Badeslade and J. Roque*, London 1739 (repr. as in n. 54, vol. II), pls 13–14, 15–16, 17–18: Kiveton; 34: 'One of the Seats of the Duke of Dorset'; 40–42, 43–4: Bulstrode; 47–8, 49, 50: Belvoir Castle; 51–2: Averham Park; 53–4: Boghengieght; 55–6, 57–8: Wentworth; 59–60, 61–2: Exton Park; 65–6: Ham House; 69–70: Marston; 73–4: Heanton Satchville; 75–6: Four Oaks Hall; 77–8: Totteridge Park; 84–5: Southill; 86–7: Belton House; 92–3: Wokingham; 94–5: Mount Edgecumbe; 98–9: Totteridge; 100–101: Shardeloes; 102–3: Pilewell; 104–5: Tring; 106–7: Stanford Hall; 108–9: Ravenfield. On the bird's-eye view, see J. Harris, 'The Country House on Display: a Foreword', in *Vitruvius Britannicus*, repr. as in n. 54, I, pp. i–iv, esp. pp. ii–iii.

56. A. Hamber, 'The Use of Photography by Nineteenth-Century Art Historians', in Roberts (as in n. 31), pp. 89–123, esp. p. 110.

57. J. Ruskin, *The Stones of Venice*, London (1st edn 1851–53), 2nd edn, vol. I (1858), 'Preface', p. x.

58. Ibid., vol. III, London 1867, p. 169.

59. J. Snyder, 'Nineteenth Century Photography of Sculpture and the Rhetoric of Substitution', in Johnson (as in n. 31), pp. 21–35, esp. p. 23.

60. R. Lieberman, 'Thoughts of an Art Historian/Photographer on the Relationship of His Two Disciplines', in Roberts (as in n. 31), pp. 217–48, esp. p. 240.

61. *Art and its Images* (as in n. 16), p. 27.

62. J. Montagu, 'The "Ruland/Raphael Collection"', in Roberts (as in n. 31), pp. 37–58, esp. p. 40.

63. Ibid., p. 43 and fig. 4.

64. Ibid., p. 40.

65. See E. H. Gombrich, 'Raphael's *Stanza della Segnatura* and the Nature of its Symbolism', in his *Symbolic Images*, New York 1972, pp. 85–101, esp. pp. 85–6.

66. W. Benjamin, 'The Work of Art in the Age of Mechanical Reproduction' (1936), in his *Illuminations*, ed. and transl. H. Arendt, New York 1968, pp. 217–51, esp. pp. 224, 243.

67. N. Lynton, 'Portraits from a Pluralist Century', in *Painting the Century: 101 Portrait Masterpieces 1900–2000*, exh. cat. London 2000, pp. 7–47, esp. p. 46 n. 13.

68. J. Hillis Miller, *Illustration*, London 1992, p. 22.

69. C. H. Smyth, *Mannerism and Maniera* (1962), Vienna 1991, on diversity in *maniera* painting: 'But in black and white reproductions diversity is partly suppressed, because colour so often plays a role in it. Colour in *Maniera* still needs to be properly valued and explored.'

70. A. Gell, *Art and Agency: An Anthropological Theory*, Oxford 1998.

71. G. Dillon, 'Prefazione/Preface', in *L'istoriato: libri a stampa e maioliche italiane del Cinquecento*, exh. cat. Biblioteca Apostolica Vaticana, Faenza 1993, pp. 7–8, 9–10, esp. p. 9.

72. Dillon (as in n. 71), p. 9.

73. J. Nadal, *Evangelicae historiae imagines*, Plantin, Antwerp 1593; *Adnotationes et meditationes in Evangelia*, Plantin, Antwerp 1596. See U. Thieme and F. Becker, *Allgemeines Lexikon der bildenden Künstler*, 37 vols, Leipzig 1907–50, XXXV, pp. 537–8, on the Wierix brothers Anton (1552–?1624), Hieronymus (1553–1629) and Jan (1549–1615). Anton Wierix cut 58 plates, Hieronymus 26, and Jan engraved 17 plates. A further 21 were shared between the brothers Adriaen and Jan Collaert (Antwerp 1560–1618, 1566–1628 respectively, *AKL*, as in n. 50, vol. XX, 1998, pp. 272–3), and Karel van Mallery (Antwerp 1571 – after 1635, *AKL, Bio-bibliographischer Index* (as in n. 52), IV, 2000, p. 287).

74. On these engravings and the texts they generated see P.-A. Fabre, 'La Légende, cadre ou marge? Voire/lire les Evangelicae Historiae Imagines' in *Cadres et marges*, ed. B. Rougé, Paris 1995, pp. 45–51; P. Rheinbay, 'Nadal's Religious Iconography Reinterpreted by Aleni for China', in *"Scholar from the West": Giulio Aleni S.J. (1582–1619) and the Dialogue between Christianity and China*, ed. T. Lippiello and R. Malek, Brescia and Sankt Augustin 1995, pp. 323–31, esp. p. 324.

75. Harris (as in n. 53), p. 140.

1

Seventeenth-century illustrations for the chapters on motion in Leonardo's *Trattato*

Juliana Barone

The difficulties in assessing the reception of theoretical ideas include not only the complexities of perception and comprehension at work in the period being studied, but also (unavoidably) those of our contemporary perspective. However, a key to understanding how Leonardo's ideas were 'seen' in the seventeenth century is provided by two sets of illustrations of the human figure in editions of his *Trattato della pittura*. In fact, variations in the contemporary sets of illustrations supplied respectively by Nicolas Poussin (1594–1665) and Stefano della Bella (1610–64) provide clear and first-hand evidence of profoundly different interpretations of Leonardo, evidence that has been largely ignored up to now.

An 'official' view of Leonardo's ideas was established by the *editio princeps* of his *Trattato*, published in Paris in 1651 by Raphaël Trichet Du Fresne, which contains a set of engravings of (in some respects revised) copies by Charles Errard after a set of drawings by Nicolas Poussin (see Figures 1.1, 1.2).[1] Aspects of this 'official' view were questioned at the time, but an explicitly different view was to be offered only with the 1792 edition of the *Trattato*, published in Florence by Francesco Fontani. According to Fontani, his edition was much closer to Leonardo's theory of painting than the *editio princeps*. Fontani's edition, published under the title *Leonardo ridotto alla sua vera lezione*,[2] brought to light a little-known interpretation of Leonardo (see Figure 1.3), that of Stefano della Bella (see Figure 1.4). Despite Fontani's edition, however, it was not until the beginning of the nineteenth century, with the edition printed by Guglielmo Manzi in 1817 of the Codex Urbinas Latinus 1270[3] that the 'official' view of Leonardo established in 1651 was made obsolete.

In this essay I will look at the two seventeenth-century interpretations of Leonardo, by Poussin and Stefano, and focus on their respective sets of illustrations of the human figure for chapters excerpted from Book Three of the Codex Urbinas,[4] a text compiled from Leonardo's original manuscripts soon after the artist's death. The abridged version of the Codex Urbinas, commonly referred to as Leonardo's *Trattato*, was compiled later in the sixteenth century, and was in circulation in manuscript copies, some of which contain illustrations based on those in the Codex Urbinas.[5] Many of the sections transcribed from Book Three of the Urbinas deal extensively with human motion.

My enquiry aims primarily to shed light on the discrepancies between their respective visual interpretations of Leonardo's analyses of figures in motion, but also seeks to reassess the value of these illustrations of the human figure in the *Trattato* as visual demonstrations of his theoretical principles. Unlike many others of Leonardo's scientific illustrations, the illustrations of the human figure have not usually been considered in close relationship with the text. Yet a comparison of Poussin's and Stefano's approaches to illustrating the *Trattato* text reveals that they responded to the text in different ways. The different degrees to which the two sets of illustrations conform with the text convey meaning; they allow us to assess the different messages the sets were intended to convey. A common reference point for the examination of Poussin's and Stefano's illustrations is provided by the Codex Urbinas, which was the prototype for all copies of the abridged *Trattato*.

Of the two sets of illustrations, Poussin's is by far the better known. The correspondence between Cassiano dal Pozzo and Galeazzo Arconato reveals the former's efforts to acquire an accurate text of Leonardo's *Trattato*, which, once obtained, was to be illustrated by Poussin.[6] In a letter to Abraham Bosse, Poussin clarifies the extent to which he participated in the illustrations; his contribution was limited to the human figures.[7] Poussin's original drawings are currently believed to be those pasted in the manuscript H 228 inf., now in the Biblioteca Ambrosiana in Milan, and were probably executed around 1635.[8] The most likely copy of the *Trattato* to have served as Poussin's source is the Codex Barberinus 4304,[9] one of the manuscript copies derived from the Urbinas.

Some preliminary questions need to be addressed before embarking on an examination of the two sets of illustrations. The first concerns the authorship of the illustrations in the MS Riccardianus 2275 in the Biblioteca Riccardiana in Florence,[10] which was used for Fontani's edition. None of the accounts of Stefano della Bella, from the seventeenth to the early twentieth century, makes any reference to a copy by him of the *Trattato*.[11] However, there are positive indications within the manuscript supporting an attribution to della Bella, such as the watermark (a sun with eight rays), which is similar to those found in some of Stefano's Florentine drawings,[12] and, even more telling, the monogram on the manuscript's title page. The letters 'SDB', with the 'D' intertwined with the other two letters, correspond exactly to monograms found in a large number of della Bella's works.[13]

The purpose of Stefano's copy is uncertain. No commission for it is known and there is no dedication or any other evidence to suggest a patron. The most likely hypothesis is that Stefano both transcribed and illustrated the *Trattato* for his own use.[14] This is consistent with the date of the manuscript, 1630, which places it in Stefano's early period,[15] when he had just begun his career as an independent artist and was still seeking patronage, and with the fact that other artists in Florence at the time, such as Francesco Furini, were also making copies of the *Trattato* for their own use.[16] Regarding the *Trattato* copy Stefano used as his source, it has been suggested that it was the Pinellianus D 467. This is, however, questionable, since it is highly unlikely that della Bella had access to the Pinellianus manuscript.[17] So far, there is no conclusive evidence as to the copy he employed, but, as the copies then in circulation were all derived from an abridged version of the Urbinas, the one that Stefano used must have been very similar to Poussin's source.

Given that Poussin's and Stefano's sets of illustrations were produced almost at the same time and are derived from very similar versions of the *Trattato*, the question arises why the sets show markedly different interpretations of Leonardo's theoretical principles. It could be argued that these differences result from differences in purpose: Poussin's set was commissioned and designed for publication, whereas Stefano's was not. However, it will here be suggested that this only partially explains the two sets' very different interpretations of Leonardo's ideas on motion. In order to throw light on this issue, I will address Leonardo's concept of motion and examine the text–image relationship in Poussin's and Stefano's manuscripts; then I will consider the likely reasons for, and implications of, these two artists' respective approaches to Leonardo.

The issue of motion is frequently addressed in Leonardo's writings, in contexts ranging from shadows on moving objects to the investigation of the human body.[18] In particular, the topic of human motion is, as has been pointed out, extensively dealt with in Book Three of the Codex Urbinas, numerous chapters of which were transcribed in the abridged *Trattato*. Leonardo explains that there are three kinds of motion: *moto locale* (local motion), which is 'da loco a loco', that is, from one location to another; *moto azzionale* (motion of action), which is 'in se medesimo senza mutazione di loco', that is, motion within the figure, without change in location; and *moto composto d'azzionale col locale* (compound motion), which is a combination of both.[19] Later on, Leonardo discusses *moto locale*, of which he distinguishes nine kinds. For *moto azzionale* and *composto* he gives examples and also makes clear that he considers these types of movement infinite.[20] Movements during the course of a single event are infinitely varied because they occur in space, and space is infinitely divisible. Leonardo considers motion to be a *quantità continua* (continuous quantity).[21]

A typical illustration of this idea can be seen in Leonardo's sketch of a 'hammering man' on a sheet at Windsor Castle (Figure 1.5).[22] The quick sequence of the actions of the man, either raising or bringing down his hammer, suggests the course of movement in space and successfully conveys Leonardo's idea of motion as a dynamic and continuous process. A close parallel can be seen between this drawing and the vivid little figures in the Urbinas, which seem to take into account both the text and the drawings of Leonardo's manuscripts. For instance, the two lively figures in the Urbinas illustration for a chapter on powerful movements (CU 278) suggest the kinds of motion referred to by Leonardo in Book Three (see Figure 1.6). This illustration shows a first figure in the initial position of the movement (a), about to throw a spear, and its contained, potential motion implies a subsequent change in location and therefore a movement in space that is about to be completed in the second figure (b). The combination of the figures' *moto azzionale* and *moto locale* results in *moto composto*.

The question of motion occupies a prominent place in most of Leonardo's drawings. It can be traced back to his earliest studies such as, for example, the *recto* and *verso* of the sheet *A Child with a cat* in the British Museum.[23] Both the rapid drawing and the apparent indifference to neatness contribute to the impression of the instability of the figures' poses and suggest their potential motion. But it is in Leonardo's later drawings, from those for *The Battle of Anghiari* onwards, that he specifically addresses the question of the body and imminent motion. A striking example is the well-known study of *The Rearing Horse*, also at Windsor.[24] The *pentimenti* of its head (turned up, or flung back, or turned forward) and those of its chest and legs have been seen as part of Leonardo's search for its pose; however, they can also be viewed as an attempt graphically to convey the motion of the horse in its full dynamism. With regard to the human figure, the emphasis on the rendering of movement can be clearly noticed in the figures in action at the bottom of another sheet for *The Battle of Anghiari* (see Figure 1.7).[25] The two foreground figures on the left suggest either two consecutive stages of a single movement (in a way comparable to the hammering man sketch), or two similar movements by two different men; whichever is the case, both imply the ideas of potential and actual motion in space. So also do the figures in the middle ground; yet in this case it is not a sequence of poses (or a possible sequence) that evokes movement. It is mostly the figures' forceful twisting and bending – the disruption of their balance – that visually demonstrates Leonardo's ideas on motion and dynamism. Similarly, in the Urbinas illustrations in which the figures do not imply a sequence of poses, as in the chapter showing two figures demonstrating two different types of movement (CU 279), it is through the disruption of balance that Leonardo's sense of the kinetics of the human body is conveyed (see Figure 1.8).

Nicolas Poussin's set of illustrations for Leonardo's chapters on motion does not entirely match the *Trattato* text and differs significantly from the illustrations offered in the Urbinas and in Stefano della Bella's manuscript. The most immediately obvious difference is the number of figures that Poussin provides. Although his figures cover most of the examples referred to in the text, and illustrated in the Urbinas and by Stefano, there are some telling divergences. For instance, in the section where three figures are referred to in the text (H 228 197.196; CU 306; Ricc 201), and illustrated in the Urbinas and in Stefano's manuscript, Poussin reduces them to just two, both of them now showing more balanced poses; the third figure, exemplifying an unstable pose, is missing. Similarly, he does not provide any illustration for the section on the forceful bending and lateral twisting of the body (H 228 204; CU 313; Ricc 208), which explicitly and uniquely describes the contrast in the heights of the limbs, and which is illustrated in the Urbinas and in Stefano's set. Neither does Poussin provide two figures to show the contrast between the initial and final positions of a forceful motion (H 228 181; CU 278; Ricc 185), analysed in the text and again illustrated in the Urbinas (see Figure 1.6) and in Stefano's set. On the other hand, he does provide illustrations – for which no precedents exist in any copy of the abridged *Trattato* – for two sections on the equilibrium of stationary figures (H 228 201, 203; CU 310, 312; Ricc 205, 207), one of which is illustrated here (Figure 1.9). Poussin tended to ignore chapters dealing with unstable or contrasting poses, and favoured instead those that addressed static and decorous ones. Poussin's omissions underline the visual message he wanted his set of illustrations to convey.

Even when Poussin does not alter the number of figures or illustrations, the way he depicts the poses of the figures is indicative of the visual message of his set. A case in point is his illustration for one of the sections on violent motion (H 228 182; CU 279; Ricc 186) (see Figure 1.2). Although in this case Poussin does depict two figures to exemplify two different types of movements, so that the figures conform in number to those referred to in Leonardo's text, he clearly reduces their imbalance. He eliminates the figures' forceful bending and twisting, mentioned in the text and illustrated in the Urbinas (see Figure 1.8) and in Stefano's manuscript (see Figure 1.4), and reduces the impression that it is the powerful disruption of equilibrium that generates motion. Consequently, Poussin's figures lack any sense of potential motion and inherent dynamism. Instead, they give the idea of a frozen instant within motion, a suspended pause. The continuous quality of Leonardo's motion is rendered discontinuous in Poussin's figures, making them differ in essence from what is stated in the *Trattato*.

Stefano's illustrations are closer than Poussin's to the *Trattato*'s analysis of motion. Della Bella does not make changes to the number of individual figures, nor does he introduce significant alterations in the poses. A case in point is his illustration for the chapter on powerful movements, which deals with the contrast between the initial and final positions of a figure (Ricc 185). Stefano, following the *Trattato* text but unlike Poussin, does depict the two positions, even though they refer to the motion of one figure only. The first figure, clearly twisted to the left, evokes both the initial and a potential motion; the second one, leaning to the right, away from its centre of gravity, leads towards the final position and suggests that movement has occurred in space.

The same holds for della Bella's illustration for another chapter on violent motion, in which two figures illustrate two different types of movement (Ricc 186) (see Figure 1.4). Unlike Poussin's restriction of their poses (see Figure 1.2), Stefano's figures very much demonstrate their instability, their forceful twisting and bending, suggesting potential motion in space in a way similar to the Urbinas figures (see Figure 1.8). Throughout Stefano's manuscript, his figures illustrate the disruption of balance – which according to Leonardo is the mark of and condition for a powerful movement – and della Bella's set of illustrations thus accords with the *Trattato*.

The divergence which emerges from an examination of Poussin's and Stefano's illustrations is not a merely extrinsic one, due to the adaptation or otherwise of the figures for publication, but rather it rests on a fundamental difference in the two artists' interpretations of the concept of motion. While in Stefano's manuscript there is accordance with the *Trattato*'s concerns, in Poussin's there is a disjunction, which is unlikely to have occurred by chance. Poussin's figures, rather than rendering the kinetics of the human body, are characteristically immobile, statuesque.

The disjunction between text and illustration in Poussin's set and his break with Leonardo's logic of the movement of the human body raise the question of what his illustrations are based on, and of whether, besides the *Trattato* itself, there might have been other sources for his illustrations of the human figure. It is well known that the antique played a central role in Poussin's art, particularly in the 1630s, the period during which he worked on the *Trattato* illustrations. Therefore it is unsurprising that his response to the antique can be recognized in his *Trattato* illustrations (see Figure 1.9), which a number of scholars have associated with two antique sculptures: the Farnese *Hercules* and the Belvedere *Antinous*.[26] Similarities are apparent in visual terms, and there is early evidence that Poussin was familiar with these statues. A sketchbook[27] shows that he was involved in taking measurements of the Belvedere *Antinous*,[28] and some of his paintings, such as *The Choice of Hercules between Vice and Virtue*,[29] reveal a close borrowing from the Farnese *Hercules*.[30] The role of the antique in Poussin's illustrations becomes even clearer when we consider how he dealt with his sources.

Poussin's work on the *Trattato* illustrations involves a process of *electio* (selection). This manifests itself in his choices of the passages to illustrate, of the figures to depict, of the poses of these figures and of his antique models.[31] Apart from the *Hercules* and *Antinous*, Poussin also seems to have utilized other antique sculptures present in Rome in the seventeenth century as models. The group of *Castor and Pollux*, now in the Prado,[32] for example, might have provided a model for his two-figure composition (the illustration in the Codex Urbinas is made up of three) for a passage on balance (H 228 197.196); in particular, the left-hand figure closely resembles the figure on the left in Poussin's illustration.[33] The Borghese *Gladiator*, prominently displayed in Rome following its excavation in 1611,[34] also seems to have provided Poussin with references. The pose of this statue (especially that of the legs) comes to mind when we look at two of Poussin's figures in the act of throwing a spear (H 228 182; 261), and at one of his figures in the act of swinging a club (H 228 181), although yet again Poussin attenuates the dynamism of his likely source. In instances where the *Hercules* and *Antinous* statues could not offer a model for the poses in Poussin's illustrations, he looked at other antique statues, readjusting them to conform with the proportions of the *Antinous*, so as to guarantee a sense of unity across his illustrations.

Poussin's process of *electio* accords with his working methods at the time. His mythological and religious paintings of the 1630s and 1640s show his tendency to move from sixteenth- and seventeenth-century variants to antique sources while working on a painting. This is, for example, the case with his likely use as sources of both Raphael's *Judgement of Paris* (known to us from a Raimondi engraving) and of a Roman sarcophagus illustrating the judgement of Paris for his *Apollo and the Chariot of Phaeton*; and, to give another example, with his indebtedness to both Guercino's *Arcadian Shepherds* and a Hellenistic cameo of Minerva in dispute with Neptune for his *Arcadian Shepherds* in the Louvre.[35] This tendency to move from variants back to antique sources can also be found in Poussin's *Trattato* illustrations. There are, however, differences. Whereas the sixteenth- and seventeenth-century sources of his paintings might themselves have been indebted to ancient compositions, the same is not likely to be true of Leonardo's original illustrations. Poussin's reinterpretation of the illustrations in terms of ancient models therefore creates a gap between image and text. In reinterpreting the illustrations to conform to classical taste, he undermines their function as illustrations.

Such a disjunction between image and text does not exist in Stefano della Bella's set of illustrations, nor does he introduce references extrinsic to the text. Moreover, a concurrence with Leonardo's ideas is favoured by the graphic style of Stefano's illustrations. His tiny, vividly alive figures, rapidly delineated by a spirited outline, retain Leonardo's sense of inherent dynamism of the human body and greatly contrast with Poussin's figures, modelled with broad washes that indicate their solid sculptural quality. This difference in technique is not primarily due to the fact that Stefano's set of drawings, unlike Poussin's, was not commissioned or intended for publication. Rather, the differences between Poussin's and Stefano's illustrations are largely due to qualities inherent in their respective styles.

Some drawings attributed or closely related to Poussin and not intended for publication show a technique similar to that of his *Trattato* illustrations. A case in point is the drawing of Castor and Pollux (see Figure 1.10),[36] which reveals graphic qualities analogous to those of his illustrations and a comparable degree of finish. Several compositional studies of the 1630s, such as those for *The Adoration of the Magi*, *The Saving of the Young Pyrrhus* and *The Rape of the Sabines*,[37] support this observation. Even though these drawings are less highly finished than the *Trattato* illustrations, the washes indicate the sculptural quality of the figures and serve to arrest their poses in a frozen moment. The static quality of Poussin's *Trattato* illustrations is not exclusive to this set, but rather was an aspect of his style at the time.

Stefano's illustrations likewise conform to his own graphic style and they, too, are best understood in the broader context of his work. The sense of the dynamics of motion evoked in his *Trattato* illustrations is traceable in a significant number of his drawings, which, in their turn, also evoke Leonardo's ideas and graphic modes for representing movement. Della Bella's *Holy Family with the lamb* drawing,[38] for example, not only conjures up Leonardo's Madonna studies, and particularly those of the *Madonna with St Anne*,[39] but also shows that Stefano is thinking about the relation of the figures in terms of the dynamics of their forms. The constant redrawing of their outlines and the dense pen work communicate the inherent kinetics of the bodies. Also, in his drawing *Boy with a lamb* (Figure 1.11),[40] the innumerable, successive *pentimenti* of the lamb's legs and head and of the boy's legs combine to convey the group's self-generating dynamism. To give two further examples, in the drawing *Horseman with a sword*,[41] the rapidity with which the group is drawn and the different positions of the horseman's arm and sword express a comparable sense of dynamism, as does the rapid drawing *Galloping horseman* (Figure 1.12).[42] In the latter, even without either dense pen work or successive *pentimenti*, a similar kinetic effect is achieved through a spirited outline and through the position of the figures. The extreme positioning of the horseman out of his centre of gravity, and in the opposite direction to the horse's movement, is in accordance with Leonardo's principle of motion based on the dynamics of action and compensatory reaction, either within the same figure or within the composition.

The divergence in the visual messages of these two sets of illustrations rests on different interpretations of Leonardo's concept of motion, to which variations in the figures and in the type of poses selected in each set contribute significantly. In Poussin's illustrations, movement becomes a matter of rhetorical motion rather than of real dynamism, while in Stefano's case movement conveys a sense of the kinetics of the human body. While the former sought a reference (the antique) outside the *Trattato*, any outside references della Bella brought into his set of *Trattato* illustrations were adapted from Leonardo's principles of movement. That is not to say that Stefano's illustrations are not reinterpretations as well, or that Poussin, in his turn, was not influenced by Leonardo.[43] The point is that their approaches and visual responses to Leonardo were notably different, and that Stefano's *Trattato* illustrations accord much more closely with Leonardo's principle of human motion than do those by Poussin.

As we have seen, it was Poussin's interpretation that served as the basis for the *Trattato's editio princeps*, published in Paris in 1651 (see Figure 1.1). This edition, which came out in Roland Fréart de Chambray's French translation in the same year, became the 'official' and primary form in which Leonardo's theoretical ideas were made available in the seventeenth century. By contrast, Stefano's interpretation was not to be made public until 1792, in the edition published in Florence by Francesco Fontani (see Figure 1.3).

Clues to the choices of visual messages offered in these editions emerge from their prefaces. In Chambray's edition in French, the approval of Poussin's interpretation of Leonardo is clear. He posits that his edition of the *Trattato* had two 'pères', Leonardo and Poussin, and that the latter was responsible for bringing to light 'la partie la plus essentielle' of the treatise, which would otherwise have been unintelligible.[44] In Du Fresne's preface to the edition in Italian, too, attention is drawn to the role played by Poussin; one of Du Fresne's main points of interest is the antique, a preference which indexes both approval for Poussin's interpretation and the artistic values of the time. Du Fresne not only recalls the 'beauty of both Romes' ('bellezze dell'una e dell'altra Roma') and the contemporary that 'would have brought Rome to Paris' ('havrebbe portare Roma a Parigi') but he also draws attention to what he calls the attempt 'to have restored' ('di haver restituito') Leonardo's *Trattato* 'to its original purity' ('alla sua prima purità').[45] We should remember that this attempt, in visual terms, relied on Poussin's illustrations as redrawn by Charles Errard, whose taste for the antique prompted Du Fresne to comment that 'the soul of one of the earliest masters had transmigrated to him' ('fusse passata in lui l'anima di qualch'uno di quei primi maestri').[46] Du Fresne thus confirmed that Leonardo was to be approached via the antique. Even though there are some differences between Poussin's and Errard's illustrations,[47] Poussin's visual message regarding Leonardo's concept of human motion is taken up and consolidated in the 1651 edition.

Against this 'official' view of Leonardo, the 1792 edition was brought to light with the title *Leonardo da Vinci ridotto alla sua vera lezione*, as we have seen. In his preface, Fontani claimed that his edition presented Leonardo's principles more faithfully than did the edition of 1651. His claim was mostly based on the supposedly more accurate text he was offering, which, in fact, is not very different from that of 1651.[48] His emphasis on the text can be understood as an expression of his philological interests;[49] it is via his appraisal of this version of Leonardo's text that Fontani comes to praise Stefano's illustrations. Fontani's claim for the greater accuracy of his text was based on the fact that it had been transcribed by the '*rinomato* Stefano della Bella', who had also furnished it 'with small figures in his manner, thus in a way making practice of the precepts he so rightfully admired'.[50] Fontani also drew attention to the fidelity and precision with which Stefano's drawings had been interpreted and engraved for the printed edition (see Figures 1.3 and 1.4), by della Bella's admirer, 'our' painter Giuseppe Fabbrini, almost certainly the Florentine Giuseppe Antonio Fabbrini.[51] Fontani was the first to make Stefano's visual message widely available, and thus to disseminate a visual interpretation of Leonardo much closer to the text of the abridged *Trattato* and to Leonardo's original illustrations copied in the Codex Urbinas than was the 'official' one, which since its publication had eclipsed other visions of Leonardo's text.

The point, however, is less to ask whether there is a 'vera lezione' than to show that there are different 'lezioni'. To perceive and reassess contemporary – but different – interpretations of Leonardo in the seventeenth century helps to disclose aspects of the reception of his theoretical ideas that are frequently overlooked, and to give valuable insights into seventeenth-century attitudes. Poussin's and Stefano's contrasting illustrations are not only consistent with qualities inherent in the art of these two artists, but also offer insights into wider issues germane to the milieu in which their respective interpretations of Leonardo were appreciated or disregarded. In other words, there was a pluralistic picture of Leonardo, and if one were to rephrase the claim 'Leonardo da Vinci ridotto alla sua vera lezione', one could say that through both Poussin's and Stefano's illustrations for the *Trattato*, Leonardo was condensed into two seventeenth-century 'lezioni' – both of which are crucial to our understanding of how he was 'seen' at that time.

Acknowledgements

A short version of this paper appeared in the *Gazette des Beaux-Arts*, CXXXVIII, 2001, pp. 1–14. Some of the material presented here was considered in my doctoral thesis at Oxford University, 'Leonardo on motion: seventeenth-century views'.

I am very grateful to my supervisor, Professor Martin Kemp, for his support and perceptive comments. The illustrations were partly funded by a grant from the Graduate Committee of Oxford University.

Notes

1. R. Trichet Du Fresne ed., *Trattato della pittura di Lionardo da Vinci, novamente dato in luce, con la vita dell'istesso autore ...* , Paris 1651; R. Fréart, Sieur de Chambray, transl. and ed., *Traitté de la peinture de Leonard de Vinci donné au public et traduit d'italien en françois par R. F. S. D. C.*, Paris 1651. Drawings by Charles Errard based on Poussin's with the addition of landscape backgrounds, served as models for the engravings, executed by René Lochon, in the *editio princeps*.

2. A literal translation could be 'Leonardo reduced to his true reading', but 'a correct reading of Leonardo' comes closer to the meaning of the Italian title; see F. Fontani ed., *Trattato della pittura di Lionardo da Vinci ridotto alla sua vera lezione sopra una copia a penna di mano di Stefano della Bella con le figure disegnate dal medesimo*, Florence 1792.

3. The manuscript is housed in Rome, Biblioteca Vaticana. The existence of the Codex Urbinas was first reported in an inventory of the books of the Della Rovere in Castel Durante, at the time of the death of Francesco Maria, last duke of Urbino, in 1631. As part of the bequest of Francesco Maria's library to Urban VIII, the Urbinas was transferred to the Vatican in 1657, during the pontificate of Alexander VII, where it remained ignored until around 1797, the year in which it was given the catalogue number 1270 by the librarian Guglielmo Manzi. Since then this manuscript has been called 'Codex Urbinas Latinus 1270' and considered the earliest and most complete version of Leonardo's notes on painting. The chapters of this manuscript are not numbered; the numeration in this essay follows that proposed by Pedretti and Vecce (as in n. 5, below).

4. The title of this Book as in the Codex Urbinas Latinus 1270, fol. 103r, is 'Comincia dei vari accidenti et movimenti de l'uomo'. An additional part of this title, not here transcribed, was crossed out in the manuscript and the following words were added to the original title: 'et proportione di membra'.

5. For the Urbinas and its abridged copies, see C. Pedretti, *Leonardo da Vinci on Painting: A Lost Book (Libro A)*, Berkeley and Los Angeles 1964; idem, 'Belt 35: A New Chapter in the History of Leonardo's Treatise on Painting', in *Leonardo's Legacy* (International Symposium, Los Angeles 1966), ed. C. D. O'Malley, Berkeley and Los Angeles 1969, pp. 149–70, and *The Literary Works of Leonardo da Vinci Compiled and Edited from the Original Manuscripts by Jean Paul Richter. Commentary by Carlo Pedretti*, 2 vols, Oxford 1977, I, pp. 12–31; and C. Pedretti and C. Vecce, *Leonardo da Vinci: Libro di pittura*, 2 vols, Florence 1995, I, pp. 11–82. The manuscript will hereafter be referred to as Urbinas (in text references) or 'CU' in references to specific chapters.

6. The Dal Pozzo–Arconato correspondence was published by E. Carusi, 'Lettere di Galeazzo Arconato e Cassiano dal Pozzo per lavori sui manoscritti di Leonardo da Vinci', *Accademie e Biblioteche d'Italia*, III, 1930, pp. 503–18 (reprinted by K. T. Steinitz in *Leonardo da Vinci's Trattato della Pittura: A Bibliography of the Printed Editions 1651–1956*, Copenhagen 1958, pp. 218–29).

7. The letter was published by A. Bosse in *Traité des pratiques géométrales et perspective enseignées dans l'Académie Royale de Peinture et Sculpture*, Paris 1665; pp. 128–9.

8. This manuscript will hereafter be referred to as 'H 228'. For the identification of Poussin's original set, see A. Blunt, *The French Drawings in the Collection of His Majesty the King at Windsor Castle*, Oxford and London 1945, pp. 48–9; K. T. Steinitz, 'Poussin illustrateur de Léonard de Vinci et le problème des répliques de l'atelier de Poussin', in *L'Art et la Pensée de Léonard de Vinci* (Congrès International, Val de Loire 1952), Paris and Algiers 1953–54, pp. 339–60 (published in English in *The Art Quarterly*, XVI, 1953, pp. 40–55); T. D. Kamenskaya, 'K voprosu o rukopisi "Traktata o zivopisi" Leonardo da Vinci i jeje illustracjach v sobranii Ermitaza', *Trudy Gosudarstvennogo Ermitaza*, I, 1956, pp. 48–59 (English résumé by J. Białostocki, 'Recent Research: Russia II', *Burlington Magazine*, XCIX, 1957, pp. 421–5, esp. p. 425); Steinitz (as in n. 6), p. 76, and 'Trattato Studies II', *Raccolta Vinciana*, XIX, 1962, pp. 223–54; T.D. Kamenskaya, 'Le

Manuscrit du "Traité de la peinture" de Léonard de Vinci au Musée de l'Ermitage', *Raccolta Vinciana*, XIX, 1962, pp. 255–8; K. T. Steinitz, 'Early Art Bibliographies: Who Compiled the First Art Bibliography?', *Burlington Magazine*, CXIV, 1972, pp. 829–37, esp. p. 830; and W. Friedlaender and A. Blunt, 'The Illustrations to Leonardo da Vinci's *Trattato della Pittura*', in their *The Drawings of Nicolas Poussin: Catalogue Raisonné*, 5 vols, London 1963, IV, pp. 26–33, 204–10. For the dating of Poussin's set, see Blunt (as above), p. 49; J. Białostocki, 'Poussin et le "Traité de la Peinture" de Léonard: notes sur l'état de la question', in *Nicolas Poussin* (C.N.R.S., Colloques internationaux, Sciences humaines, Paris 1958), ed. A. Chastel, 2 vols, Paris 1960, I, pp. 133–40, esp. p. 137; Friedlaender and Blunt (as above), p. 26; and J. Bell, 'Cassiano dal Pozzo's Copy of the Zaccolini Manuscripts', *Journal of the Warburg and Courtauld Institutes*, LI, 1988, pp. 103–25, esp. p. 117.

9. See Białostocki, 'Poussin et le "Traité"' (as in n. 8), p. 137; Friedlaender and Blunt (as in n. 8), p. 26; and A. Félibien, 'Vie de Poussin', in *Vies de Poussin*, ed. S. Germer, Paris 1994, pp. 151–265, esp. p. 166.

10. This manuscript will hereafter be referred to as 'Ricc'.

11. See F. Baldinucci, 'Stefano della Bella', in Baldinucci's *Notizie dei professori del disegno da Cimabue in qua*, ed. F. Ranalli, 7 vols, Florence, 1845–47, repr. 1974–75, IV, pp. 602–19; J. von Sandrart, *Academia nobilissimae artis pictoriae*, Nuremberg 1683, ch. XXIII, p. 197, and ch. XXV, p. 359; A. Félibien, 'Septième Entretien', in his *Entretiens sur les vies et sur les ouvrages des plus excellens peintres anciens et modernes; avec la vie des architectes*, 6 vols, Trevoux 1725, III, pp. 385–7; F. Le Comte, 'Catalogue d'Etienne de la Belle Florentin', in his *Cabinet des Singularitez d'architecture, peinture, sculpture et gravure. Ou introduction à la connoissance des plus Beaux Arts, figurés sous les Tableaux, les Statues & les Estampes*, 3 vols, Brussels 1702, II, pp. 393–406; P. J. Mariette, 'Della Bella (Stefano)', in *Abécédario et autres notes inédites de cet amateur sur les arts et les artistes*, ed. Ph. De Chennevières and A. De Montaiglon, 6 vols, Paris 1851–60, II, pp. 68–85; C.-A. Jombert, *Essai d'un catalogue de l'oeuvre d'Etienne de la Belle, peintre et graveur florentin. Disposé par ordre historique suivant l'année où chaque pièce a été gravée. Avec la vie de cet Artiste, traduite de l'Italien, & enrichie de notes*, Paris 1772; M. Faucheux, 'François Langlois, dit de Chartres', *Revue universelle des arts*, VI, 1857, pp. 314–30, esp. pp. 321–8 (in part republished in A. De Vesme with introduction and additions by P. Dearborn Massar, *Stefano della Bella: Catalogue Raisonné*, 2 vols, New York 1971, text vol., pp. 34–6); and A. De Vesme, 'Etienne Della Bella', in de Vesme's *Le Peintre-graveur italien*, Milan 1906, pp. 66–332.

12. For the watermarks in Stefano's drawings, see T. Ortolani, *Stefano della Bella: aggiornamento del catalogue raisonné di A. De Vesme e Ph. D. Massar*, Milan 1996, pp. 100–1.

13. Stefano's monogram can be seen, for instance, on the bottom right of the etching serving as the frontispiece of A. Cavalcanti's *Esequie del Serenissimo Principe Francesco celebrate in Fiorenza il dì 30 d'Agosto 1634*, Florence 1634. See A. Forlani Tempesti, *Stefano della Bella: incisioni scelte e annotate*, Florence 1972, repr. 1983, no. IX, n.p., and *Mostra di incisioni di Stefano della Bella*, exh. cat. Florence 1973, pp. 20–21, no. 5.

14. This hypothesis was first put forward by Fontani, in the preface to the 1792 edition of Leonardo's *Trattato* (as in n. 2), and later supported by De Vesme and Massar (as in n. 11), p. 5.

15. The numbers '16' and '30' flanking Stefano's monogram indicate that the manuscript was written in 1630. For Stefano's activities around this time, see Baldinucci (as in n. 11), pp. 602–7; and De Vesme and Massar (as in n. 11), pp. 3–15.

16. Furini's copy of the *Trattato* is housed in Modena, Biblioteca Estense, Fondo Campori, app. 803, segn. 5.3.28. For a description of his copy, see Steinitz (as in n. 6), p. 66; A. R. Masetti, 'Il casino Mediceo e la pittura fiorentina del Seicento, 1', *Critica d'Arte*, IX, 50, 1962, pp. 1–27, esp. pp. 25–6 n. 40; A. Forlani Tempesti, 'Un libro su Stefano della Bella', *Paragone*, XXIV, 279, 1973, p. 72 n. 4; and Pedretti, *The Literary Works* (as in n. 5), pp. 15–17.

17. For the hypothesis that Stefano used the Pinellianus manuscript, see J. P. Richter, *The Literary Works of Leonardo da Vinci Compiled and Edited from the Original Manuscripts*, 2 vols, London, New York and Toronto 1939, I, p. 7 n. 7, entry 'e', and Steinitz (as in n. 6), pp. 53–4, 174–5. For arguments against this hypothesis, see De Vesme and Massar (as in n. 11), pp. 4–5. The manuscript was part of Gian Vincenzo Pinelli's library when the majority of its holdings was acquired by Cardinal Borromeo in 1609 and transferred in the same year to the Ambrosiana, Milan, where it remains.

18. Many of Leonardo's original notes on human motion are lost, but some of them can still be found in his manuscripts such as A, E, L, Madrid II, and Codex Atlanticus. Luca Pacioli, in the introductory letter (dated 1498) to his *De divina proportione*, Venice 1509, fol. 2r, is the first writer known to have referred to Leonardo's book on painting and human motion.

19. See Codex Urbinas, fol. 111r–v. The original text is lost; see Pedretti and Vecce (as in n. 5), II, pp. 265–6. For the English translation of the terms, see Pedretti, *The Literary Works* (as in n. 5), p. 66, and M. Kemp and M. Walker eds, *Leonardo da Vinci On Painting*, New Haven and London 1989, pp. 132–3, 314.

20. Codex Urbinas, fol. 111r–v; see Kemp and Walker (as in n. 19), p. 132. For *moto locale*, Leonardo initially mentions three examples: rising, falling and moving horizontally. Then he refers to several others: slowness and speed, straight and twisting motion and another related one, jumping. For *moto azzionale* Leonardo mentions rowing, and for *moto composto* dancing, fencing, playing, sowing and ploughing. The original text is lost; see Pedretti and Vecce (as in n. 5), II, pp. 265–6.

21. See Codex Urbinas, fol. 110v. The original text is lost; see Pedretti and Vecce (as in n. 5), II, pp. 264–5.

22. This sheet (RL 19149v) is one of those loose ones bound in a volume that was part of Leoni's collection. See J. P. Richter, *The Notebooks of Leonardo da Vinci*, 2 vols, 1st edn 1883, repr. New York 1970, I, pp. XXV, 6, 102, 299, and K. Clark and C. Pedretti, *The Drawings of Leonardo da Vinci in the Collection of Her Majesty the Queen at Windsor Castle*, 3 vols, London and New York 1969, III, p. 57.

23. London, British Museum. See A. E. Popham and P. Pouncey, *Italian Drawings in the Department of Prints and Drawings in the British Museum: The Fourteenth and Fifteenth Centuries*, London 1950, pp. 58–60, no. 99r–v; and A. E. Popham, *The Drawings of Leonardo da Vinci*, ed. M. Kemp, London 1994, p. 106, no. 12, and p. 107, no. 13.

24. Windsor, Royal Library (RL 12336). This horse is thought to be a study for the one on the right in the cartoon for *The Battle of Anghiari*, though in the cartoon the position of the neck has been altered. See the introduction by Kemp to his edition of Popham's catalogue (as in n. 23), pp. 29–30; Clark and Pedretti (as in n. 22), I, p. 31; and C. Pedretti, *I cavalli di Leonardo: studi sul cavallo e altri animali di Leonardo da Vinci dalla Biblioteca Reale nel Castello di Windsor*, Florence 1984, pp. 54–62.

25. See Popham, ed. Kemp (as in n. 23), p. 142, no. 194; and G. Nepi Sciré, 'La battaglia di Anghiari', in *Leonardo & Venezia*, exh. cat. Milan 1992, pp. 256–85, esp. pp. 262–3.

26. See Steinitz, 'Poussin illustrateur …' (as in n. 8), p. 345; Steinitz (as in n. 6), p. 72; and Białostocki, 'Poussin et le "Traité"' (as in n. 8), p. 137. On *Hercules*, see L. Hautecoeur, 'Poussin illustrateur de Léonard de Vinci', *Bulletin de la Société de l'Histoire de l'Art Français*, 1913, pp. 223–8, esp. p. 225. On Poussin and the antique see C. Dempsey, 'Poussin and Egypt', *The Art Bulletin*, XLV, 1963, pp. 109–19; R. Wittkower, 'The Role of Classical Models in Bernini's and Poussin's Preparatory Work', in Wittkower's *Studies in the Italian Baroque*, London 1975, pp. 104–14; A. Blunt, 'Dessins d'après l'antique et copies de dessins de maîtres', in his *Les dessins de Poussin*, Paris 1988, pp. 143–65; C. Dempsey, 'The Greek Style and the Prehistory of Neoclassicism', in E. Cropper, *Pietro Testa 1612–1650: Prints and Drawings*, exh. cat. Philadelphia 1988, pp. xxxvii–lxv; and F. Sénéchal, 'Fortune de quelques antiques Farnèse auprès des peintres à Rome au début du XVIIe siècle', in *Poussin et Rome*, ed. O. Bonfait, Paris 1996, pp. 31–45. On Poussin's paintings of the 1630s see M. Bull, 'Poussin and the Antique', *Gazette des Beaux-Arts*, CXXIX, 1997, pp. 115–30.

27. Two measurement drawings of the Belvedere *Antinous* are found in a sketchbook now in the Bibliothèque de l'École des Beaux-Arts in Paris, fol. 27r. The drawing on the right-hand side was attributed to Poussin in G. Kauffmann, '*La Sainte Famille à l'escalier* et le problème des proportions dans l'oeuvre de Poussin', in *Nicolas Poussin*, ed. A. Chastel (as in n. 8), I, pp. 141–50, esp. pp. 143–4, but this attribution was questioned by P. Rosenberg and L.-A. Prat in their *Nicolas Poussin 1594–1665: catalogue raisonné des dessins*, 2 vols, Milan 1994, II, pp. 1016–17, entry R. 904. However, it is very likely that Poussin carefully studied this statue. Not only was the Belvedere *Antinous* mentioned in all accounts of the most famous statues in Rome and extensively reproduced and copied, but the two measurement drawings of this statue are by an artist very closely connected with Poussin's circle. Moreover, there is no doubt that the two etchings depicting this statue published by Bellori as being from Poussin's original drawings were at least based on drawings by an artist very close to Poussin. For the *fortuna* of this statue, see F. Haskell and N. Penny, *Taste and the Antique*, New Haven and London 1981, pp. 141–3. For contemporary references to Poussin's drawing after this statue, see G. P. Bellori, 'Nicolò Pussino', in Bellori's *Le vite de'pittori, scultori e architetti moderni* (1st edn 1672), ed. E. Borea, Turin 1976, pp. 419–81, esp. pp. 426, 472; and Félibien (as in n. 9), p. 160. For clear associations with the figure of *Antinous*, see Poussin's illustrations in H 228, fols 50v and 73r according to its original pagination; and for associations with the figure of *Hercules*, see the illustrations on fols 21r and 49v there. These illustrations were published by Friedlaender and Blunt (as in n. 8), as '259', '268', '251' and '258' respectively.

28. Rome, Musei Vaticani (Belvedere Courtyard). See Haskell and Penny (as in n. 27), pp. 141–3.

29. Stourhead (Wiltshire), National Trust. See C. Wright, *Poussin, Paintings: A Catalogue Raisonné*, London 1984, p. 192, no. 116; and D. Sparti, 'La Maison de Nicolas Poussin via del Babuino, à Rome', in *Nicolas Poussin (1594–1665)* (Actes du colloque organisé au Musée du Louvre, Paris 1994), ed. A. Mérot, 2 vols, Paris 1996, I, pp. 45–77.

30. Now in Naples, Museo Nazionale. See Haskell and Penny (as in n. 27), pp. 229–32. For the study of this statue in Poussin's circle, see the measurement drawing of the *Hercules* now in Budapest, Szépművészeti Muzeum (inv. 2883). This drawing bears the inscription 'Posino' and, although it is not currently attributed to Poussin, it has been considered very close to the measurement drawings of the *Antinous* in the sketchbook in Paris. For this drawing, see Rosenberg and Prat (as in n. 27), II, pp. 824–5, entry R. 208.

31. For Poussin and the antique see n. 26.

32. See Haskell and Penny (as in n. 27), pp. 173–5.

33. For Poussin's illustration, see p. 27 above. It is worth noting that the *Castor and Pollux* group was reproduced in a drawing after the antique attributed to Poussin, although with slight variations in the proportions and poses of the figures, whose imbalance (especially that of the figure on the left) seems to be reduced. This drawing is now in the Musée Condé, Chantilly; see Blunt (as in n. 26), pp. 126–7, 145–6. Recently, the attribution of this drawing to Poussin has been drawn into question in P. Rosenberg and L.-A. Prat, *Nicolas Poussin: la collection du Musée Condé à Chantilly*, Paris 1994, pp. 162–3.

34. Now in the Louvre, Paris. For the *fortuna* of this statue, see Haskell and Penny (as in n. 27), pp. 221–4. This sculpture is also drawn on a sheet now in Windsor, *Bassi Rilievi Antichi*, III, fol. 8329v, which was part of Cassiano dal Pozzo's Museo Cartaceo, and which Poussin might have known.

35. Poussin's *Apollo and the Chariot of Phaeton* is in Berlin, Gemäldegalerie. In Poussin's lifetime the Roman sarcophagus was in the Villa Medici, Rome, where it remains; the Hellenistic cameo, then in the Farnese collection, Rome, is now in the Museo Nazionale, Naples. For an analysis of Poussin's variants and sources, see Bull (as in n. 26), pp. 115–30.

36. For this drawing, see nn. 32 and 33 above.

37. The first of these drawings is found in the Musée Condé, Chantilly, the other two are at Windsor, in the Royal Collection. See Blunt (as in n. 26), p. 43, fig. 24; p. 48, fig. 31; p. 50, fig. 33.

38. Paris, Musée du Louvre, Département des Arts Graphiques. See F. Viatte, *Musée du Louvre, Cabinet des Dessins: inventaire général des dessins italiens*, II: *Dessins de Stefano della Bella 1610–1664*, Paris 1974, p. 87, no. 120.

39. See, for example, the study of the *Virgin and Child with St Anne* in London, British Museum. For this drawing, see Popham, ed. Kemp (as in n. 23), p. 139, no. 175.

40. See *Disegni di Stefano della Bella, 1610–1664, dalle collezioni del Gabinetto Nazionale delle Stampe*, ed. M. Catelli-Isola, exh. cat. Rome 1976, pp. 39–40, fig. 98.

41. Ibid., pp. 34–5, fig. 71a.

42. See Viatte (as in n. 38), p. 145, no. 214.

43. For a discussion of Leonardo's influence on Poussin, see J. Białostocki, 'Une idée de Léonard réalisée par Poussin', *Revue des Arts*, IV, 1954, pp. 131–6; idem, 'Poussin et le "Traité"' (as in n. 8); Friedlaender and Blunt (as in n. 8), esp. p. 30. Although these scholars convincingly demonstrate the influence of the one artist on the other, they do not address the issue that figurative motifs derived by Poussin from the *Trattato* embody a concept of motion different from Leonardo's.

44. R. Fréart de Chambray, 'A Monsieur le Poussin, Premier Peintre du Roy', in Leonardo, ed. Fréart de Chambray (as in n. 1), n.p.

45. R. Trichet Du Fresne, 'Al molto illustre et eccellentissimo signore, il Signor Pietro Bourdelot, primo medico della Serenissima Regina di Svetia', in Leonardo, ed. Trichet Du Fresne (as in n. 1), n.p.

46. See n. 1 (above). For Errard, see J. Thuillier, 'Propositions pour Charles Errard, peintre', *Revue de l'art*, XL–XLI, 1978, pp. 151–72.

47. In Errard's copies of Poussin's illustrations the shading of the figures is very pronounced, emphasising their heavy proportions. On the other hand, several details were added, which gave this set a more decorative character, and some new illustrations were provided. For a

discussion of the attribution of these 'new' illustrations, see E. Cropper and C. Dempsey, 'Painting and Possession: Poussin's *Self-Portrait* for Chantelou and the *Essais* of Montaigne', in their *Nicolas Poussin, Friendship and the Love of Painting*, Princeton 1996, pp. 177–215, esp. pp. 190–2. For Poussin's criticism of Errard's handling of his illustrations, see Poussin's letter to Bosse, published by Bosse (as in n. 7), pp. 128–9.

48. Differences in form between the texts of the two editions are much more frequent than differences in content. To point out one example, chapter 162 of the 1651 edition corresponds to chapters 162, 163 and 164 of the 1792 edition; however, this change in chapter lengths does not affect the content. There are no significant variations in content that could account for the discrepancies between the two sets of illustrations.

49. See C. Fantappiè, 'Fontani, Francesco', in *Dizionario biografico degli Italiani*, XLVIII, Rome 1997, pp. 744–7.

50. Leonardo, ed. Fontani (as in n. 2), 'Prefazione dell'editore', p. XI: 'con piccole figure alla sua maniera, riducendo quasi così alla pratica quei precetti che ei meritamente tanto apprezzava'.

51. Ibid., p. XI: 'stimolai frattanto il Sig. Giuseppe Fabbrini valente nostro Pittore, e grande estimatore delle cose di Stefano a dilucidare, ed incidere quegli stessi di lui schizzi e figure con la più precisa esattezza e verità, siccome fece col maggior impegno per animarmi a riprodurre con la più spedita e possibile celerità il libro di Lionardo'. For Giuseppe Antonio Fabbrini (b. Florence c. 1748 – d. after 1793), see A. G. de Marchi, 'Fabbrini, Giuseppe Antonio', in *Dizionario biografico degli Italiani*, XLIII, Rome 1993, pp. 665–7.

1.1   Engraving after Nicolas Poussin, *A man throwing a stone* (detail), Leonardo's *Trattato*, 1651 edition

1.2   Nicolas Poussin, *Demonstration of violent motion: a man throwing a spear and another throwing a stone*, drawing in Milan, Biblioteca Ambrosiana, MS H 228 inf.

1.3   Engraving after Stefano della Bella, *A man in the act of throwing* (detail), in Leonardo's *Trattato*, 1792 edition

1.4   Stefano della Bella, *Two men in the act of throwing*, drawing in Florence,
Biblioteca Riccardiana, MS Riccardianus 2275

1.5   Leonardo da Vinci, *Notes on the geometry of optics*, detail incorporating the 'hammering man', Royal Library, Windsor

1.6   After Leonardo da Vinci, *Demonstrating violent movement: two stages of a man throwing a spear*, drawing in Rome, Biblioteca Apostolica Vaticana, Codex Urbinas Latinus 1270

1.7   Leonardo da Vinci, *Study for The Battle of Anghiari*, drawing, Venice, Gallerie dell'Accademia

1.8   After Leonardo da Vinci, *Demonstration of two kinds of movement: a man throwing a spear and another throwing a stone*, drawing in Rome, Biblioteca Apostolica Vaticana, Codex Urbinas Latinus 1270

1.9   Nicolas Poussin, *Illustration of the equilibrium of stationary figures: a man standing on one leg*, drawing in Milan, Biblioteca Ambrosiana, MS H 228 inf.

1.10   Nicolas Poussin (or his circle), *Castor and Pollux*, drawing, Chantilly, Musée Condé

1.11   Stefano della Bella, *Boy with a lamb*, drawing, Rome, Istituto Nazionale per la Grafica

1.12   Stefano della Bella, *Galloping horseman*, drawing, Paris, Musée du Louvre, Département des Arts Graphiques

2

'The outer man tends to be a guide to the inner': the woodcut portraits in Vasari's *Lives* as parallel texts

Sharon Gregory

Giorgio Vasari is perhaps best known as the author of the *Lives*, a book of artists' biographies first published in Florence in 1550. A second edition of the book, revised and expanded, appeared in 1568. In a passage in the second edition devoted to Flemish artists, Vasari commented on a letter he had received from a Flemish correspondent, Domenicus Lampsonius, who begged him to 'add to [the *Lives*] three treatises on sculpture, painting and architecture, with drawings of figures, in order to explain and teach matters of the arts'.[1] Vasari made it clear that this had not been his intention; rather, he had wanted to produce a book about artists, about their lives and works. For that reason he also provided the second edition of the *Lives* with portraits of the artists.

Vasari had supplied for both editions of the *Lives* designs for title pages and endpieces that were intended to elucidate the primary purpose of the book. In the title page for the first edition, published in 1550, the figures of Apollo and Eternity support a stage set with the curtain opening onto a view of Florence, the city Vasari believed had for centuries produced the most excellent artists. The endpiece is an allegory of Fame and the Arts. Fame, with a lighted torch and a trumpet, flies through the air above female personifications of the three arts of *disegno* (painting, sculpture, architecture). At their feet lie dead men. Title page and endpiece together enclose the text, like visual embodiments of Vasari's Preface and Conclusion. In both these passages, Vasari stated his intention to 'protect artists from second death through the written word' and to free them from 'dust and oblivion'.[2] The 1568 edition of the *Lives* saw the introduction of a new title page and a new endpiece. The endpiece is an elaboration and clarification of the first version: now, as Fame blows her trumpet, she actually awakens the dead artists to judgement. A Latin inscription, provided by Vasari's adviser Vincenzo Borghini, expresses the idea that as long as Vasari's history lived it could never be said that the artists had truly died, nor that their works had remained buried.[3]

Other scholars have explored the meaning of the title pages and endpieces of both editions of the *Lives* as visual analogues to statements in the text – a means of announcing the import and purpose of the *Lives*.[4] I believe that the artists' portraits, which appeared for the first time in the 1568 edition, can, in a similar fashion, also be read as parallel texts.

In Renaissance Italy, the main purpose of collections of lives of illustrious men and women was, as it had been in antiquity, to provide models of moral behaviour to be imitated by the reader.[5] The genre of exemplary biography, established by ancient writers such as Cicero, Plutarch and Suetonius, was re-established for the Renaissance by Petrarch, in his *De viris illustribus*. These examples and many written during the Quattrocento were available in manuscript and in published form in Vasari's time.[6] Their subjects were typically persons of great stature: rulers and pontiffs, warriors, philosophers and saints. It has been amply demonstrated by scholars including Patricia Rubin and Paul Barolsky that Vasari's intention was to create a similar heroic biography for the visual artist; indeed, Vasari himself states in the *Lives* that the purpose of history is 'to teach men men how to live and make them prudent'.[7]

One of Vasari's friends and advisers, the historian Paolo Giovio, had in the 1520s begun collecting portraits of illustrious historical figures. In the 1530s he began to build a villa at Como, intended in part as a home (the 'Museum') for his collection, which by the time of his death in 1552 numbered over 400 portraits. The portraits were displayed with pieces of parchment below, on which eulogies were written.[8] Giovio published two volumes of the eulogies, in 1547 and 1551, without illustrations, though he stated that he would have liked to include them.[9] It seems that Vasari, too, partly as a result of Giovio's influence, had intended to illustrate the first edition of the *Lives* with portraits of the artists, but was unable to do so, perhaps due to a combination of lack of time and financial constraints.[10] In the 1568 edition he achieved this goal, and his book became part of the humanist tradition of illustrated biographies.[11]

In the second edition of the *Lives*, there are 144 oval portraits, each at the beginning of the respective artist's biography. Each portrait is enclosed within an elaborate architectural frame. In addition there are eight empty frames, heading the biographies of Pietro Cavallini, Giovanni da Ponte, Barna da Siena, Duccio, Taddeo di Bartolo, Antonio da Correggio, Pietro Torrigiano and Marco Calavrese. Vasari explains in the Preface to the first part of the *Lives* that he was unable to find any surviving portraits of these artists.[12]

There are six variants of the frame, the blocks for which were used repeatedly with new portraits inserted into them. The frames contain allegorical figures and other attributes referring to the skills of the artists portrayed within them: some refer to painting, sculpture or architecture alone; some to a combination of two of these arts; some to all three arts of *disegno*.[13] For example, the frame surrounding the self-portrait of Vasari, painter and architect, contains a female figure shown in the act of painting; below, *putti* hold devices of architecture. The frame around the portrait of the architect Cronaca, however, contains a reference to architecture alone, in the form of an allegorical figure on the pediment. The relationship between individual portrait and frame can sometimes be puzzling; for example, Lorenzo Ghiberti's portrait was printed within a frame signifying painting. Such anomalies were apparently the fault of the printer. In 1568, the same year that the second edition of the *Lives* was published, the Giunti press in Florence also issued a volume containing solely the portraits in their frames, the *Ritratti de' più eccellenti pittori, scultori et architetti* … . In this extremely rare book, many of the anomalies have been corrected, presumably by Vasari or Borghini: Ghiberti, for instance, is now ensconced in the frame appropriate to a sculptor.[14]

The woodcut portraits, their frames and the title page and endpiece for the *Lives* were cut in Venice. Unfortunately, we do not know the identity of the woodcutter. In the *Lives* Vasari refers only to a 'maestro Cristofano'. A blank space was left after the name, indicating that Vasari may have hoped to find out the surname and fill it in later. The surviving correspondence between Vasari and Cosimo Bartoli, who was in Venice and acted as go-between, is no more illuminating.[15] H. W. Frey thought the artist in question might be Cristofano dell'Altissimo, a painter sent in 1552 by Duke Cosimo to copy some of the portraits of illustrious men in Paolo Giovio's Museum, but this is improbable, not least because Vasari was in charge of that project and so knew the artist's surname: indeed, elsewhere he refers to him by his full name.[16] Gaetano Milanesi thought the block cutter might have been Cristoforo Coriolano (Christopher Lederer); the blank left by Vasari had been filled in with the name of Coriolano in the Bolognese reprinting of the *Lives* in 1647.[17] Paul Kristeller suggested that the woodcutter could have been either Coriolano or Cristoforo Chrieger (Cristoforo della Guerra).[18] Most recent scholars tend to ascribe them to Coriolano, though this attribution is by no means certain.

The fact that the blocks were cut in Venice suggests that no craftsman of sufficient ability could be found in Florence. Vasari had faced a similar situation during the preparation of the 1550 edition, published by Torrentino in Florence. In January of that year, Pierfrancesco Giambullari, who was helping to see the book through publication in Vasari's absence, wrote to Vasari in Rome to ask his opinion of a print that had been made after Vasari's design by a German artist at Torrentino's press. If Vasari was not pleased with it, the alternative was to send the design to Venice to be cut. In the event, the title page and endpiece were both cut in Venice, though we do not know by whom.[19]

One of the most perplexing aspects of the portraits in the second edition of the *Lives* is that in five instances the portrait of one artist was copied and cut again on another block. In the case of the pairs comprised of the portraits of Luca della Robbia and Cecca, and of Giuliano Bugiardini and Spinello Aretino, the portraits face in the same direction, but in the other three pairs (Paolo Romano and Cosimo Rosselli, Girolamo da Carpi and Daniele da Volterra, and Girolamo da Treviso and Giovannantonio Sodoma) they are mirror images.[20] In the reversed pairs, the woodcutter presumably pasted the first version of the woodcut portrait onto the block and cut directly through it, resulting in the reverse image. In each of these five pairs, the second portrait is of a markedly inferior quality, appearing very schematic. The hair and beards in most of the woodcuts appear curly and springy, typical of Vasari's drawing style, while in the copy versions these features are arranged in ill-considered clumps. The ears, too, become distorted in the copies. It seems to me that these copies can hardly have been cut by the hand responsible for the remainder of the woodcuts. It is possible that the Florentine Giunti employed a woodcutter, considerably less skilful than Cristofano, and used him to provide the copies when some portraits were discovered, for whatever reason, to be missing. On the other hand, these spurious portraits also appear in the corrected volume of *Ritratti*, which may indicate that neither Vasari nor Borghini saw any need to correct them.

In the preface to the *Lives*, Vasari stated that the woodcut portraits he had gathered would be a better guide to artists' likenesses than could be provided by descriptions,[21] and the scholarship surrounding them has focused on their accuracy as portraits. In 1966, Wolfram Prinz identified most of Vasari's sources for the 144 portraits, calculating that 95 of them have some claim to be considered authentic likenesses.[22] Charles Hope later argued that, even in most of the remaining cases, Vasari looked to sources that were at least contemporary with the individuals depicted, in which their portraits might reasonably have been expected to appear.[23] It should be noted, however, that the sources for some 61 of the portraits have not yet been identified.[24] In the cases where such identifications have been made, it seems that Vasari was not always scrupulously careful, as sometimes the portrait of the wrong artist was used as a likeness. For example, as Hope pointed out, the woodcut of Alfonso Lombardi resembles the self-portrait of Titian now in the Prado, though it is not an exact copy.[25] Hope suggested that Vasari in this instance simply gave his publisher the wrong drawing, and that the portrait at the head of Titian's Life is 'presumably someone else'. However, the woodcut of Titian (see Figure 2.1) is also taken from a self-portrait, now in Berlin (Figure

2.2). Vasari's woodcut reproduces Titian's physiognomy closely (in reverse), although the resemblance is disguised by Vasari's changes to Titian's costume.

Given the elaborate allegorical meanings associated with title pages, endpieces and even the frames for the portraits, it seems reasonable to suppose that the portraits might also have been intended by Vasari to fulfil a similar function – not merely to record likenesses. Of the 83 portraits for which the sources are known, some 25 (over a quarter) have been altered in some way. Vasari seems, by means of these changes, to have invested some of these woodcuts with visual clues that were intended to convey meaning – meaning related to the content of the biographies.

It must be stressed that in his Life of Marcantonio Raimondi Vasari states that all the drawings for the portraits were made by Vasari himself or by his assistants under his supervision.[26] The surviving evidence corroborates Vasari's statement. The surviving sheets of preparatory drawings, in the Uffizi, contain heads of Lorenzo di Bicci and Orcagna (no. 638F), Andrea Tafi and Gaddo Gaddi (no. 642F recto) and Giottino (no. 642F verso). These drawings served as models for those sent to Venice for use by the woodcutters. They are typical of Vasari's technique for chalk drawings, and the captions are also in Vasari's hand. As Licia Ragghianti Collobi noted, comparison of these drawings with the corresponding woodcuts clearly shows that the woodcutter was faithful to every detail in the drawings, down to the smallest buttons of the garments.[27] Therefore, it is reasonable to suppose that the woodcuts accurately reflect Vasari's intentions for the portraits: neither the physiognomy of the individuals represented nor their attire was altered by the craftsman who cut the blocks.

Physiognomy and clothing were Vasari's two main devices for adding meaning to a portrait. Vasari's knowledge and use of physiognomy was not unusual. Several treatises on physiognomy appeared in the fourteenth and fifteenth centuries, many based on ancient texts such as pseudo-Aristotle's *Physiognomica*. The first discussion of physiognomy in a work of art theory was a chapter in Pomponius Gauricus's *De sculptura*, published in Florence in 1504. For example, the association of leonine features with heroic portraits was apparently already widespread. Peter Meller has argued that, among Quattrocento artists, Uccello, Donatello, Alberti and Verrocchio were influenced by the 'physiognomical doctrine'. Among Vasari's contemporaries, Baccio Bandinelli and Benvenuto Cellini were also certainly aware of physiognomic theory, and Cellini made explicit use of leonine features in his bronze portrait bust of Duke Cosimo de' Medici (Florence, Bargello).[28]

Clothing provided information about social status that would have been instantly comprehensible to contemporaries. Vasari's awareness of the importance of appropriate dress is revealed in the Life of Bastiano da Sangallo, where he criticizes the artist Jacone's brutish behaviour and clothing in contrast to Vasari's own cultivated manners and velvet apparel, concluding that 'the outer man tends to be a guide to the inner, and to reveal what our minds are'.[29] Vasari sometimes used clothing in the portraits to provide information about the artist portrayed, signalling themes that would be confirmed in the text of his biography. Not all of the changes he made to his sources can be described as meaningful in this way; some were surely simple attempts to avoid the ridiculous effect of bizarre costumes. For example, in the source for the woodcut of Jacopo Palma il Vecchio, Palma's *Adoration of the Magi* (Milan, Brera), the man from whom Vasari drew the portrait wears an exotic tall, furry hat, while Vasari's version of the headgear is a simple unadorned cap.[30] But other instances reveal much more interesting transformations that cannot be so easily explained. Vasari altered details of the clothing in at least 16 other portraits, and it is very likely that similar changes were made in additional cases where the original source is no longer known. I will discuss only a few of these instances here.[31]

A straightforward example is the identification of an artist with the religious order to which he belonged by means of showing him in clerical costume. Thus, Lorenzo Monaco, Fra Angelico, Fra Bartolommeo and Fra Giovanni Montorsoli all appear in their monastic habits. Significantly, Fra Filippo Lippi does not (see Figure 2.3). Vasari cited a self-portrait of Fra Filippo in the frescoes in Prato cathedral, in which he noted that the painter wore a friar's habit.[32] Another self-portrait of Filippo clothed in his monastic habit can be seen in his *Coronation of the Virgin* in the Uffizi. Vasari used this painting as his source for the friar's portrait but, instead of the actual self-portrait by Fra Filippo, he used the portrait of the kneeling donor, Francesco Maringhi (see Figure 2.4). Vasari was probably misled by the inscription beside Maringhi ('is perfecit opus') thinking that it referred to the painter as opposed to the patron. Maringhi was a canon of San Lorenzo and chaplain of the convent at Sant'Ambrogio, and in the *Coronation* he also wears clerical robes. In his Life of Fra Filippo, Vasari recorded the friar's sexual exploits, claiming that 'he was a slave to his amorous appetite'.[33] Vasari's stories may in the main have been true. It seems that Fra Filippo, appointed to the chaplaincy of a convent in Prato, improperly shared his house with seven nuns from 1456–1458. One of the nuns, Lucrezia, bore him a daughter and a son (the painter Filippino Lippi). Later he and Lucrezia left their religious communities, but Filippo continued to wear his habit and signed his paintings as Frater Philippus. Vasari, on the other hand, seems to have believed that the friar had at the age of 17 'boldly thrown off his monastic habit'.[34] Therefore when he came to design the woodcut portrait of Fra Filippo, he removed the clerical clothing and substituted secular attire, though the friar still displays the tonsure.

Two other figures also wear clerical garments: Sebastiano del Piombo and Donato Bramante. Wolfram Prinz was disturbed by Sebastiano's clerical cloak and cap and thought that Vasari had inappropriately used the portrait of a bishop or a cardinal for his woodcut.[35] But Vasari expressly tells us that when Sebastiano was appointed to the office of the Piombo, he took up the friar's habit.[36] The office of the Piombo, a papal appointment given to a celibate man, entitled its bearer to wear the bishop's *mozzetta*.[37] This must also be the reason for the habit worn by Bramante (who, as Vasari noted, was appointed to the same office) in his woodcut portrait, probably based on the supposed portrait of Bramante as Euclid in Raphael's *School of Athens*.[38] One of Vasari's primary themes in the *Lives* is the high social status that artists were able to attain. In these two examples he alludes in the woodcut portraits to an artist's having received an important papal appointment; and in both instances the fact was also noted in the artist's biography.

Clothing could also reveal Vasari's view of an artist's character. Vasari's Life of Piero di Cosimo describes the painter as a talented observer of the natural world but also as a solitary, abstracted, misanthropic man who lived a life 'more beastly than human'.[39] Piero ate only when he was hungry, instead of at the proper hour; he allowed his garden to grow without pruning; and he 'liked to see everything wild like his own nature'.[40] The source for Vasari's portrait woodcut is not known, but it is surely significant that the woodcut itself shows Piero dressed in very rustic clothing – a simple smock and an outdoor labourer's or gardener's hat (see Figure 2.5). Similar floppy felt hats can be seen in Andrea del Sarto's lost *Parable of the Vineyard* in SS. Annunziata in Florence (the design of which is recorded in an anonymous drawing),[41] and in a drawing by Girolamo Muziano of the *Noli me tangere*, with Christ appearing to Mary Magdalen in the guise of a gardener. This drawing was in Vasari's 'Libro de' disegni'.[42] Vasari frequently expressed reservations about artists who withdrew from society and who lived in a manner more plebeian than refined. Alluded to in the woodcut, this is made explicit in Piero's biography, where Vasari complained that Piero should 'have made known his great talent in such a way that he would have been adored; whereas instead, on account of his bestial life, he was thought to be mad'.[43] Further, according to Vasari, Piero was inclined to become abstracted and to daydream, to the extent that when a subject was being discussed, it was often necessary to recount the argument for him, as his mind had in the meantime wandered. Vasari says that he was 'always building castles in the air'.[44] Thus Vasari's portrait shows Piero with his eyes half closed, as though lost in dreamy and unproductive thought.

An interesting comparison can be made between Piero's biography and portrait and those of Leonardo da Vinci. In their Lives, Vasari draws pointed parallels between the two artists: both are said to have been obsessed with the natural world, to have painted fantastic monsters and to have failed to discipline their talent. Vasari claims that Piero used to look at the stains on walls and find there battle scenes and landscapes – something that Leonardo in his notebooks actually recommends.[45] However, while Piero, in Vasari's opinion, led his life in an uncivilized manner, Leonardo was the very model of the courtly artist, urbane and sociable. Whereas Piero died alone, his body being found later at the foot of the stairs, Leonardo died, according to Vasari, in the arms of the King of France.

Vasari's Life of Leonardo concentrates on his intellectual pursuits and scientific study of nature: even in his youth, he would confound his mathematics teacher with difficult questions; at a more mature age, he turned his attentions to the properties of herbs, the motions of the heavens and equine and human anatomies.[46] Vasari wrote that 'there was infused in that brain such grace from God, and a power of expression in such sublime accord with the intellect and memory that served it ... that he vanquished with his discourse and confuted with his reasoning every valiant wit'.[47]

Vasari's woodcut portrait of Leonardo (Figure 2.6) was probably based upon a likeness of the artist that had been reproduced by Cristofano dell'Altissimo from a painting in Paolo Giovio's collection (Figure 2.7). The painted likeness had its original source in a red chalk drawing of Leonardo that was then in the collection of Francesco Melzi. It shows Leonardo in profile, with a long white beard. Unlike its source, however, Vasari's woodcut provides Leonardo with a cap and also with a decidedly piercing gaze, in contrast to Piero's dreamy expression: both serve to underline Leonardo's resemblance to depictions of Aristotle and other ancient philosophers.[48] For example, the pen and ink drawing of a philosopher by the young Michelangelo, now in the British Museum, is very similar. The cap and long beard are also features of the portrait of Bastiano da Sangallo, of whom Vasari wrote:

he would speak with great gravity, slowly and sententiously, so that a company of good artists gave him the name of Aristotle, which, moreover, sat upon him all the better because it appeared that according to an ancient portrait of that very great philosopher and confidant of nature, Bastiano closely resembled him.[49]

Social status and laudable attributes of character are also alluded to in the portrait of Michelangelo, shown wearing an elaborate and expensive costume of fur and brocade. Michelangelo is presented as a gentleman artist, capable of being on good terms with popes and princes. His attire is notable because of its extreme improbability: surely this cannot be the dress adopted by an artist who was notoriously parsimonious, and who cared so little about clothing or personal comfort that he was described by both Vasari and Condivi as wearing dogskin buskins on his legs for months at a time, so that when he finally took them off, his own skin came off with them.[50]

Brocade in particular seems to have been associated with courts and the nobility. In their portraits, the courtly rulers of northern Italian cities are frequently seen in brocaded garments. For example, the members of the inner court of the Gonzaga family wear brocade in Mantegna's frescoes in the Camera Picta (Mantua, Palazzo Ducale); so do Galeazzo Maria Sforza in the portrait by Piero del Pollaiuolo (Florence, Uffizi), Ludovico Maria Sforza in the painting attributed to Boltraffio (Milan, private collection) and Lionello d'Este in the Pisanello portrait in Bergamo (Galleria dell'Accademia, Carrara). Closer to home for Vasari was Bronzino's famous portrait of Eleonora da Toledo with her son Giovanni (Florence, Uffizi). When in 1549 Duke Cosimo I and Eleonora commissioned Bronzino to paint their portraits, to be sent to Cardinal Granvelle, they allowed that, for the sake of convenience and speed, Eleonora should *not* be shown wearing a rich brocade, but that her dress should be of 'some other patterned cloth which will make a fine show'.[51]

In letters of the 1520s and 30s, the poet Pietro Aretino revealed his passion for rich brocade fabrics and the associations of high rank that they held for him. In one instance he thanked Federigo Gonzaga, Duke of Mantua, for his gift of sumptuous cloth, pleased that a nobleman should judge him 'worthy to wear the clothing of princes'.[52] The wearing of brocade by persons of lesser status could be a matter for derision. In his Life of the early-fifteenth-century Florentine sculptor and painter Dello di Niccolò Delli, Vasari described the artist going to work in Spain, where he became honoured and wealthy. When he returned to Florence and rode through the goldsmiths' quarter wearing brocade, he was mocked by his childhood friends for his pretensions.[53]

Another letter by Aretino sheds light on the symbolic value of brocade as an indicator of nobility of character. Writing to thank another patron for his gift of rich clothing, he stated that it 'comprised a gift more fitting to your greatness than to my lowliness, which nevertheless does not blush to be seen wearing such garments, thanks to the *virtù* which elevates it … '.[54] In other words, though brocade could not normally be worn by people of the lower classes, genius and virtue could elevate one's station and permit this form of dress.

Michelangelo's nobility of character was stressed repeatedly in Vasari's life of the artist. Not only was Michelangelo born to an ancient family, but he was also 'an exemplar sent by God to the men of our art, that they might learn from his life the nature of [noble] character … '.[55] Vasari noted that, despite Michelangelo's frugality, he was not avaricious and generously gave away many works of art. He helped the poor, secretly provided dowries and enriched his servants, on one occasion giving his servant Urbino 2000 crowns all at once, 'an act such as is generally left to great emperors and pontiffs'.[56] He counted among his friends many great persons, a number of whom were listed by Vasari.

The only other artist to be dressed in brocade is Vasari's friend Michele da Sanmichele, who is, significantly, also described as being of noble character if not of noble birth. He was 'honourable in his every action' and 'more courteous than any man has ever been, to such an extent that he no sooner heard the needs and desires of his friends than he sought to gratify them ... nor did any person ever do him a service that was not repaid many times over'.[57] Vasari provided a personal anecdote: he once gave Michele a drawing, and later Michele sent to Vasari's mother 'a quantity of *robe* [a word that can mean 'goods' or actual 'clothing'] beautiful and honourable enough to be the gifts of a very rich nobleman'.[58] Vasari then listed a number of noblemen and princes who were Michele's friends; the only artist to be included among these prestigious persons was Michelangelo himself. Thus, brocade in Vasari's woodcut portraits seems intended to indicate both the very high social standing of an artist, as borne out by his personal associates, and also the artist's profound nobility of character.[59]

Clothing could even be a clue to the stylistic nature and content of an artist's work. Andrea Mantegna, for example, strove to emulate antique statuary, to the extent that, as Vasari has his teacher Squarcione say, his figures looked 'like marble statues'.[60] The source Vasari cited for his woodcut was a portrait on Mantegna's grave in Sant'Andrea in Mantua.[61] While the bronze relief on the grave portrays Mantegna with a completely bare chest, Vasari provided him with draperies: in his woodcut portrait, Mantegna wears a toga (see Figures 2.8 and 2.9). Mantegna's antiquarian interests are clearly evident from his paintings, and it seems that they led Vasari to consider it appropriate to associate him with this ancient Roman garment.

In seven of the woodcut portraits, the artists wear fur collars. In three of these cases (the portraits of Cronaca, Simone Mosca and Michelangelo), Vasari's precise source is no longer known. In the other four cases, the fur collar was added by Vasari.[62] All are artists for whom Vasari seems to have had exceptional esteem, a category which, of course, also includes Michelangelo. Among them is the French stained-glass painter Guillaume de Marcillat, Vasari's first teacher in the visual arts. Lorenzo Ghiberti and Masaccio are the sculptor and painter who helped to initiate Vasari's second age of art, and Polidoro da Caravaggio was an esteemed pupil of Raphael. A study of the biographies of the seven fur-clad artists reveals that they had much in common. All are described by Vasari as being absolute masters of their primary field of activity. All had studied and learned from works of art that they had seen in Rome, and all except Marcillat had, according to Vasari, contributed in important ways to the rediscovery and revival of antiquity.[63] Vasari's esteem for these artists and his assessment of their contributions to the history of art through their studies in Rome can be contrasted with his opinion of the only artist from whom he deliberately removed a fur collar: Titian. In the self-portrait in Berlin, Titian wears a mantle with a fur collar and chains bearing the insignia of the knighthood granted to him by Charles V. Neither is present in Vasari's woodcut (see Figures 2.1 and 2.2). In his biography of Titian, and elsewhere, Vasari states that Titian, as excellent as he was, would have been a much greater artist had he spent more time in Rome studying the work of great ancient and modern masters.[64]

In most instances where Vasari's source for a portrait is known, he made no major changes to it. As his sartorial adjustments were usually significant, it seems reasonable to assume that where changes occur in other aspects of the portraits – the position of the subject's head, or his physiognomy – some intimation about the subject may likewise have been intended by Vasari.

In a few of the portraits, the heads are seen in profile, whereas Vasari's sources were either sculptural (thus presenting a variety of possible views) or two-dimensional images showing the face in three-quarter view. For example, Vasari's source for the portrait of Lorenzo Ghiberti was almost certainly the bronze self-portrait head on the Gates of Paradise. Wolfram Prinz postulated a lost painting of Ghiberti as Vasari's source.[65] However, Vasari's woodcut shares so many characteristics with the bronze bust that such a hypothesis is unnecessary: both have the firmly set mouth and small chin, the bald crown surrounded by a fringe of hair and the sharply arched eyebrows that cause pronounced creases in the flesh of the forehead. In order to have seen the bronze head in profile, as the woodcut presents it, Vasari would have had to adopt an unusual viewing point, standing pressed against the wall of the Florentine Baptistery. A profile portrait, in the context of the printed book of the Cinquecento, was almost certain to bring to mind the numerous representations of antique portrait medals that illustrated volumes by scholars such as Andrea Fulvio and Enea Vico.[66] Vasari shared with many of his contemporaries an interest in antique medals and in artists who revived their manufacture, and he expressed his admiration for Vico's books.[67] Vasari praised Ghiberti for having been the first sculptor to look closely at antique works of art and, by imitating them, to aid in the revival of the good aspects of ancient sculpture.[68] His representation of Samson on the Gates of Paradise was, according to Vasari, as good as anything made in the time of the ancients; indeed, the doors as a whole were 'the most beautiful work in the world, whether ancient or modern'.[69] It is probably more than coincidental that Vasari also mentioned that Ghiberti had made portrait medals of his friends, in emulation of ancient examples.[70]

A similar change in viewpoint may be observed in the case of Baldassare Peruzzi, whose self-portrait drawing, Vasari's probable source, shows a three-quarter view rather than the profile of Vasari's woodcut. Vasari comments on Peruzzi's antiquarian interests, noting that he had studied antique remains in Rome and had even begun a book on Roman antiquities with a commentary on Vitruvius, a copy of whose writings he had illustrated with small drawings in the margins.[71]

Luca della Robbia is also shown in profile. Vasari's source for Luca's portrait may have been, as Wolfram Prinz thought, a sculptural work, but it is more likely that it was the drawing in Vasari's 'Libro', identified by him as a Luca della Robbia self-portrait, made while looking in a mirror.[72] Licia Ragghianti Collobi has suggested that this self-portrait can be identified as the metalpoint drawing at Chatsworth (no. 704), now attributed to Lorenzo di Credi, of a man in three-quarter view; the resemblance, encompassing the style of headdress, the arched eyebrow, the hooked nose and the jowls, is close.[73] If this drawing was the source for the woodcut, the profile view was Vasari's contribution. Whereas Vasari made claims about reviving and equalling antiquity on behalf of Ghiberti and Peruzzi, he made no such claim for Luca della Robbia. On the other hand, Luca was the inventor of a new technique of terracotta glazing, and created a method of working in sculpture that was, as Vasari commented, completely unknown to the ancient world. 'By inventing this art', wrote Vasari, 'he gained immortal glory and everlasting fame.'[74] His invention may also have gained him a medallic portrait in the *Lives*.

Circumstantial evidence that innovation beyond ancient achievement was a criterion sufficing for a profile portrait is provided by Vasari's comments about Antonello da Messina, also shown in profile in the woodcuts. Vasari, unfortunately, failed to cite a source for his portrait, so that we have nothing to compare it to and cannot be certain that the profile aspect is Vasari's intervention. Nevertheless, it is worth mentioning that Antonello was credited by Vasari with the introduction of oil painting to Italy. He was

greatly honoured in his obsequies by the craftsmen [in Venice], by reason of the gift bestowed by him on art in the form of the new manner of colouring ... There is no writer to be found who attributes this manner of colouring to the ancients, and if it could be known for certain that it did not exist among them, this age would surpass all the excellence of the ancients by virtue of this perfection.[75]

The profile views in these woodcut portraits, where not taken from sources rendering the subject in profile, may be pointers to the artists' abilities either to revive antiquity or to surpass it through technical innovation.

In other portraits, the alteration of the source may be subtle but decisive in terms of the viewer's response to the subject. The woodcut portrait of Francesco Salviati was derived from his self-portrait in the fresco of the *Triumph of Furius Camillus* in the Sala dell'Udienza of Florence's Palazzo Vecchio (see Figures 2.10 and 2.11). Salviati represented himself looking back over his shoulder to meet the viewer's gaze. Vasari altered the portrait so that in his woodcut Salviati is seen from the front; the angle of his head is also changed so that instead of looking downward at the viewer in a bold and confident way, he now looks upward. The result of this angle of view, in combination with the placement of his pupils in the very corners of his eyes, is that Salviati seems to look out at the viewer furtively, as if he is at the same time attempting hurriedly to turn away. Salviati is given a swarthy complexion by means of dark shadowing on his face but also through the startling brightness of the whites of his eyes, a characteristic that can fruitfully be compared with the protagonist of Dürer's engraving, *Melencolia* (which Vasari knew).[76] In fact, Vasari's portrait of Salviati seems to aim to emphasize the melancholic and solitary aspects of his friend's character, to which he made several allusions in his biography. Vasari stated that Salviati's inability to get along with officials in the court of Duke Cosimo was largely due to the fact that 'Francesco was by nature melancholy.'[77] He was equally unable to succeed at the French court because he was 'melancholy, abstinent, sickly and morose'.[78] In sum, 'Francesco was affectionate by nature, but suspicious, credulous, acute, subtle and penetrative … in the end this nature of his, so irresolute, suspicious and solitary, did harm to no one but himself.'[79] Vasari altered Salviati's portrait in such a manner as to closely reflect these very character traits.

Vasari's woodcut portrait of Jacopo Pontormo almost certainly derives from one of the depictions of him by his pupil Bronzino (see Figures 2.12 and 2.13). Bronzino depicted Pontormo next to Christ's shoulder in the *Christ in Limbo* of 1552 (Florence, Santa Croce), and again several years later in the fresco of the *Martyrdom of St Lawrence* (Florence, San Lorenzo). The fresco, of 1567–69, was painted too late to have served as the source for Vasari's woodcut. An additional portrait, now lost but cited by Vasari, was added by Bronzino to Pontormo's frescoes in the choir of San Lorenzo, left unfinished at Pontormo's death in 1557.[80] This was presumably Vasari's actual source. Since the portrait in Bronzino's later fresco of the *Martyrdom* resembles that in *Christ in Limbo* in all respects except that Pontormo's beard has turned white, it seems reasonable to assume that the portrait in the choir was similar to both. Wolfram Prinz, who otherwise refrained from making statements about the emotional content of Vasari's portrait woodcuts, noted that in this woodcut Vasari has given us an excellent image of the aged, angst-ridden Pontormo.[81] The emphasis is probably Vasari's, since in Bronzino's surviving paintings Pontormo is shown with a mild expression, devoid of the anxious lines in the forehead and the staring eyes with which Vasari depicted him. In his biography of Pontormo, Vasari described the old artist as solitary and eccentric; he went up to his bedroom by means of a stepladder that he could pull up after him so that he could not be followed.[82] Pontormo was, like Piero di Cosimo, 'solitary beyond all belief', and so afraid of death that he would not hear it mentioned.[83] The baleful expression in Vasari's portrait woodcut is a clear guide to his view of Pontormo's personality – towards the end of his life, Pontormo descended into an anxious and misanthropic way of life.

Physiognomy is also relevant to understanding the portrait of Rosso Fiorentino (Figure 2.14). Prinz was unable to identify Vasari's source for this portrait but, during a conference at the Warburg Institute in 1995, Jeroen Stumpel convincingly suggested that it may have been a drawing by Andrea del Sarto, later used for one of the apostles in his fresco of the *Last Supper* (see Figure 2.15).[84] Like the woodcut, the drawing shows a man in profile, with short, slightly wavy hair and a beard. The resemblance is most striking in the furrowed forehead that creates a small lump at the eyebrow, the shape of the eye itself and the pronounced cheekbone. Stumpel was unable to explain the alteration of features such as Rosso's nose (which is made larger and more blunt) and his beard (which is made longer), except to speculate that this was the fault of the woodcutter. But, as we have noted, the woodcutters seem to have followed Vasari's designs with unfailing accuracy. If this drawing was Vasari's source, as I believe it to have been, then I suspect that the changes instead constitute a deliberate reference to Rosso's leonine, choleric temperament. In Renaissance physiognomic theory, a strained prominent brow, a blunt, fleshy, obtuse nose and pronounced cheekbones with swelling facial muscles (all present in Vasari's woodcut) were considered to be signs of a leonine character – a great soul given to great deeds and to magnanimity, but also prone to fits of rage.[85]

We learn from Vasari's biography that Rosso was 'endowed with a most beautiful presence … he was always, however poor in circumstances, rich in spirit and grandeur'.[86] King Francis I enjoyed the company of Rosso, who was 'imposing in person, with red hair in accordance with his name, and serious, considerate and very judicious … in his every action'.[87] Rosso lived there 'like a nobleman, with a good number of servants and horses, giving banquets and showing all manner of extraordinary courtesies to all his acquaintances and friends'.[88]

But, in Vasari's account of his life, Rosso was prone to bouts of anger. He had left Italy after causing a row during mass, when a priest struck one of his assistants. And, rich as he was in France, he was robbed and rashly accused an innocent friend of the crime, having him arrested and tortured. When the accused issued a writ of libel against Rosso, he 'perceived that he had not only accused his friend falsely, but had also stained his own honour … he therefore resolved to kill himself by his own hand rather than be punished by others'.[89] Rosso's appearance in Vasari's woodcut reflects his character – imposing, gracious, but rash and impetuous – both the positive and the negative attributes of the leonine man.

As we have seen, in the woodcut illustrations Vasari was concerned to provide visual analogues to the text. This has been shown both with respect to the title pages and endpieces of both editions of the *Lives*, and now also with respect to the woodblock portraits included for the first time in the edition of 1568. Thus the woodcuts can by no means be seen as merely decorative additions to the book; they were for Vasari a vital part of the fabric of the entire work, and an essential component of his project for promotion of the visual arts and their practitioners. They reinforce the message of the biographies, presenting artists as moral and social exemplars.

Acknowledgements

My essay is based upon a chapter in my PhD thesis, 'Vasari, Prints and Printmaking', London, Courtauld Institute of Art, 1999. My research was generously funded by the Social Sciences and Humanities Research Council of Canada, and the Commonwealth Scholarship Commission in the United Kingdom. Papers on this subject were presented at the Universities Art Association of Canada Annual Conference in Montreal (1996), at the Annual Conference of the Renaissance Society of America in Vancouver (1997) and at the Leonardo da Vinci Society Symposium in London (1999). I am grateful for advice offered by several people, including my PhD adviser Patricia Rubin, David McTavish, Martin Kemp, Charles Hope and Rodney Palmer.

Notes

1. G. Vasari, *Le Vite de' più eccellenti pittori scultori e architettori nelle redazioni del 1550 e 1568*, ed. R. Bettarini and P. Barocchi, 6 vols, Florence 1966–87 (hereafter Vasari-BB), VI, pp. 228–9: 'In altre poi mi ha pregato … che io ci faccia tre trattati della scultura, pittura et architettura, con disegni di figure, per dichiarare secondo l'occasioni et insegnare le cose dell'arte'. Vasari's comment on Lampsonius's letter (which has not survived) appears in a passage following the 'Life of Giulio Clovio'.

2. J. Kliemann, 'Su alcuni concetti umanistici del pensiero e del mondo figurativo vasariani', in *Giorgio Vasari: tra decorazione ambientale e storiografia artistica*, Florence 1985, pp. 73–82. Vasari-BB, I, pp. 9–10: 'dalle … penne delli scrittori … per difenderli il più che io posso da questa seconda morte e mantenergli più lungamente che sia possible nelle memorie de' vivi'; VI, p. 411: 'per … fare immortali questi artefici gloriosi, che io semplicemente ho tolti alla polvere e alla oblivione'.

3. 'HAC SOSPITE NVNQVAM HOS PERIISSE VIROS, VICTOS AVT MORTE FATEBOR': 'I shall claim with this breath these men never perished, nor have been conquered by death.' A document in Borghini's hand explains the meaning of the inscription; see J. Kliemann, cat. no. VII-60g, in *Giorgio Vasari: principi, letterati e artisti nelle carte di Giorgio Vasari*, ed. C. Davis, M. Davis, L. Corti and J. Kliemann, exh. cat. Florence 1981 (hereafter Davis et al.), pp. 238–42, especially p. 239.

4. For the 1568 edition, see Kliemann (as in n. 3), pp. 238–42, and M. Warnke, 'Die erste Seite aus den "Viten" Giorgio Vasaris: der politische Gehalt seiner Renaissancevorstellung', *Kritische Berichte*, V, 1977, pp. 5–28, esp. p. 16.

5. E. Cochrane, *Historians and Historiography in the Italian Renaissance*, Chicago 1981, pp. 15–20, 393–404.

6. Ibid., pp. 393–9. For printed editions of numerous categories of biography, see P. Rubin, *Giorgio Vasari: Art and History*, New Haven and London 1995, pp. 161–2 nn. 68–70.

7. Rubin (as in n. 6), pp. 155–61; P. Barolsky, *Michelangelo's Nose*, University Park 1990; Vasari-BB, III (Preface to the Second Part), p. 4: 'il che è proprio l'anima dell'istoria, e quello che invero insegna vivere e fa gli uomini prudenti … '.

8. L. Klinger, 'The Portrait Collection of Paolo Giovio', PhD thesis, Princeton 1991; a useful short history is P. L. de Vecchi, 'Il Museo Gioviano e le "Verae Imagines" degli uomini illustri', in *Omaggio a Tiziano: la cultura Milanese nell'età di Carlo V*, Milan 1977, pp. 87–96.

9. *Elogia veris clarorum virorum imaginibus apposita quae in Musaeo Ioviano Comi spectantur*, Venice 1547, and *Elogia virorum bellica virtute illustrium veris imaginibus supposita quae apud Musaeum spectantur*, Florence 1551. See also Kliemann (as in n. 3), p. 239.

10. Evidence to this effect has been presented by W. Prinz, in 'La seconda edizione del Vasari e la comparsa di "vite" artistiche con ritratti', *Il Vasari*, XXI, 1963, pp. 1–14, esp. pp. 5–7; and C. Davis, cat. no. VII-31, in Davis et al. (as in n. 3), pp. 213–15, esp. p. 214.

11. See P. O. Rave, 'Paolo Giovio und die Bildnisvitenbücher des Humanismus', *Jahrbuch der Berliner Museen*, I, 1959, pp. 119–54.

12. Vasari-BB, II (Preface to Part One), p. 32: 'e se d'alcuno mancasse il ritratto, ciò non è per colpa mia, ma per non si essere in alcuno luogo trovato'. He reiterates this disclaimer in two of the Lives of these artists: ibid. (Life of Pietro Cavallini), p. 189: 'Il ritratto suo non si è mai trovato per diligenza che fatta sì sia: però non si mette'; ibid., IV (Life of Correggio), p. 54: 'Ho usato ogni diligenzia d'avere il suo ritratto: e perché lui non lo fece e da altri non è stato mai ritratto, perché visse sempre positivamente, non l'ho potuto trovare.'

13. The portraits and their frames were first analysed by W. Prinz, in *Vasaris Sammlung von Künstlerbildnissen*, Florence 1966. Additional clarification of the meaning of the frames was provided by C. Davis, cat. no. VIII-11, in Davis et al. (as in n. 3), pp. 258–9.

14. The significance of the *Ritratti* was discussed by Davis (as in n. 13), pp. 258–9. Of the only two copies of the book known to me, one is in the Harvard Rare Book Library (Houghton Typ 525 68.866) and the other at Villa I Tatti in Florence (Biblioteca Berenson SPC N 6923.V32 1568).

15. Vasari-BB, V (Life of Marcantonio), p. 25: 'Per ultimo basta vedere gl'intagli di questo nostro Libro dei ritratti de' pittori, scultori et architetti, disegnati da Giorgio Vasari e dai suoi creati, e stati intagliate da maestro Cristofano [...], che ha operato et opera di continuo in Vinezia infinite cose degne di memoria'. For letters from Cosimo Bartoli to Vasari, see K. Frey, *Der literarische Nachlass Giorgio Vasaris*, II, Munich 1930, p. 107 (19 August 1564), and pp. 347–8 (13 September 1567).

16. H. W. Frey, *Der literarische Nachlass Giorgio Vasaris*, III, Munich 1940, p. 52 n. 3. Cristofano dell'Altissimo was sent to Como in 1552 and stayed until 1558. Vasari provided in the 1568 edition of the *Lives* a list of the portraits copied for Cosimo's collection. In his discussion of the members of the Accademia del Disegno (Vasari-BB, VI, p. 239) Vasari noted: 'È stato anco discepolo, prima del Puntormo e poi del Bronzino, Cristofano dell'Altissimo pittore, il quale ... fu mandato dal signor duca Cosimo a Como a ritrarre dal Museo di monsignor Giovio molti quadri di persone illustri ... '.

17. G. Vasari, *Le vite de' più eccellenti pittori, scultori et architettori scritte da Giorgio Vasari pittore aretino con nuove annotazioni e commenti*, ed. G. Milanesi, 9 vols, Florence 1878–85, V, p. 441 n. 2.

18. U. Thieme and F. Becker, *Allgemeines Lexikon der Bildenden Künstler*, 37 vols, Leipzig 1907–50, VI, p. 533 (Chrieger) and VII, pp. 415–16 (Coriolano).

19. For the letter from Giambullari of January 1550, see K. Frey, *Der literarische Nachlass Giorgio Vasaris*, I, Munich 1923, p. 247. Cosimo Bartoli wrote on 23 February 1550 to say that two woodcuts had arrived from Venice (ibid., p. 265).

20. Prinz (as in n. 13), p. 36, discovered four of these pairs; the Girolamo da Treviso – Sodoma repetition was first noted in S. Gregory, 'Vasari, Prints and Printmaking', PhD thesis, London, Courtauld Institute of Art 1999, p. 101 n. 109.

21. Vasari-BB, II, p. 32: 'E nel discrivere le forme e le fattezze degl'artefici sarò breve, perché i ritratti loro, i quali sono da me stati messi insieme con non minor spesa e fatica che diligenza, meglio dimostreranno quali essi artefici fussero quanto all'effigie che il raccontarlo non farebbe giamai.'

22. Prinz (as in n. 13), p. 40.

23. C. Hope, 'Historical Portraits in the "Lives" and in the Frescoes of Giorgio Vasari', in *Giorgio Vasari: tra decorazione ambientale e storiografia artistica*, Florence 1985, pp. 321–38.

24. By my count, the sources for 83 portraits can be identified. Many were discovered by Prinz; other sources have been suggested by L. Ragghianti Collobi, in 'Il "Libro de' Disegni" ed i ritratti per le "Vite" del Vasari', *Critica d'Arte*, XVIII, 1971, pp. 37–64. These scholars sometimes disagree; I discuss their observations in more detail in Gregory (as in n. 20), pp. 101–2 n. 110. See also D. Franklin, 'The Source for Vasari's Portrait of Morto da Feltre', *Print Quarterly*, XIV, 1997, pp. 79–80. Franklin has additionally proposed a more likely source for Vasari's portrait of Ridolfo Ghirlandaio, in 'Towards a New Chronology for Ridolfo Ghirlandaio and Michele Tosini', *Burlington Magazine*, CLX, 1998, pp. 445–55, esp. p. 447. I have found the source for the portrait of Giovanni Antonio Sogliani precisely where Vasari said his self-portrait could be found: in Sogliani's *Adoration of the Magi*, painted for S. Domenico in Fiesole (Vasari's woodcut is based on the man with hands folded in prayer behind the young magus on the left). See the Life of Sogliani, Vasari-BB, IV, p. 440.

25. Hope (as in n. 23), p. 337.

26. Vasari-BB, V (Life of Marcantonio Raimondi), p. 25: the portraits were 'disegnati da Giorgio Vasari e dai suoi creati'.

27. For the portraits see Ragghianti Collobi (as in n. 24), figs 37, 41, 45; for comments on the fidelity of the reproductions see ibid., p. 58.

28. P. Meller, 'Physiognomical Theory in Renaissance Heroic Portraits', in *Studies in Western Art*, vol. II: *The Renaissance and Mannerism*, Princeton 1963, pp. 53–69; A. Chastel, *The Myth of the Renaissance 1420–1520*, Geneva 1969, 'Physiognomy and Portraiture', pp. 145–6, esp. p. 145.

29. Vasari-BB, V, p. 404: 'il di fuori suole essere indizio di quello di dentro e dimostra quali sieno gl'animi nostri'.

30. For reproductions of these images, see Prinz (as in n. 13), p. 130.

31. Other examples are discussed in greater detail in Gregory (as in n. 20), pp. 104–15. To summarize changes made to the known portrait sources, two instances involve the removal or addition of clerical attire; in three cases, Vasari added hats; in four cases he added a shirt collar resembling a ruffle of lace or linen; in another four cases he added fur collars. To one portrait he added a garment resembling a toga; to another a chain with a cross pendant around the neck. In another case he removed chains from around the neck and also removed a fur collar.

32. Vasari-BB, III (Life of Fra Filippo Lippi), p. 337. Vasari mistakenly cited the *Feast of Herod* as the scene in which he appears 'in a prelate's black habit'; the self-portrait is actually in the *Mourning over the Body of St Stephen*.

33. Vasari-BB, III, p. 331: 'et era tanto perduto dietro a questo appetito [venereo]'.

34. Ibid., p. 329: 'animosamente si cavò l'abito d'età di anni XVII'.

35. Prinz (as in n. 13), p. 135.

36. Vasari-BB, V (Life of Sebastiano), pp. 95–6.

37. Ragghianti Collobi (as in n. 24), p. 50.

38. Vasari-BB, IV (Life of Bramante), p. 80. It is not certain that Raphael's fresco was Vasari's source; however, the woodcut resembles the figure of Euclid far more than it does any other known portrait. If this was his source, then Vasari also raised the head slightly to provide a viewpoint somewhat less foreshortened than the head of Euclid in the fresco.

39. Vasari's Life of Piero (Vasari-BB, IV, pp. 59–71) refers constantly to the painter's solitariness and abstraction; for his 'bestial' life, see p. 61: 'teneva una vita da uomo più tosto bestiale che umano'.

40. Ibid., pp. 61–2: 'si contentava veder salvatico ogni cosa come la sua natura'.

41. The anonymous drawing after Andrea's fresco is reproduced in J. Shearman, *Andrea del Sarto*, 2 vols, Oxford 1965, I, pl. 37.

42. For Girolamo Muziano's drawing, see L. Ragghianti Collobi, *Il 'Libro de' disegni' del Vasari*, 2 vols, Florence 1974, II, pl. 431.

43. Vasari-BB, IV, p. 62: 'E se Piero non fusse stato tanto astratto e avesse tenuto più conto di sé nella vita che egli non fece, arebbe fatto conoscere il grande ingegno che egli aveva, di maniera che sarebbe stato adorato, dove egli per la bestialità sua fu più tosto tenuto pazzo.'

44. Ibid., p. 60: 'fare suoi castelli in aria'.

45. Ibid., p. 62. For Leonardo's notation, see M. Kemp and M. Walker eds, *Leonardo da Vinci, On Painting*, New Haven and London 1989, p. 222. S. Fermor, in *Piero di Cosimo: Fiction, Invention, and Fantasia*, London 1993, pp. 26–8 and 35–6, shows how Vasari's Life of Leonardo provides a counterpoint to that of Piero.

46. Vasari-BB, IV (Life of Leonardo), pp. 16, 19, 27.

47. Ibid., p. 17: 'era in quello ingegno infuso tanta grazia da Dio et una dimostrazione sì terribile, accordata con l'intelletto e memoria che lo serviva … che con i ragionamenti vinceva e con le ragioni confondeva ogni gagliardo ingegno'.

48. The resemblance of the Melzi drawing of Leonardo (Windsor 12726) to portraits of Aristotle was pointed out by J. Roberts in *Leonardo da Vinci*, exh. cat. London 1989, p. 46. Patricia Rubin observed that Vasari's Life of Leonardo was the life of a philosopher, in her 'What Men Saw: Vasari's Life of Leonardo da Vinci and the Image of the Renaissance Artist', *Art History*, XIII, 1990, pp. 35–46. She drew attention to the similarity between the Leonardo portrait and images of sages in fifteenth-century world chronicles.

49. Vasari-BB, V (Life of Bastiano da Sangallo), p. 393: 'Nel che fare parlando egli con gravità, adagio e sentenziosamente, gli fu da una schiera di virtuosi artefici posto il sopranome di

Aristotile: il quale gli stette anco meglio, quanto pareva che, secondo un antico ritratto di quel grandissimo filosofo e secretario della natura, egli molto il somigliasse.'

50. Vasari-BB, VI (Life of Michelangelo), p. 122: 'Alle gambe portò invec[c]hiando di continuove stivali di pelle di cane sopra lo ignudo i mesi interi, che, quando gli voleva cavare, poi nel tirargli ne veniva spesso le pelle'; A. Condivi, *Vita di Michelagnolo Buonarroti*, ed. G. Nencioni, Florence 1998, p. 63: 'più volte ha dormito vestito e con li stivaletti in gamba, quali ha sempre usati sì per cagion del granchio, sì per altri rispetti, e è stato qualche volta tanto a cavarsegli, che poi insieme con li stivaletti n'è venuta la pelle, come quella della biscia.'

51. Letter from Pagni to Riccio, 21 October 1549, in G. Pieraccini, *La stirpe de' Medici di Caffaggiolo*, 3 vols (vol. 2 in 2 pts), Florence 1924–25, II, pt I, p. 56.

52. Letter of 11 May 1529, in P. Aretino, *Il primo libro delle lettere*, ed. F. Nicolini, Bari 1913, p. 19: 'Né mi son tanto rallegrato del dono per la ricchezza sua, quanto de l'avere voi, che principe sète, giudicatomi degno di portare gli abiti dei principi.' Aretino describes the clothes, which included a black velvet robe with a lining of cloth-of-gold, and a brocade jerkin.

53. Vasari-BB, III, p. 40.

54. Letter of 21 January 1530, to Count Massimiano Stampa, in Aretino (as in n. 52), pp. 23–4: ' ... dono conveniente a la grandezza vostra più che a la bassezza mia, la quale non si vergogna a esser vista ornata di robbe tali per amor de la vertù che l'alza ... '.

55. Vasari-BB, VI (Life of Michelangelo), pp. 4–5, for Michelangelo's noble birth; and p. 122: 'Certamante fu al mondo la sua venuta ... uno esempio mandato da Dio agli uomini dell'arte nostra, perché s'imparrassi da lui nella vita sua i costumi, e nelle opere come avevano a essere i veri et ottimi artefici.'

56. Ibid., pp. 113–15: 'donò [to Urbino] scudi dumila in una volta, cosa che è solita da farsi per i Cesari e' Pontefici grandi'.

57. Vasari-BB, V (Life of Michele da Sanmichele), p. 374: 'Fu Michele di costumatissima vita et in tutte le sue cose molto onorevole'; p. 375: 'Fu dunque Michele cortese sopra quanti uomini furono mai, con ciò fusse che, non si tosto sapeva il bisogno e desiderio degl'amici, che cercava di compiacergli, se avesse dovuto spendere la vita; né mai alcuni gli fece servizio che non ne fusse in molto doppii ristorato.'

58. Ibid.: 'trovò il San Michele aver molto innanzi mandato a sua madre ... una soma di robe così belle et onorate, come se fusse stato un ricchissimo signore'.

59. That Vasari's use of brocade was not meant to refer only to personal wealth is evident from its absence in the portraits of other wealthy artists, notably, for example, Raphael and Titian.

60. Vasari-BB, III (Life of Mantegna), p. 549: 'non avevano quelle pitture somiglianza di vivi ma di statue antiche di marmo'.

61. Vasari visited Mantua in 1542, and may have seen Mantegna's grave at that time. However, he mentioned the bronze portrait only in 1568; see Vasari-BB, III, p. 555.

62. The sources are cited by Prinz (as in n. 13), pp. 72–5, 114–15, 125–6. I disagree with Prinz concerning Ghiberti's portrait, as I will explain later.

63. Vasari-BB, III (Life of Ghiberti), pp. 75–6, 88; ibid. (Life of Masaccio), pp. 124, 128; ibid., IV (Life of Guillaume de Marcillat), pp. 221, 223; ibid. (Life of Cronaca), pp. 234, 236; ibid. (Life of Polidoro da Caravaggio and Maturino), pp. 456–60; ibid., V (Life of Simone Mosca), pp. 337–8.

64. Life of Titian, Vasari-BB, VI, p. 157: 'se Tiziano in quel tempo fusse stato a Roma et avesse veduto le cose di Michelagnolo, quelle di Raffaello e le statue antiche, et avesse studiato il disegno, arebbe fatto cose stupendissime ... '.

65. Prinz (as in n. 13), pp. 72–3.

66. Vico published several books of engravings of ancient medals, beginning with *Imagini con tutti i riversi trovati et le vite de gli imperatori*, Parma 1548, including addresses to the reader by Antonio Zantani. Andrea Fulvio's *Illustrium imagines*, Rome 1517, purports to contain reproductions of ancient coins, though many are the author's inventions.

67. For Vasari's interest in medals, see for example the Life of Gentile da Fabriano and Pisanello, Vasari-BB, III, p. 368; Life of Francesco Francia, ibid., p. 582; and Life of Valerio Vicentino ... and Other Engravers of Cameos and Gems, ibid., IV, pp. 619–30. He cites Vico's books in the Life of Marcantonio Raimondi, ibid., V, p. 11.

68. Vasari-BB, III (Life of Ghiberti), p. 88: 'fu il primo che cominciasse a imitare le cose degli antichi Romani, delle quali fu molto studioso, come esser dee chiunche disidera di bene operare'.

69. Ibid., p. 94: 'e tutte bellissime: come uno Sansone ignudo che … mostra quella perfezzione che maggior può mostrare cosa fatta nel tempo degli antichi'; p. 100: 'si può dire che questa opera abbia la sua perfezzione in tutte le cose, e che ella sia la più bella opera del mondo e che si sia vista mai fra gli antichi e' moderni'.

70. Ibid., p. 77: 'Diletossi anco di contraffare i conii delle medaglie antiche, e di naturale nel suo tempo ritrasse molti suoi amici.'

71. Vasari-BB, IV (Life of Peruzzi), p. 324. For his self-portrait drawing, see Ragghianti Collobi (as in n. 24), pl. 350.

72. Vasari-BB, III (Life of Luca della Robbia), p. 58.

73. Ragghianti Collobi (as in n. 24), fig. 15 and pp. 40 and 60 n. 3.

74. Vasari-BB, III, p. 58: 'Onde ne venne aricchito il mondo e l'arte del disegno d'un' arte nuova, utile e bellissima, et egli di gloria e lode immortale e perpetua.'

75. Vasari-BB, III (Life of Antonello), pp. 308–9: 'Fu dagl'artefici nell'essequie molto onorato per il dono fatto all'arte della nuova maniera di colorire … La qual cosa tanto più debbe essere in pregio, quanto manco si trova scrittore alcuno che questa maniera di colorire assegni agl'antichi. E se si potesse sapere che ella non fusse stata veramente appresso di loro, avanzarebbe pure questo secolo l'eccellenza dell'antico in questa perfezzione.'

76. Vasari describes the print in his discussion of Dürer's prints in the Life of Marcantonio Raimondi; see Vasari-BB, V, p. 6. The idiosyncratic spelling of 'Melencolia' is Dürer's, as it appears on the engraving.

77. Vasari-BB, V (Life of Francesco Salviati), p. 522: 'Era Francesco di natura malinconico … '.

78. Ibid., p. 528: Salviati did not enjoy life in France 'per esser di natura tutto contraria a quella degli uomini in quel paese essendo che, quanto vi sono avuti cari et amati gli uomini allegri, gioviali, che vivono alla libera e si trovano volentieri in brigata et a far banchetti, tanto vi sono, non dico fuggito, ma meno amati e carezzati coloro che sono, come Francesco era, di natura malinconico, sobrio, malsano e stitico.'

79. Ibid., p. 533: 'Era il Salviati amorevole di natura, ma sospettoso, facile a credere ogni cosa, acuto, sottile e penetrativo … ma finalmente quella sua sì fatta natura irresoluta, sospettosa e soletaria non fece danno se non a lui.'

80. Vasari-BB, VI (Of the Academicians), p. 236.

81. Prinz (as in n. 13), p. 139: 'Vasari gibt mit dem Vitenbild ein vorzügliches Bildnis des alten, angstvollen, und todesfürchtigen Pontormo.'

82. Vasari-BB, V, p.328: 'ha più tosto cera di casamento da uomo fantastico e soletario che di ben considerata abitura: con ciò sia che alla stanza dove stava a dormire e talvolte a lavorare si saliva per una scala di legno, la quale, entrato che egli era, tirava su con una carrucola, a ciò niuno potesse salire da lui senza sua voglia o saputa'.

83. Ibid., pp. 333–4: 'quasi sempre stette da sé solo … fu tanto pauroso della morte, che non voleva, non che altro, udirne ragionare … fu oltre ogni credenza solitario'.

84. 'The Accidental Portrait: Drawings after the Model in the Studios of Andrea del Sarto and Pontormo', paper presented at the conference 'The Image of the Individual c.1400–1500', Warburg Institute, London, 10 March 1995.

85. See Meller (as in n. 28).

86. Vasari-BB, IV (Life of Rosso), pp. 473–4: 'Rosso era … dotato di bellissima presenza … e sempre, per povero ch'egli fosse, fu ricco d'animo e di grandezza.'

87. Ibid., p. 486: 'Rosso … era grande di persona, di pelo rosso conforme al nome, et in tutte le sue azzioni grave, considerato, e di molto giudizio.'

88. Ibid., p. 487: 'il Rosso con buon numero di servidori e di cavalli viveva da signore e facea banchetti e cortesie straordinarie a tutti i conoscenti e amici … '.

89. Ibid., p. 490: 'parendogli non solo avere falsamente vituperato l'amico, ma ancora mac[c]hiato il proprio onore, et il disdirsi o tener altri vituperosi modi lo dichiarava similmente uomo disleale e cattivo. Per che deliberato d'uccidersi da se stesso più tosto che esser castigato da altri, prese questo partito … '.

TIZIANO DA CADOR
PITTORE.

2.1   Portrait of Titian, woodcut, from Vasari, *Le Vite de' più eccellenti pittori scultori e architettori*, 1568 edition

2.2   Titian, *Self-portrait*, c. 1562, oil on canvas, Berlin, Gemäldegalerie

2.3   Portrait of Fra Filippo Lippi, woodcut, from Vasari, *Le Vite de' più eccellenti pittori scultori e architettori*, 1568 edition

2.4   Fra Filippo Lippi, *Coronation of the Virgin* (detail), 1439–47, tempera on panel, Florence, Galleria degli Uffizi

PIERO DI COSIMO PITTOR
FIORENTINO

2.5   Portrait of Piero di Cosimo, woodcut, from Vasari, *Le Vite de' più eccellenti pittori scultori e architettori*, 1568 edition

2.6   Portrait of Leonardo da Vinci, woodcut, from Vasari, *Le Vite de' più eccellenti pittori scultori e architettori*, 1568 edition

LEONARDVS DAVINCI

2.7   Cristofano dell'Altissimo, *Portrait of Leonardo da Vinci*, c. 1552–58, oil on panel, Florence, Vasari Corridor, Galleria degli Uffizi

2.8   Andrea Mantegna, *Self-portrait*, before 1506, bronze relief, Mantua, Sant'Andrea

2.9   Portrait of Andrea Mantegna, woodcut, from Vasari, *Le Vite de' più eccellenti pittori scultori e architettori*, 1568 edition

FRANCESCO SALVIATI
PIT. FIORENTINO.

2.10   Portrait of Francesco Salviati, woodcut, from Giorgio Vasari, *Le Vite de' più eccellenti pittori scultori e architettori*, 1568 edition

2.11   Francesco Salviati, *Triumph of Furius Camillus* (detail), 1543–45, fresco,
Florence, Sala dell'Udienza, Palazzo Vecchio

IACOPO DA PVNTORMO PIT.
FIORENTINO.

2.12   Portrait of Jacopo Pontormo, woodcut, from Vasari, *Le Vite de' più eccellenti pittori scultori e architettori*, 1568 edition

2.13   Agnolo Bronzino, *Martyrdom of St Lawrence* (detail), 1567–69, fresco, Florence, San Lorenzo

2.14   Portrait of Rosso Fiorentino, woodcut, from Vasari, *Le Vite de' più eccellenti pittori scultori e architettori*, 1568 edition

2.15   Andrea del Sarto, *Head of a man*, c. 1520–26, black chalk on white paper,
Florence, Gabinetto Disegni e Stampe degli Uffizi

3

'Of little or even no importance to the architect': on absent ideals in Serlio's drawings in the Sixth Book, on domestic architecture

Vaughan Hart

The Bolognese architectural theorist Sebastiano Serlio (1475–1554) is well known for having produced one of the most easy to use, and hence widely studied, of the illustrated treatises on architecture published in vernacular languages in the sixteenth century.[1] Indeed his was the first-ever wide-ranging, fully illustrated architectural treatise. Before Palladio only the Roman author Vitruvius and the Renaissance master Leon Battista Alberti can be said to have rivalled Serlio's influence on those wishing to design buildings *all'antica* – in the antique manner. Twenty years or so after Serlio's death, the Mantuan antiquarian and art dealer Jacopo Strada eulogized the author for having 'renewed the art of architecture and made it easy for everyone. Indeed, he did more with his books than even Vitruvius had done before him, in that Vitruvius is obscure and not so easily understood by everyone'.[2]

The most important of the 'Books' (or chapters) Serlio produced after he left Italy for France was his sixth, concerned as it is with the design of domestic architecture ranging from peasant hut to royal palace, following the order first utilized by Francesco di Giorgio.[3] Although never published in his lifetime, this work of Serlio's survives in two variant manuscript versions and a set of trial woodcuts. One manuscript is held in the Bayerische Staatsbibliothek, Munich, and the other in Columbia University in New York.[4] This sixth book represents the first-ever attempt to illustrate a complete range of domestic architectural models matched to social status, first for the countryside and then for the city. This range went far beyond the few examples of Italian villas which close Serlio's third book (published in Venice in 1540), or those which Filarete and Francesco di Giorgio illustrated, or Alvise Cornaro discussed in his manuscript on domestic architecture of the common citizen written in the 1520s.[5] The surviving so-called Vienna manuscript of Serlio's seventh book records that he had studied Pliny the Younger's description of his Roman villa, Serlio designing a semi-circular *sala* 'in imitation' of one built by Pliny.[6] But in the absence of any surviving antique villa other than in ruined form, or of a description by Vitruvius of how to apply the architectural orders to domestic buildings (only briefly dealt with in Vitruvius's sixth book), Serlio's house designs are highly inventive yet practical. This is especially the case concerning his un-precedented drawings of dwellings for the poor. Soon after its production, the Columbia manuscript of Book VI passed through the hands of Jacques Androuet Du Cerceau and set the tone for his famous survey of the French château, the *Livre d'architecture* published in Paris in 1559 and 1561.[7] The manuscript was equally an influence on Philibert De l'Orme's domestic designs, illustrated in his *Premier tome* published in Paris in 1567. In the collected editions of Serlio's books of 1584 and 1600 the place of the sixth book was destined to be filled by his (unnumbered) book on gates, the *Libro extraordinario* (first published in Lyons in 1551), and by the time of the 1618–19 collected edition this additional book had, not surprisingly, been mistaken for the missing Book VI.

Serlio's sixth book was for the most part structured around a hierarchy of contemporary social types centred on the king. He frequently praises the French king, noting on François I that 'his magnanimity, wisdom and power can be clearly seen in many buildings arranged by his Majesty in his fine kingdom' (Munich MS, fol. 66v).[8] But the book did not attempt to house harmoniously any royalist 'ideal' society, as this praise might suggest, in either the rural projects or those in the city. Certainly there had been a healthy enough tradition of utopian speculation amongst Renaissance architectural theorists. But whereas Alberti had made recommendations concerning the ideal layout of cities,[9] Serlio includes no such discussion in Book VI. Whereas the 'utopian' pioneer Filarete had illustrated an ideal urban layout (called 'Sforzinda'), Serlio proposes no overall plan in his text or figures.[10] This is despite illustrating in the so-called 'Book VIII' (surviving in manuscript form only)[11] an ancient *cardo-decumanus*-style military city, following Niccolò Machiavelli's illustration of a Roman camp published in 1521 and Albrecht Dürer's model of an ideal city published in 1527. Whereas Francesco di Giorgio had drawn the figure of a man as an ideal outline for a walled town, Serlio has no such anthropomorphic images; and whereas Thomas More, whose *Utopia* had been published in 1516, had emphasized uniformity in his walled utopian city (called 'Aircastle') through regulation three-storey façades and collective ownership, Serlio expressed a diversity of domestic forms, wealth and private ownership. Serlio's houses are clearly defined in the drawings with boundary gates, walls and, on occasion, moats. Thus his drawings emphasized the divisions of society as he found it. Even Serlio's famous stage scenes in Book II (published in Paris in 1545), which are often taken as images related to the Urbino 'Ideal City' painting attributed to the circle of Piero della Francesca, are less than ideal in their typology. The 'comic scene' of private houses contains a brothel and inn, and the temple at the scene's focus is in a state of decay. The 'tragic scene' of houses of noblemen follows antique convention in forming a setting for 'violent and gruesome deaths' (fol. 68r),[12] whilst the 'satiric scene' of rustic huts forms one for licentious characters.

Moreover, despite Serlio's now-recognized evangelical bias and his passing reference to the fractiousness of Papal government when observing that the Papal states 'are the hot-bed and nest of fractiousness' (fol. 12v),[13] his text took no explicit political, religious or moral stance. Having described the activities of the tyrant, he concludes, 'But why should I go over these subjects which are of little or even no importance to the architect?' (fol. 27v).[14] Given the tendency towards utopianism that was Serlio's inheritance as an architectural-treatise writer, his rejection of the relevance of political theory, evident in his graphic models through their juxtaposition and conflicting characteristics, needs some explaining. In this essay, by examining Serlio's drawings I propose to clarify the reciprocal relationship between Serlio's rejection of political theory and his selection and presentation of graphic models.

It might be observed at the outset that the models illustrated in Serlio's sixth book are exclusively secular, ignoring both individual houses for priests and communal monasteries; as a result these models avoid any accusation of sectarianism. Serlio's book has therefore been characterized as owing something to the reforming quest for a universal (or non-sectarian) system of knowledge pursued by his Italian friends, men such as Achille Bocchi, Giulio Camillo and Alessandro Citolini.[15] Their aspirations had found particular expression in the use of images in Camillo's famous memory system, with its Neoplatonic ambition towards religious and political unity.[16] Despite recent comparisons by Mario Carpo between Serlio's treatise and Camillo's method, Serlio's drawings in Book VI were much more practical (or non-utopian) in their universal appeal than were Camillo's.[17] The hierarchical arrangement inherited by Serlio from Francesco di Giorgio echoed the easily memorized grades in Camillo's memory 'theatre' in pedagogical methodology alone. Serlio's gradation of domestic 'types' owed as much to the rise of systematization in the natural sciences and the study of language as promoted in particular by the Evangelical Alessandro Citolini, a witness to Serlio's will of 1528.[18]

It was earlier pointed out that Serlio's domestic models are monarchical in character rather than republican, in line with his French patronage at the time of working on the sixth book. However, the universal applicability of these models is further emphasized by the fact that his city projects include, ambiguously, a communal building (a *Podestà*; see Figure 3.1) and a palace for a governor serving an alien ruler (Figure 3.2). Here again no specific recommendations are made in drawn or written form concerning the ideal layout of streets, squares or even a city which these public buildings might serve and help structure. The craftsman's and merchant's city dwellings could certainly be built in rows,[19] a fact represented in the drawings by potentially blank party walls, and would therefore have suited a partnership of builders or a wealthy developer. However, Serlio's more noble urban houses in Book VI, for wealthy merchants, gentlemen, princes and kings, are illustrated and described as unique, freestanding projects, defined as they are by clear boundaries, this time with windows on all sides.[20] Serlio's only interrelated designs in his treatise are for the 'idealized' Roman military camp in 'Book VIII' which, in contrast, is completely divorced from contemporary urban realities and expectations of commodity. The projects in Book VI, rather than forming any such continuous new urban fabric, are for the most part applicable to all available sites of sufficient size in the city. Serlio's city house of the *condottiero* (Figure 3.3), although intended for a gentleman by rank, is to be built amongst those of the poorest folk and the peasants of higher rank (see fol. 57v).[21] This recommendation serves to emphasize the displacement between the neatly arranged social hierarchy of Book VI and the urban mix of most European cities which the book does not attempt to reform but to work within.

This realism extends to Serlio's treatment of contemporary social types. Previous commentators have glossed over the conflicting nature of these types by presenting them as combining a republican and monarchical system similar to that found in Venice.[22] However, in the sixth book Serlio adopts a pragmatic strategy towards the contemporary problems of social organization and the diversity of political systems which the architect might encounter, whether monarchical, republican, papal, or communal. He had himself experienced the oppressive presence of the Cardinal Legate in Papal Bologna, under Julius II's rule following the fall of the Bentivogli in 1506.[23] This may have led him to remark that governors 'administer justice more rigorously [or 'violently' in the Columbia manuscript] than the *Podestà*, particularly in the regions where I was born, and sometimes through their administration they provoke some of the people to armed riot' (fol. 61v).[24] Nevertheless, in the city models Serlio provides the architect with a model for a fortified house suitable for a governor serving an alien ruler, the equivalent of the tyrant prince of the countryside models. Serlio had also experienced at first hand the tyranny of Cesare Borgia in the Romagna region and, like Machiavelli in Florence, recognized the instability of a government not based on the goodwill of the people. He echoes both Alberti and Machiavelli concerning the best defence for a prince in noting that

The noble prince who is liberally minded, just and kind to his subjects and who fears God, has no need of fortresses; the hearts and minds of his subjects will be his protection and impregnable bastion. I myself witnessed this with Francesco Maria, Duke of Urbino. He had been driven out of his State and the walls of Urbino had been destroyed such that if he had returned he could not have lived there safely, and yet when God willed it he retook his State by force of arms and slept securely in a thus unwalled Urbino, guarded by his subjects. On the other hand, as for the cruel, greedy tyrant, who steals other people's goods, who rapes virgins, wives and widows, who dispossesses his subjects, all the fortresses in the world could not protect him. But Heavens above, there are some today who, although their dominion may be quite small, all the same they play the tyrant over it. Nonetheless, since I have to discuss the habitations of all ranks of men which are to be built outside the city, now is the moment when I must discuss that of the tyrant prince (fol. 27v).[25]

The idea of conflict is thus built into the very concept of Book VI, finding form in the illustrations of fortified houses for the *condottiero* and the tyrant which reflect those of Serlio's master, Baldassare Peruzzi. Both *condottiero* and tyrant destabilized royal authority, as Alberti and later Machiavelli had emphasized, and as Serlio himself notes in explaining why the *condottiero*'s city house should be in the poorer part of town, that is 'distant from the Palace, so that the Palace would not be able to attack the patron of the house easily were he to perform an act of disobedience' (fol. 57v).[26] The inclusion of both factious types in Book VI dramatically underlines the political contradictions and lack of utopianism of the work as a whole. In the city projects the isolated rusticated fortress of the *condottiero* (see Figure 3.3) is directly followed by the open loggias, shops, staircases and civic clocktower of the public magistrate's chambers (the model *Podestà*; see Figure 3.1).

Serlio's pragmatism concerning the need for, and design of, fortifications is in contrast to earlier architectural theorists. Although Alberti had discussed the house of the tyrant and the fortress in his treatise, here the ultimate protective power is attributed to beauty; for 'what other human art might sufficiently protect a building to save it from human attack? Beauty may even influence an enemy, by restraining his anger and so preventing the work from being violated' (VI.2).[27] We have seen that Francesco di Giorgio linked his fortifications directly to Vitruvian anthropomorphism in designing them in human shape, evoking the harmonies of microcosm and macrocosm, whilst Filarete not suprisingly ignored the tyrant's fortress when illustrating house types in his utopia. In contrast, when Serlio illustrates model gates for fortified cities in Book VII (published in Frankfurt in 1575), their design and inclusion amongst common 'situations' an architect might encounter is justified once again by him entirely on practical grounds. For he laments that 'the foremost leaders of Christians, who ought to be trying to keep peace amongst themselves, are in fact the very men who are continually causing and inciting new wars'.[28]

The Serlian architect was thus not expected to transform the poverty and contradictions of men, as in previous theoretical incarnations, but to practise in contemporary circumstances and respond to a wide range of social groups. Serlio's drawings in Book VI comprise a representative diagram of European society, excepting priests – who are excluded, as was previously suggested, to avoid sectarianism. Serlio sets out for the first time to accommodate decorously the 'meanest hovel of a poor peasant', yet with no substantial improvements to the commodity of the peasant house of his day; he acknowledges but chooses to omit 'the humble hut of the poor beggar', and defines the poorest of peasants to be housed by him as a 'poor man living off his own labours with his small household, who has a little land and who needs at least one room to sleep in and in which to have a fire' (fol. 1v).[29] Hence despite his status as 'peasant', Serlio's smallholder has farm animals and land, is self-sufficient and thus not reliant on a feudal lord for either cottage or protection – the text emphasizes that Serlio's peasant houses are particularly vulnerable to being commandeered by passing soldiers. Serlio's peasant is expected to pay for the construction of his house himself, either with the services of an architect or, again somewhat inexplicably, directly from a copy of Book VI.[30] The feudal or patrician models of property ownership common throughout Europe at this time are at no point acknowledged by Serlio in his descriptions of the lower-order country houses. Rather, as the drawings emphasize, these houses are physically and economically independent from one another and, more significantly, from the country houses for the nobility illustrated subsequently. Throughout the drawings in Book VI the expression of an individual's status through property size and degree of ornament (or decorum) is regulated by a free market or by the variable means of the social grades, rather than by any idealized central economic and legal power in the form of a feudal overlord, commune or mercantile landlord. A prominent example of contemporary housing built by a mercantile landlord is the Fuggerei at Augsburg, constructed for the workers of the Fugger family around 1543. Serlio's independent rural projects, like their city counterparts, do not form any such 'ideal' community and owe little to French feudal and mercantile traditions or to examples of charitable housing in Lyons and Venice, as has been claimed.[31] Rather, once again they are non-specific designs perfectly adaptable to contemporary models of ownership – whether communal, feudal or freehold. Thus, as Serlio boasts, these rural houses 'could serve for every country' (fol. 3v).[32]

Serlio's aim is here again to furnish the European architect with adaptable graphic models and 'general rules' ('regole generali'), avoiding utopian prescription on the one hand and over-universality on the other.[33] These graphic models were intended less for slavish copying than as starting points for invention within an established architectural language. The illustration of alternative models for the same project in Book VI serves to underline the importance for Serlio of the architect's creative judgement as opposed to a dependence on absolute rules. Serlio's user-friendly combination of clear illustrations and accompanying vernacular text was principally aimed at the context-dependent architect rather than at the abstract political theorist or architectural scholar. The clarity and adaptability of Serlio's woodcut models in his published works easily explains the success of these throughout Europe, and the drawings in the unpublished Book VI were designed with the same criteria in mind. Indeed if this work was intended to be published with the illustrations following the text on a separate, facing page (copying the manuscript arrangement), this would have departed from the layout of Serlio's previous books and that of architectural literature to date (which on certain pages had put text and image together). The layout in Serlio's manuscript might be seen to enhance the status of the image, and to represent a step in the development of the future architectural pattern books in which a range of optional models was presented without need of any textual (and theoretical) elaboration.

On the influence of context, Serlio makes clear in Book VI that this would determine a design as much as the above-mentioned 'general rules', since the available resources of the patron and the physical qualities of the site had to be accepted by the Serlian architect. This notion was justified with reference to the first men who, Serlio relates, had, 'depending on the region', 'made use of the materials which they found most suitable' (fol. 1r).[34] Context might even mould ornament to the point of licentiousness. This was especially true with Serlio's famous Mannerist gates in the *Libro extraordinario*, which are excused by him as having been determined by 'the country where I am living' (fol. 2r).[35] In this way Serlio's recommended 'mean' or middle path in the choice of ornament and style could not be defined by any abstract ideal but rather by the norms of a particular context, and was left to the all-important judgement of the architect.[36] The variables of context thus rendered the absolute relative. Although his urban models were illustrated in ideal circumstances without boundary restrictions and on regular flat sites, Serlio conceived that these general models should be fully adaptable to the actual physical and stylistic conditions as found. This fact was emphasized by the inclusion of 'Parisian-style' variants amongst the merchant houses illustrated in Book VI (see Figure 3.4).

In much the same way that the physical and social imperfections of the world were thus accommodated by Serlio in the 'inventions' ('invenzioni') in Book VI, in Book VII he deals with a range of unusual, but predictable enough, architectural 'situations' ('accidenti'). His unprecedented concept of 'situations' includes solutions as to how, on non-rectangular or sloping sites, courtyards and arcades could act as devices to make asymmetrical plans acquire regularity by changing their axis or level. By studying these graphic models the task of the Serlian architect was thus, like a painter or sceno-grapher, to give the imperfect an *appearance* of perfection through an economy of means: the pedestal would correct the antique column's shortness, the rectangular courtyard would mask the site's irregular boundary and the arcade would correct its slope. This disguise aimed to satisfy the eye rather than restore to the work any inherently perfect form of ornament or plan, which were thereby demoted as essential qualities of any approved building.[37]

Of course this need to adapt to circumstance runs throughout Serlio's own life and work in the wake of his repeated displacement, first from Rome following the Sack, then from Venice following a failure of patronage and finally from Paris and Fontainebleau following the loss of his court appointment. Serlio's drawings record this adaptability. Where the woodcuts in Book IV, published in Venice, had incorporated Venetian windows and palazzo façades, Book VI gave explicit French-style models. And where his work in Venice had implicitly celebrated the achievements of that Republic (albeit one largely administered by the nobility), his work in France was evidently intended to embody a faith in the monarchical structure of French society. This is most apparent in the case of Serlio's two built houses, Ancy-le-Franc and the Grand Ferrare, both illustrated in Book VI. Whilst the fourth book was, according to his Venetian copyright application, to be issued 'for the honour of this famous State',[38] its first edition was in fact dedicated to Ercole d'Este of Ferrara. The second edition was dedicated to Alfonso d'Avalos and appeared in 1540, the same year as Book III with its dedication to François I. Ironically D'Avalos was Lieutenant General in Italy of the Holy Roman Emperor, Charles V, the arch-rival of François in the Italian wars that Serlio laments. Both warring monarchs are thus openly cultivated as patrons by Serlio in the same year. Even Serlio's drawings of model palaces for a king (see Figure 3.5) seem to have been added to the sixth book due to current circumstances rather than any abstract ideal; having defined in the (Munich) preface the book's range, covering designs for both peasant and prince, he adds almost as an afterthought that 'I shall also discuss Royal houses since I am in the service of the Most Christian King, HENRI' (fol. 1r).[39] In fact, in the description of his intended books found in the introduction to Book IV, written in 1537 whilst he was still in Republican Venice, the domestic models anticipated in the sixth book stop at residences for princes.

Serlio is not, of course, a theorist without ideals. When illustrating his public and grand domestic architecture he frequently emphasizes the civil and moral virtues of Roman magnanimity and decorum, and the virtues of what amounts to a Protestant- (or Calvinist-) based moderation. But the embodiment of these ideals in works of architecture was not expected to lead to any particular reform of society. If a utopia is to be found in Serlio's work as a whole, it lies in his project in 'Book VIII' for the self-contained Roman consular army camp that might have been built for Trajan which he himself acknowledges is an architectural fantasy with little relationship to his own time. Equally what Serlio described as the Emperor Trajan's 'clemency' yet 'severity' evidently provided him with a lost, antique model of strong leadership, rather like Machiavelli's ideal Prince, a model which Serlio considered had been lacking in the Italy of his youth. Amongst the overwhelmingly practical models of Book VI, this archaeological idealism is restricted to the concluding grandiose palace plans (which foreshadow the ancient house illustrated in Daniele Barbaro's *Vitruvius*).[40] These plans – and especially the one based on an amphitheatre (Figure 3.5) – are, however, excused as theoretical exercises to instruct architects, and more particularly to urge François I to build, and perhaps to commission Serlio himself. Serlio's nostalgia at the outset of this book for what he terms the 'rustic Prince' ('rustico principe') or for the rich peasant surrounded by 'great numbers of people living in harmony, in obedience to a single head of the household' (fol. 2v),[41] such as he witnessed in his youth in Italy but which had now vanished due to the quarrels of 'proud spirits' bent on revenge, repeats the timeless myth of paradise lost. Likewise in Book III, concerning the Naples villa Poggio Reale and its new Spanish masters, Serlio laments, 'O the pleasures of Italy, how you have been ruined by your discords!' (p. CL).[42] Like most displaced people, Serlio no doubt dreamed of a new age of peace and union implicit in the ideal of the Golden Age. It was this ideal which designs for such harmonious villas celebrated and which Serlio's uniting of opposing stylistic qualities in his engravings of rustic and delicate gates in the *Libro Extraordinario* may have symbolized. But, like Machiavelli before him, Serlio accepted the contemporary tyrant and *condottiero*, and housed them in projects devoid of the anthropomorphic and aesthetic idealism of previous architectural theorists. He planned the tyrant's guard house using the same Vitruvian (yet non-human-based) principles of proportion and harmony he employed elsewhere for the king's chambers, and the orders feature on the fortified gates illustrated in Book VII.[43] The buildings constructed from Serlio's model drawings were not expected by him to 'perfect' the fallen world by embodying proportions considered divine or otherwise. A further symptom of his practical non-utopianism is that no ideal human form is represented by Serlio, despite its status in previous illustrated Vitruvian treatises.

To conclude, at no point in the text of the sixth book is the modest Serlian architect exalted to realize the universal harmony of Neoplatonists such as Serlio's friend Camillo or of mystics such as his French patron Marguerite of Navarre; or to tame hostile forces through the beauty of ornament as Alberti had proposed; or to resolve the contradictory forms of contemporary government through interrelated urban types as Filarete had implied in his ducal city; nor is he urged to apply human proportions as a guarantor of divine harmony as Francesco di Giorgio had illustrated. In contrast Serlio's many direct references to Franchino Gaffurio's concept of 'harmonious discord' ('discordia concordante')[44] represent a striking change in emphasis from previous architectural treatises. This might be especially understandable in the wake of the Sack of Rome, and a growing acknowledgement by Serlio of the failure of the High Renaissance masters to deliver a better world – detectable in his interest in licentious forms and models remote from their work, especially in the *Libro extraordinario*.[45] It is almost as if Serlio identifies personally with the irregular house and the redundant column in his seventh book, as no theorist had before him, finding ordered solutions to their shortcomings such as those he had found for himself in less than ideal circumstances. His many references to his own past experiences might suggest this link between biography and pragmatic architectural theory, rather as Machiavelli's experiences in Florence had informed his 'Realpolitik'.

In the absence of a single princely patron (as found in Filarete's treatise), and of designs for model houses for priests, Serlio's range of secular domestic models illustrated in Book VI are not offered as jigsaw pieces capable of realizing any universal social or spiritual order. Rather, they relate to the fallen world of man. We should no doubt take him at his word that, as he put it in his dedication of the fifth book to Marguerite of Navarre, 'true temples' are the 'hearts of devout Christians',[46] in contrast to the collection of material temples illustrated in this book – a collection which he calls a mere 'representation' ('representazione') of the house of God (fol. 1v). In the earthly pragmatism so evident in his drawings, Serlio followed Machiavelli rather than More, and as a consequence the aspirations of the architect were advanced technically but limited politically, in what was seen by Serlio as his 'modern times'.[47] Indeed Serlio's graphic models anticipate the down-to-earth architectural pattern book, in both their range and their optional characteristics. For although he lacked the systematic rationalism of later theorists like Vignola, Serlio introduced through these drawings the now commonplace concept of the architect as the 'selector' of one of any number of possible models, in contrast to Alberti who had emphasized the individuality of each particular design created by the divinely inspired architect.[48] In this respect Serlio is clearly amongst the first moderns.

Notes

1. See in general W. B. Dinsmoor, 'The Literary Remains of Sebastiano Serlio', *The Art Bulletin*, XXIV, 1942, pp. 55–91 [pt 1], pp. 115–54 [pt 2]; J. Onians, *Bearers of Meaning: The Classical Orders in Antiquity, the Middle Ages, and the Renaissance*, Cambridge 1988; C. Thoenes ed., *Sebastiano*

Serlio, Milan 1989; M. Carpo, 'The Architectural Principles of Temperate Classicism: Merchant Dwellings in Sebastiano Serlio's Sixth Book', *Res*, XXII, 1992, pp. 135–51; M. Carpo, *Metodo ed ordini nella teoria architettonica dei primi moderni: Alberti, Raffaello, Serlio e Camillo*, Geneva 1993; H.-W. Kruft, *A History of Architectural Theory from Vitruvius to the Present*, 1st edn Munich 1985; English edn London 1994, pp. 73–9; S. Serlio, *Sebastiano Serlio on Architecture*, I [Books I-V], transl. V. Hart and P. Hicks, New Haven 1996; V. Hart and P. Hicks eds, *Paper Palaces: The Rise of the Renaissance Architectural Treatise*, New Haven 1998, pp. 140–57, 170–85; S. Frommel, *Sebastiano Serlio*, Milan 1998; and A. Payne, *The Architectural Treatise in the Italian Renaissance: Architectural Invention, Ornament, and Literary Culture*, Cambridge 1999.

2. Opening letter in S. Serlio, *Il Settimo Libro d'architettura di Sebastiano Serlio Bolognese*, Frankfurt 1575, sig. Aiiiir: ' … ch' egli hà restituito l'Architettura, e fatta la facile ad ogniuno: & hà giouato egli più con li suoi libri, che non fece gia mai perlo avanti Vitruvio: percio che egli, per esser difficile, non era inteso cosi facilmente da ogniuno'.

3. See Onians (as in n. 1), p. 176.

4. Munich, Bayerische Staatsbibliothek, Codex Icon. 189, ca. 1547–54. Facsimile: M. Rosci and A. M. Brizio eds, *Il trattato di architettura di Sebastiano Serlio*, 2 vols, Milan 1966; a translation by Peter Hicks and myself of Rosci's commentary is available at <http://www.serlio.org>). Transcription with figures: F. P. Fiore ed., *Sebastiano Serlio, Architettura civile, libri sesto, settimo e ottavo nei manoscritti di Monaco e Vienna*, Milan 1994. Translation: S. Serlio, *Sebastiano Serlio on Architecture*, II [Books VI–'VIII'], transl. V. Hart and P. Hicks, New Haven, forthcoming. New York, Avery Architecture Library, Columbia University, AA.520.Se.619.F, ca. 1541–47/9: facsimile: M. N. Rosenfeld ed., *Sebastiano Serlio: On Domestic Architecture*, New York 1978; republished New York 1996. On the history of these MSS, see Carpo, 'The Architectural Principles' (as in n. 1), p. 136 nn. 9, 10. See also M. N. Rosenfeld, 'Sebastiano Serlio's Late Style in the Avery Library Version of the Sixth Book on Domestic Architecture', *Journal of the Society of Architectural Historians*, XXVIII, 1969, pp. 155–72.

5. The second version of Cornaro's treatise was written around 1550–53; see Rosenfeld, *On Domestic Architecture*, 1978 edn (as in n. 4), p. 44. Di Giorgio's treatise illustrated only plans of houses, not façades.

6. Vienna, Österreichische Nationalbibliothek, Cod. ser. nov. 2649, ca. 1541–50, Project XVI fol. 5r [corresponding to Book VII, pp. 38–9]. A transcription with figures can be found in Fiore (as in n. 4). See M. N. Rosenfeld, 'Sebastiano Serlio's Drawings in the Nationalbibliothek in Vienna for his Seventh Book on Architecture', *The Art Bulletin*, LVI, 1974, pp. 400–409.

7. See D. Thomson, *Renaissance Paris: Architecture and Growth 1475–1600*, London 1984, p. 18; Rosenfeld, *On Domestic Architecture*, 1996 edn (as in n. 4), p. 5.

8. 'La grandezza de l'animo del quale, il sapere et il potere, si vede espresso in mol<t>i edificii ordinati da sua maiestà … nel suo bel regno.' All subsequent quotations from Book VI are from the Munich MS (see n. 4).

9. V.4; see Leon Battista Alberti, *On the Art of Building in Ten Books*, ed. and transl. J. Rykwert, N. Leach and R. Tavernor, Cambridge MA 1988, pp. 122–4.

10. See L. Giordano, 'On Filarete's *Libro architettonico*', in Hart and Hicks, *Paper Palaces* (as in n. 1), pp. 51–65.

11. Munich, Bayerische Staatsbibliothek, Codex Icon. 190, ca. 1546–54: transcription with figures in Fiore (as in n. 4). See J. G. Johnson, *Sebastiano Serlio's Treatise on Military Architecture*, Michigan 1985 (facsimile of Ph.D. thesis, University of California, Los Angeles 1984). See also Dinsmoor (as in n. 1), pp. 83–91; P. Marconi, 'L'VIII Libro inedito di Sebastiano Serlio, un progetto di città militare', *Controspazio*, I, 1969, pp. 51–9, and IV–V, 1969, pp. 52–9. Onians has also claimed that Serlio intended this work to form a 'Book VIII' in his sequence, see Onians (as in n. 1), pp. 263, 276–80. See also Rosenfeld, *On Domestic Architecture*, 1978 edn (as in n. 4), p. 28. See also V. Hart, 'Decorum and the Five Orders of Architecture: Sebastiano Serlio's Military City', *Res*, XXXIV, 1998, pp. 75–84.

12. ' … morti violente, & crudeli'.

13. ' … dove è il segio et il nido delle parzialità'. In the Columbia MS, Project LX,R, for the *condottiero* in the city, Serlio notes 'the discords and civil wars … especially in the lands and cities under the yoke of the Pope'. See M. Tafuri, *Venice and the Renaissance*, Cambridge MA 1989 edn, pp. 62–70; Carpo, 'The Architectural Principles' (as in n. 1), p. 139 n. 22. But see also Fiore (as in n. 4), pp. XIII–XIV, and Frommel (as in n. 1), p. 18. Serlio represents his designs for the house (the Grand Ferrare) of the Cardinal of Ferrara, Ippolito d'Este, amongst those for 'illustrious Princes' in the Munich MS, fol. 14v, and those for 'gentlemen' in the Columbia MS XI,[N,13A].

14. 'Ma che vo io discorrendo queste cose che poco o nulla importano a l'architetto?'

15. In the case of Camillo, Serlio was to make his will in the philosopher's favour (although Camillo was in fact just five years younger than Serlio), on Serlio's arrival in Venice in 1528. See Tafuri (as in n. 13), pp. 62–70, and M. Tafuri, 'Ipotesi sulla religiosità di Sebastiano Serlio', in *Sebastiano Serlio*, ed. Thoenes (as in n. 1), pp. 57–66.

16. This memory system was formulated in Camillo's MS 'Idea dell'Eloquenza' (ca. 1530s) and eventually published at Florence and Venice in 1550 with the title *L'Idea del Theatro dell'eccellen. M. Giulio Camillo*. See F. Yates, *The Art of Memory*, Chicago 1966, pp. 129–72, and Carpo, *Metodo ed ordini* (as in n. 1).

17. Carpo, *Metodo ed ordini* (as in n. 1).

18. See Frommel (as in n. 1), p. 15 n. 45 and p. 16. Citolini promoted Italian in particular as the language of literature; his *Lettera in difesa della lingua volgare* was brought out in 1540 by Francesco Marcolini, the Venetian publisher of Serlio's Books III and IV. On Serlio's theory of 'species', see Payne (as in n. 1), pp. 141–3. On Serlio's will, see Dinsmoor (as in n. 1), p. 64 n. 49. In general see Tafuri (as in n. 13), p. 61; Carpo, 'The Architectural Principles' (as in n. 1), p. 138 n. 18; and Rosenfeld, *On Domestic Architecture*, 1996 edn (as in n. 4), p. 3.

19. In the Columbia MS on Projects 'E' and 'F' in the city (Munich MS Projects V and VI), Serlio notes that using his designs 'you could build a long street of houses, all uniform'.

20. The *condottiero*'s house is 'set on its own' (fol. 57v) and the *Podestà*'s is to 'stand on its own' (fol. 59v).

21. 'È ancora necessario che questa casa sia fra gente bassa et povera et mediocre.'

22. See Rosenfeld, *On Domestic Architecture*, 1978 edn (as in n. 4), pp. 42, 47, 58; here she misunderstands the factious nature of the *condottiero*, translating him as 'capitano' and placing him in charge of the city's militia responsible for urban defence against attack from an external enemy (and not, as Serlio has it, opposing the prince himself); the alien governor is even equated to the Governor of Paris, a role created by Louis XI.

23. On Serlio's *Podestà* design related to that in Bologna, see R. Tuttle, 'Sebastiano Serlio Bolognese', in *Sebastiano Serlio*, ed. Thoenes (as in n. 1), pp. 22–9. On this design and Papal Bologna see S. von Moos, 'The Palace as a Fortress: Rome and Bologna under Pope Julius II', in *Art and Architecture in the Service of Politics*, ed. H. Millon and L. Nochlin, Cambridge, Mass. 1978, pp. 57–65.

24. 'Questi tali aministrano la giusticia più rigorosamente del podestà, et massimamente nelle contrade dove io sono nato, per le quali aministrazioni provocano tavolta una parte del populo a furore et alle armi.'

25. 'Il principe nobile di animo liberale, giusto et amatore delli suoi populi, temendo Iddio, non ha bisogno di fortezza alcuna, ma li cuori et gli animi de' suo' vassalli gli sono inespugn[a]bili ripari et bastigli[o]ni. Come ho veduto a' giorni miei Francesco Mario duca d'Urbino il quale, essendo discacciato del suo stato et abbatute le mura di Urbino, acciò che ritornandovi non potesse sicuramente abitarvi, nondimeno, quando piacque a Dio, egli per vertù d'armi riprese il stato suo, dove in Urbino così smurato sicuramente dormiva guardato da' suoi populi. Ma il tiranno crudele, avaro, rapinatore del bene di altrui, sforzator di vergini, di maritate et di vedove, ocupatore delle facultà de' suoi suditi, tutte le fortezze del mondo nol potrebbono asicurare. Ma, o Dio imortale, quale è colui ogidì che avendo pure un puoco non scio che di dominio che non tirannegi qualche puoco? Nondimeno, poich'io debbo trattare delle abitazioni di tutti li gradi degli uomini per far fuori delle città, ora è il tempo ch'io tratti di quella del principe tiranno.'

26. ' ... non sia propinqua al palazzo, a fine che per qualche disobidienzia del padrone il palazzo facilmente non l'offendesse'.

27. Alberti (as in n. 9), p. 156.

28. Serlio (as in n. 2), p. 88: ' ... li primi capi de Christiani, li quali dovriano cercare di mantenere la concordia fra di loro, son quegli, che muovono e suscitano ogni giorno nuove guerre'.

29. ' ... minima casipola del povero contadino ... la vil capanna del povero mendico ... quel povero che con la sua famigliola si va vivendo delle sue fatiche, avendo un puoco di terreno, al quale fa di mestiero una stanza almeno per dormire et per fargli del fuoco'. Serlio's models referred to Italian rather than French peasant dwellings of the period; see K. W. Forster, 'Back to the Farm: Vernacular Architecture and the Development of the Renaissance Villa', *Architectura*, IV, 1974, pp. 1–12.

30. A fact which James Ackerman acknowledges but does not accept at face value, 'superimposing' an anonymous landlord; see Ackerman 'Introduction', in Rosenfeld, *On Domestic Architecture*, 1978 edn (as in n. 4), pp. 11–15, esp. p. 12.

31. Serlio's houses for the rural poor have, however, been equated to those built by the Venetian Senate in 1528, see Rosenfeld (as in n. 30) p. 43. On French de-feudalization and more recent ownership of land by merchants, see ibid., p. 48. On charitable housing in Lyons, see ibid., pp. 48–9.

32. ' …potrà servire a tutti li paesi'.

33. The 'general rules' concerning the orders are to be found in Serlio's fourth book, the *Regole generali di architettura*, Venice 1537.

34. ' … segondo li paesi, di quella materia che trovavano al suo proposito si servivano'.

35. ' … habbiate riguardo al paese, dove io sono'.

36. See Carpo, 'The Architectural Principles' (as in n. 1).

37. See L. Lefaivre and A. Tzonis, 'The Question of Autonomy in Architecture', *Harvard Architecture Review*, III, 1984, pp. 33–5, and Kruft (as in n. 1), pp. 77–8.

38. Serlio, translated in *Sebastiano Serlio on Architecture*, transl. Hart and Hicks (as in n. 1), p. 466: ' … ad honor di questo Inclyto stato'.

39. 'Anci io trattarò delle case reggie, poiché al servizio del cristianissimo re ENRIGO io mi truovo.'

40. See Munich MS fols 61v–73r. On this archaeological character, see Rosci's commentary in Rosci and Brizio (as in n. 4), p. 82.

41. ' … di gran numero di persone con gran concordia star sotto ubidienzia di un sol padre di famiglia'.

42. 'O delitie Italiane come per la discordia uostra siete estinte.'

43. Moreover the real, sixteenth-century military fort had evolved into a geometric bastion which contemporary theorists such as Girolamo Maggi and Giovan Battista Bellucci suggested required little or no ornament. On Serlio's ability as a military architect, see N. Adams, 'Sebastiano Serlio: Military Architect?', in *Sebastiano Serlio*, ed. Thoenes (as in n. 1), pp. 222–7.

44. Serlio's concept of 'harmonious discord' echoes Gaffurio's famous phrase 'Harmonia est discordia concors' ('Harmony is a concordant discord') proclaimed in his 1508 *Angelicum ac divinum opus* (and re-used for the 1518 publication of his *De harmonia musicorum instrumentorum*). See Alberti (as in n. 9), I.9 [p. 24]. See also Serlio's Book V, fol. 211v; Book VI, Munich MS fol. 74r ('discordant concord'), Columbia MS Project XLI,29; and Book VII, pp. 122, 168, 232.

45. 'Cose licenciose' are a recurrent theme in the *Libro extraordinario*; see Onians (as in n. 1), p. 281.

46. ' … i veri Tempij sono i cuori dei pietosi Christiani'. Here he is quoting from St Paul, Corinthians 6.16; see Tafuri (as in n. 13), pp. 64–5.

47. Book IV was self-consciously addressed to 'these modern times' ('questi moderni tempi'), opening letter to the readers, fol. 126r; see Carpo, *Metodo ed ordini* (as in n. 1).

48. See M. N. Rosenfeld, 'Sebastiano Serlio's Contributions to the Creation of the Modern Illustrated Architectural Manual', in *Sebastiano Serlio*, ed. Thoenes (as in n. 1), pp. 102–10, and F. Choay, *The Rule and the Model: On the Theory of Architecture and Urbanism* (1st edn Munich 1985), Engl. edn: ed. and transl. D. Bratton, Cambridge MA 1997, pp. 190–1.

3.1   Sebastiano Serlio, the *Podestà*, Bayerische Staatsbibliothek Munich, Codex Icon. 189

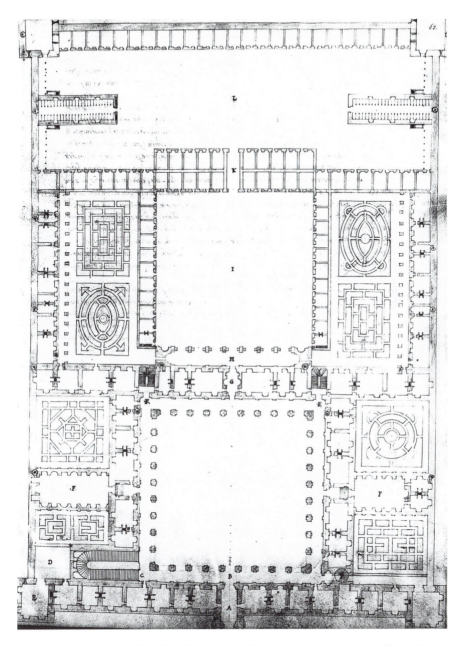

3.2   Sebastiano Serlio, the plan of the palace for a governor serving an alien ruler,
Bayerische Staatsbibliothek Munich, Codex Icon. 189

3.3   Sebastiano Serlio, the city house of the *condottiero*, Bayerische Staatsbibliothek Munich, Codex Icon. 189

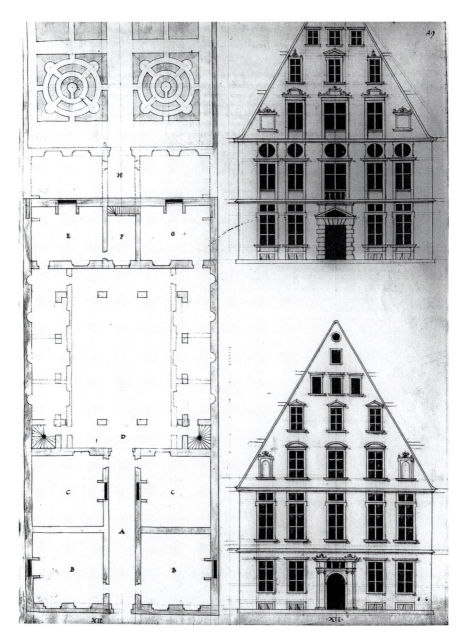

3.4   Sebastiano Serlio, the 'Parisian-style' city house of a merchant, Bayerische Staatsbibliothek Munich, Codex Icon. 189

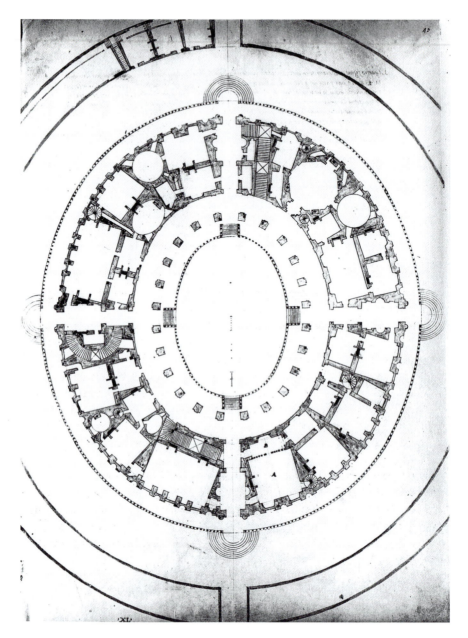

3.5   Sebastiano Serlio, a country palace for a king, based on an amphitheatre, Bayerische Staatsbibliothek Munich, Codex Icon. 189

4

'Brevity without obscurity': text and image in the architectural treatises of Daniele Barbaro and Andrea Palladio

Robert Tavernor

Introduction

Leon Battista Alberti (1404–72) wrote the first architectural treatise since antiquity. Composed in Latin in the mid-fifteenth century, and entitled *De re aedificatoria*, it is concerned with how and why architects and their patrons should design and build.[1] Alberti's scholarship and admiration for classical antiquity – its authors, institutions and buildings – led him to consult and scrutinize *De architectura*, the only surviving treatise from the ancient world, which had been written in the first century BC by the Roman architect Vitruvius. The ten main chapters or 'Books' of *De architectura* provided Alberti (and all subsequent architectural theorists and practitioners) with the primary account of architecture *all'antica*.[2] Indeed, it is likely that Alberti began his own treatise as a commentary on Vitruvius; but the obscurity of many of Vitruvius's statements about ancient buildings led him to write something entirely new, and in the process to create the first modern work of its kind.[3]

Vitruvius's *De architectura* had become difficult to comprehend because its specialized Greek and Latin terminology for architectural details no longer had any currency, and because the text referred to buildings which, by the fifteenth century, were in a ruinous condition at best and difficult to identify. Those that had survived were, in any case, mostly Imperial rather than Republican. Nonetheless, Alberti had the background and determination to make good sense of Vitruvius. He was renowned as an expert antiquarian, for he had studied classical literature and surveyed ancient buildings himself. During his lifetime Alberti designed religious and domestic buildings that were to have a fundamental influence on the subsequent development of architecture, and through a potent combination of scholarship and architectural practice he renewed the Vitruvian message.[4] He became the standard by which all subsequent architect-theorists would be measured.

Alberti's impact was limited initially because the first versions of his treatise were in manuscript form, written in Latin and without illustrations. Even the first printed editions of *De architectura* and *De re aedificatoria*, published in 1485 and 1486 respectively, were published unillustrated.[5] Thus the readership of both treatises was principally the educated elite in Italy and the rest of Europe – that is, potential patrons, and not those directly concerned with designing buildings.

The first illustrated architectural treatises

In 1511, Fra Giovanni Giocondo of Verona produced a scholarly edition of Vitruvius's *De architectura*, accompanied by 136 woodcuts and an index.[6] It proved invaluable for successive commentators on Vitruvius. Ten years later Cesare Cesariano translated Fra Giocondo's Latin edition into the vernacular, supplemented by his own commentary and illustrations, which drew on the architecture of northern Italy and, most famously, Milan Cathedral.[7] In 1544, a classical philologist, Guillaume Philandrier, published his Latin *Annotationes* on Vitruvius in Lyon, France, which he republished in 1552 accompanied by Vitruvius's text.[8]

The presentation of Alberti's *De re aedificatoria* was modified only slowly. The text was translated into vernacular dialects in the mid-sixteenth century – first Venetian (by Pietro Lauro in 1546), then Florentine (by Cosimo Bartoli in 1550 and 1565); the illustrations in these publications undoubtedly widened Alberti's appeal.[9]

The most important breakthrough was made by the artist and architect Sebastiano Serlio, under whom Philandrier had studied in Venice. Serlio wrote the *Architettura*, the first illustrated treatise on ancient architecture to be accessible to architects and patrons alike.[10] It is subdivided into seven books, which were published separately and non-sequentially – commencing with the publication of Book IV in 1537, followed in 1540 by Book III and a new edition of IV. It bears little resemblance to the treatises by Vitruvius and Alberti, primarily because Serlio designed it as a combination of words and woodcut illustrations, appropriate images being placed in close proximity to a descriptive text. Each book defines a topic, and the first five books – I 'On Geometry', II 'On Perspective', III 'On Antiquities', IV 'On the Five Styles of Building', V 'On Temples' – were finally published together in 1551.

Serlio had been introduced to ancient architecture by his master in Rome, Baldassare Peruzzi. Through Peruzzi he developed a detailed understanding of Roman – specifically Augustan – architecture, as well as an admiration for the early-sixteenth-century architecture of Donato Bramante, architect to Pope Julius II. Following the Sack of Rome in 1527, Serlio sought patronage in northern Italy – especially Venice and Padua – and eventually in France, where he became architect to the French King, François I. Serlio took with him a refined appreciation of Roman antique and modern architecture, supported by a collection of Peruzzi's drawings.

Barbaro and Palladio

One of Serlio's Venetian acquaintances, the wealthy nobleman Giangiorgio Trissino (1475–1550), whose passion for antiquity was both scholarly and practical, was instrumental in developing and promoting the architectural career of Andrea Palladio. Indeed, Trissino could probably claim to have discovered Andrea, who had worked as an apprentice on Trissino's villa at Cricoli, just outside Vicenza, around 1538. Its design was inspired by a woodcut in Serlio's Book III,[11] which Trissino adapted for his own use as an academy for young noblemen, who were taught the 'classics'. Under his guidance, Andrea was transformed from apprentice stonemason to architect. Within a decade, Palladio was practising as an independent architect, and by the time of Trissino's death he had formed a new creative alliance with another local nobleman, Daniele Barbaro (1514–70). Barbaro – as a Venetian diplomat and Patriarch-Elect of Aquileia – was in a good position to nurture Palladio further, and he used his family's social and political connections to provide Palladio with opportunities to build in Venice.

Palladio fulfilled the promise these two patrons recognized in him. He enjoyed an immensely productive professional life, recording his enthusiasm for architecture *all'antica* alongside his many building projects in *I quattro libri dell'architettura* (1570). This treatise was instrumental in the international spread of Palladianism, the only architectural movement to have been named after an architect. It influenced the shape of architecture across Europe, especially in England and her American colonies, for the next two hundred years.[12] A major factor in the popular success of the *Quattro libri* is that it appeals to the reader visually as well as intellectually. Palladio's balanced use of carefully composed woodcuts, accompanied by a direct, succinct and lucid text, has proved to be a winning combination.

Palladio referred to Vitruvius as his principal 'master and guide' in matters architectural, as he provided the starting-point for his architectural treatise.[13] The format of Palladio's volume was also undoubtedly indebted to Bartoli's 1550 *folio*-sized illustrated Italian translation of Alberti and to Serlio's volumes *in folio* of the 1530s and early 1540s, and he readily acknowledged their authority. Yet his treatise is quite different from theirs, and represents a new synthesis of antiquarian research. Palladio combined clarity and beauty of representation with brevity of textual description, and he avoided the lengthy (even tedious) descriptions that encumber Serlio's text. This new balance of word and image benefited from his collaboration on Daniele Barbaro's editions of Vitruvius, which were published in 1556 and 1567.

Daniele Barbaro and Palladio formed an influential partnership – combining erudition, intelligence and practical knowledge. Their talents are readily discernible. Barbaro was applauded in Venice in his lifetime, and recognized as an expert Latinist and erudite scholar who took a leading role in the intellectual life of the Veneto. After graduating from the University of Padua in 1540, he published two books – a commentary on Aristotle's *Rhetoric* and one on the *Nicomachean Ethics* (Venice 1544), which had been translated from Greek into Latin by his great-uncle, Ermolao Barbaro (1390–1454), and published during the latter part of the fifteenth century. As well as being an active scholar, Daniele, with his younger brother Marcantonio Barbaro, was also an enthusiastic supporter of the arts. The brothers had been patrons of Palladio since the latter part of the 1550s when he undertook the transformation of their existing castle at Maser. He turned it into the refined and exquisitely decorated Villa Barbaro, with internal frescoes by Veronese and sculptures around an external nymphaeum that were possibly designed and carved by Marcantonio himself. It is probable that, as a result of Daniele's influential support in Venice, Palladio was commissioned to design the façade of S. Francesco della Vigna. This design foreshadowed those of Palladio's most famous Venetian churches, San Giorgio Maggiore and the Redentore. The latter commission and that for the Convent of the Carità were won with the help of Marcantonio, in his capacity as Venetian senator.

Daniele was recognized as a leading designer in his own right. In 1545, with the architect Andrea Moroni, he laid out the botanical gardens (among the first in Europe to be funded publicly) at Padua.[14] In *Venezia città nobilissima* (Venice 1562), Francesco Sansovino named Daniele as one of the three best architects in Venice, alongside Sansovino's father Jacopo and Palladio; Daniele's reputation as an architect developed from his knowledge of Vitruvius and ancient architecture, and from his close working relationship with Palladio, six years his senior.[15] Palladio provided the practical experience and direct knowledge of architecture to match Daniele's erudition and scholarship. While Daniele did not express his architectural talents as completely as Alberti had done through the design of buildings, his partnership with Palladio undoubtedly influenced the development of Renaissance – and Palladian – architecture.

The Barbaro *Vitruvius*

Daniele Barbaro found eloquence in Vitruvius's writing, unlike Alberti who had lamented that the ancient text was unrefined 'and his speech such that the Latins might think he wanted to appear a Greek, while the Greeks would think that he babbled Latin'.[16] Barbaro read him quite differently, and in the preamble to Book V of his 1556 edition, responding to Vitruvius's own concern for the way that architectural books had to be written, he stated:

We see clearly that Vitruvius [...] has proposed in his mind to explain everything in a beautiful and artful manner, and in a way appropriate to the treatment of an art: who has not seen ... the wonderful order of his precepts, and who does not admire his selection of beautiful things? What division or part is lacking that is not collocated in its appropriate place? Who would take away from or add to his good evidence?[17]

Barbaro translated Vitruvius into the vernacular, and wrote a commentary that is roughly two-thirds longer than Vitruvius's own text. Two preparatory manuscripts survive in the Biblioteca Nazionale Marciana, Venice (chronologically, MS Italian 5133 and 5106), and there are three printed versions of Barbaro's commentary: two in Italian – a large *folio* edition of 1556 (at 42.5 × 29 cm it was the largest architectural publication of its time), and a more practical *quarto* edition of 1567, which has a revised text and smaller illustrations. There is also a Latin *folio* edition of 1567, which is based on Philandrier's *Vitruvius* of 1552 and was originally intended as a companion edition to the 1556 Italian *folio*.[18] They were aimed at a different group of readers. The smaller Italian edition of 1567 was less expensive than the earlier *folio* edition, and was targeted at practising and would-be architects. The Latin edition was published for a more scholarly and international audience.

The text is accompanied by illustrations, and the majority of those in the 1556 *folio* edition are attributed to Palladio. They are different from those in Fra Giocondo's *Vitruvius*, as many were extracted from their immediate reference points in the text and given a full *folio* page, or an extended page. This layout was achieved with the connivance of the publisher, 'the ingenious [Francesco] Marcolini', who even devised rotating plans of the amphitheatres at Curio for this edition.[19] While the *folio* edition has large and very legible woodcuts, inevitably it was not only more expensive but also in fact less practical than the smaller, more compact Italian *quarto* of 1567. The latter is characterized by a larger typeface and shorter line lengths, and a 'forma commoda', as the new publisher, Francesco de' Franceschi, states in his introduction to this edition.[20] Barbaro's commentary was simplified and abridged, and Palladio's illustrations considerably reduced in size and recut by Giovanni Chrieger Alemano (Johannes Krüger of Germany) for inclusion in the two 1567 editions, though in the process some images were reversed, their proportions and details changed, and the fine lines of the engravings were lost in Chrieger's coarser woodcuts.[21] Francesco de' Franceschi was undoubtedly a trusted ally of Barbaro, and they expressed mutual respect: Francesco produced the first *quarto* edition of Serlio's Books I–V and his *Extraordinary Book*, also containing woodcuts by Giovanni Chrieger, which he dedicated to Daniele in 1566, one year before Barbaro's second edition of *Vitruvius*.[22] Domenico de' Franceschi published Palladio's *Quattro libri* in 1570.

A major concern of Barbaro in his *Commentari* is to explore the appropriate relationship between the *artes* of the Quadrivium (Arithmetic, Geometry, Music and Astronomy) and architecture, a question he addresses in terms of his Aristotelian world-view. In the foreword to Book I, Barbaro argues that the Arts must be founded on a proper understanding of Nature, which can be revealed only by direct experience.[23] The individual artist imitates natural order through the mastery of number, geometry and mathematics. The intellect is innate and, as such, is variable, being determined by the *virtù* of the creative artist. The idea of *virtù* pervades Barbaro's commentary (as it does Palladio's *Quattro libri*). It was an attribute stressed by many Renaissance intellectuals. For example, in his architectural treatise, Alberti repeatedly declared the supreme importance of *virtus* for humanity.[24] It entailed that the privileged education of the few should be ultimately for the benefit of the whole of society, and that this was possible only by turning words into deeds. For Barbaro this meant turning the recorded theory of Vitruvius into something that architects and patrons of his own time would find meaningful and useful. It is not surprising therefore that he was irritated by the unidentified critics of his 1556 *Commentari* who, he laments, found his language too philosophical and lofty, and 'more theoretical than practical'.[25] Consequently, Francesco de' Franceschi was at pains to state in his publisher's introduction to the 1567 Italian edition that the benefits of Barbaro's book for readers were both 'letterate, & pratiche'.[26]

As a man of letters Barbaro had an excellent command of ancient literature, but he had also gained practical knowledge of ancient architecture by observing – perhaps even measuring and drawing – Roman ruins, alongside the highly experienced Palladio. The focus of each trip Palladio had made to Rome (his earliest had been with Trissino) appears to have been the study of its ancient buildings, with a view to representing them accurately. He wished not only to create the impression that the ruins could be made whole again, but to relay facts about their history. His conclusions were published in two guidebooks to the key monuments of Rome printed (in Rome and Venice) during his visit with Daniele Barbaro in 1554. The *Lantichita di Roma di M. Andrea Palladio. Rac[c]olta brevemente da gli Auttori antichi e moderni*, is a pocket-sized book (15 x 10 cm) that contains highly readable sections briefly describing the appearance and history of the classical ruins;[27] the other, a *Descritione de le chiese di Roma*, is similarly compact.[28] *Lantichita di Roma* proved, in particular, to be a successful and durable venture, demonstrating Palladio's ability to write without the aid of illustrations. He must, however, have appreciated that an extensively illustrated treatise on architecture could have considerable potential, as witnessed by his *Quattro libri*, prepared while he was involved with the Barbaro *Vitruvius* from the early 1550s onwards.

Palladio's *I quattro libri dell'architettura*

The Barbaro *Vitruvius* contains many reconstructions by Palladio of Greek and Roman buildings no longer in existence.[29] Barbaro did not have the architectural skills to reconstruct these himself, and he praises Palladio for 'his quickness of mind' in understanding the 'beautiful and subtle principles' of ancient architecture, for his ability to select 'the most beautiful *maniere* of the ancients in all Italy' and for the dexterity of 'his hand' in explaining their form and detail.[30] By the mid-1550s Palladio had also started work on three of the books that were to be developed into the *Quattro libri*, and a fragmentary manuscript of this earlier version survives.[31] Daniele Barbaro mentions Palladio's 'book of private houses' (of which Vasari saw a version when visiting Venice in 1566) at the end of Book VI, chapter 10, of the 1556 and 1567 Italian editions.[32]

Barbaro and Palladio most probably intended the reader to regard their books as parallel texts.[33] In surviving fragments of his early drafts for his books on architecture, written between 1554 and 1556, Palladio refers his reader to useful passages in Barbaro's *Vitruvius*.[34] And, in the published *Quattro libri*, Palladio writes that in Barbaro's *Vitruvius* one 'can easily learn about how the ornaments of the main doors of buildings should be made', considering also what Barbaro and he have 'said and shown in *disegno*'.[35] When referring to ancient basilicas and Vitruvius's own design for a basilica at Fano, Palladio says, 'I would have included the design of it here had not the Most Reverend Barbaro already done so with the greatest precision for his edition of Vitruvius.'[36] And, finally, when introducing Vitruvius's temple-types in Book IV, Palladio says that he will not provide any illustrations of them, 'since the plan and elevation of each of these appearances is illustrated in the edition of Vitruvius commented upon by Monsignor the Most Reverend Barbaro'.[37]

Palladio's treatise may have been intended, like Vitruvius's, to total ten books. For although it bears the unequivocal title 'four books', three different versions were published in 1570 – *I due libri* and *I due primi libri*, as well as *I quattro libri* – and related books were to have followed. Palladio refers specifically to books 'on antiquities', 'temples', 'baths' and 'amphitheatres'.[38] Thus, Palladio probably intended to describe every ancient building type. According to his seventeenth-century biographer Paolo Gualdo, Canon of Padua Cathedral, only death prevented Palladio from publishing drawings he had already prepared of 'Ancient Temples, Arches, Tombs, Baths, Bridges, Towers, and other public buildings of Roman antiquity'.[39] In 1581, a year after his death, Palladio's sons were preparing an expanded edition of the *Quattro libri* with a fifth book he had completed, but it was left unpublished. This information has prompted the suggestion that Palladio's completed treatise was intended to be longer still, and that an additional six books would have covered theatres, amphitheatres, triumphal arches, baths, tombs and bridges in some detail.[40] In this form it would have complemented Barbaro's *Vitruvius* completely, by providing illustrated examples of every ancient building type.

Palladio's contemporary, the Sienese architect Pietro Cataneo (1510?-74?), had similar ambitions for an encyclopaedic architectural treatise and, as the title of his *I quattro primi libri di architettura* (Venice 1554) suggests, this was conceived as a phased publication. In 1567 he published *L'architettura di Pietro Cataneo Senese* which added four new books to those already in circulation – on ornament, water resources, geometry and perspective. Palladio knew him personally and claims that Cataneo appropriated his rule-of-thumb method for proportioning column shafts.[41] Another model comparable with Palladio's endeavour is *La regola delli cinque ordini dell'architettura* (1562) by the architect Giacomo Barozzi da Vignola (1507–73).[42] Vignola's book is composed of a short introduction followed by 34 engravings describing the five orders, each with only a brief explanatory caption, as well as some ornaments of his own design. *La regola* influenced Book I of the *Quattro libri* in particular, and Palladio's design for the Corinthian capital and cornice is very similar in its details and as a composition on the page to Vignola's earlier design.[43] However, it was Sebastiano Serlio's *Architettura*, with its illustrated account of ancient and modern architecture, including Serlio's own, which provided Palladio with his most obvious general model, though there are also marked differences between their treatises, which may reflect their different backgrounds.

Defining architectural versus painterly drawings

Serlio came to architecture through painting, and he represents buildings and their fragments in a painterly way, in perspective. He was concerned with the effects of mass and depth, and his illustrations have a scenographic quality about them: he sometimes presents details as if they were fragments of stone found *in situ* strewn across the ground.

The established technical term for a theatrical presentation of a view or scene is *scaenographia* ('scenografia' in Italian). It is the third of three kinds of architectural representation, or *ideae*, that Vitruvius describes in Book I.2 of *De architectura*. They are: *ichnographia* – ichnography or ground plan; *orthographia* – orthography or vertical frontal image; and *scaenographia* – scenography or perspective. Vitruvius had described *scaenographia* as tantamount to one-point perspective: 'the shaded rendering of the front and the receding sides as the latter converge on a point'.[44] Its significance for architecture was disputed during the Renaissance. Fra Giocondo rendered it first as 'scenografia' (Fra Giocondo 1511 and 1512) and subsequently as 'sciografia' (Fra Giocondo 1522), by which he meant a building's profile or cross section. Cesariano understood the Greek terms 'skene' and 'skia' as respectively 'a small tent for making shade' and the 'use of shadow or imitation of an object illuminated', and as versions of perspective.[45] Serlio also adopted both terms; in his second book, on linear perspective, published in 1545, he stated without equivocation that by 'scenografia' Vitruvius meant perspective.[46]

In his earliest preparatory manuscript for the 1556 edition, MS Italian 5133, Barbaro translated this third type of representation as *scenografia* or *scorzo*, or in the sense of perspective.[47] By the time he had composed MS Italian 5106, however, he had begun to use other terms for the perspectival drawing, and in the Latin edition Barbaro actually goes as far as to replace Vitruvius's *scaenographia* with *sciographia*. Through this intervention and the ensuing commentary Barbaro makes it absolutely clear that 'scenographia', or perspective, is *not* an appropriate form of representation for architects.[48] He does not actually argue against its use by architects, though he does promote the superior accuracy of orthogonal projections – of elevations and related sections. In the 1567 Italian edition he is adamant that the practice of 'scenografia' should be restricted only to Vitruvius's account of painted scenes and perspective, and other theatrical devices used in theatres in Book V.[49] He reinforces this interpretation by following his account of these terms with two drawings that represent the three *ideae*. The first is a plan of a temple, which he calls a 'pianta ichnographia'; the second is composed of an elevation ('in pie della pianta precedente') of the left half of its front portico, and to its right is a section ('il profilo') through the corresponding half of the body of the building.[50]

It is uncertain what prompted Barbaro to revert, between the 1556 and 1567 editions, to Fra Giocondo's definition of this term. However, there were strong reasons why he should do so. Writing to Pope Leo X, sometime around 1519, Baldassare Castiglione and Raphael had considered perspective to be less important than plan, elevation and section when recording ancient ruins.[51] One assumes that this would have been an influential standpoint among the dominant artist-architects in the Roman circle by the second quarter of the sixteenth century – although, of course, Serlio did not subscribe to this opinion. It was an approach to architectural representation that had been firmly established by Alberti in the previous century. In his Book II.1, when relating the need fully to represent an architectural proposal using drawings and wooden models, Alberti warns the architect against the temptation to adopt painterly techniques:

the allurement of painting is the mark of no architect intent on conveying the facts; rather it is that of a conceited one, striving to attract and seduce the eye of the beholder [...]. The difference between the drawings of the painter and those of the architect is this: the former takes pains to emphasize the relief of objects in paintings with shading and diminishing lines and angles; the architect rejects shading, but takes his projections from the ground plan and, without altering the lines and by maintaining the true angles, reveals the extent and shape of elevation and side – he is one who desires his work to be judged not by deceptive appearances but according to certain calculated standards.[52]

Alberti presents this argument without direct reference to the terminology of Vitruvius, and he may have derived his viewpoint from other ancient authors. In his late-fifteenth-century critique of Pliny's *Natural History*, Daniele's great-uncle Ermolao Barbaro defined 'scenographia' as a painterly term, one that refers to a painter's representation of the whole building.[53] Daniele Barbaro appears to paraphrase Alberti (though without mentioning him by name), concluding his reasoning by stating that, with such a complete and measurable representation of the project, the architect can demonstrate accurately the full extent of his design and his good judgement; furthermore, the cost of the project can be readily calculated.[54]

Barbaro maintains and further clarifies his stance on perspective in his *La pratica della perspettiva ... opera molto profittevole a pittori, scultori, et architetti* (Venice 1568/9). This book – aimed (as its title indicates) at 'painters, sculptors and architects' – is arranged in nine parts. Only Part One describes perspective method, while the others contribute to a rounded understanding of the subject. Barbaro describes different kinds of projection, from geometrical figures and plans through stage design, the casting of shadows and the measurements of the human body to the tools to be employed, referring to diagrams already published by Albrecht Dürer and Serlio.[55] In his preface to this work Barbaro equates Vitruvius's *scaenographia* with perspective, a technique that he claims was still poorly understood by painters in his own day. Again he relates perspective to architecture only when considering the scenes and architectural ornaments used in stage design.

Palladio showed no signs of equivocation, and there is evidence that he had made up his mind about such issues early in his career. Already in 1540, he was redrawing perspective sketches of ancient monuments – as he had made them in the field or copied them from other draftsmen – as orthogonal elevations.[56] Accordingly, in his *Quattro libri* Palladio mostly makes use of orthogonal plans, elevations and sections, and employs perspective only when describing the structure of walls in Book I, chapter 9, and the complex assembly of timber joints for the historic 'Bridge on the Cismone', in Book III, chapter 7.

Serlio synthesized the architect's and painter's approach to representation in his *Architettura*. He included in it four different kinds of perspective in addition to the conventions of the orthogonal plan, section and elevation.[57] Barbaro's approach to illustration was also more varied than Palladio's, though it likewise differed from Serlio's. Barbaro employs three kinds of illustrations in his *Vitruvius*: the architectural plans, sections and elevations designed by Palladio that reconstruct whole buildings;[58] partial reconstructions or fragments of buildings that are presented as partly ruined; and drawings appropriated from other sources. Thus, in the 1567 Italian edition Barbaro presents the principal ancient building types in their totality, in plan, section and elevation, as Vitruvius recommends, and as if he were an architect presenting a building to his patron. However, when Barbaro is illustrating a part of a building in elevation – such as the side of a temple portico in Book III (Figure 4.1), a few bays of the exterior of a theatre in Book V (Figure 4.2), and a partial view of the front of the 'House of the Ancients' in Book VI (Figure 4.3) – the buildings are presented as ruined fragments, and the visible edge or edges of the fragment have a rough finish, from which vegetation has grown (see Figure 4.1).[59] By contrast, although Palladio will occasionally reveal the interior of a building by breaking through an exterior wall and leaving the exposed edge of the stonework ragged, he does not embellish the imagery with incidental foliage (see Figure 4.4). Barbaro's *Vitruvius*, unlike the *Quattro libri*, also contains illustrations derived from other sources – constructional elements, fragments of ornament, tools, machines and devices – that are usually shown scenographically, in perspective. For example, a Tuscan roof taken from Philandrier[60] is shown in perspective in Book IV, chapter 7 and two ancient fireplaces in Book VI, chapter 10 are taken from Francesco di Giorgio Martini's unpublished treatise;[61] in both these cases the redrawings were by Palladio.[62] Barbaro's approach to illustrating his *Vitruvius* is therefore somewhere between Serlio's and Palladio's. Indeed, it is probable that while initially Barbaro was influenced by Serlio's illustrations, the direct advice he received from Palladio led him to modify his approach.

It would appear that as Barbaro developed his commentary on Vitruvius, he realized that it would be pertinent not only to go beyond contemporary architectural books but to include archaeological evidence from buildings constructed after Vitruvius's time. Such evidence would provide visual proof that Vitruvius's contemporaries had indeed built along the lines of the theory described in *De architectura*. Thus Barbaro presented two distinct kinds of representation: 'signs' (that is, *segni*, plural of *segno*, which is at the root of the word *disegno*), and 'figures' (*figure*). The 'signs' record the physical facts about existing ruins, while the 'figures' were derived from Vitruvius's text and provide reconstructions of lost buildings.[63]

Palladio, in the foreword to Book IV of his *Quattro libri*, makes the distinction very clearly between what he had to reconstruct of the ancient temples using the barest physical remains and Vitruvius's text, and the ornament that he has been able to measure completely:

Vitruvius had helped me immensely in this because, by comparing what I have observed with what he teaches us, it has not proved too difficult for me to arrive at an understanding of their appearance and forms. But, as for ornaments, that is, bases, columns, capitals, cornices, and such like, I have included nothing of my own but have measured all of them myself with scrupulous care using various fragments found on the sites where the temples were.[64]

Similarly, Barbaro had described an approach he and Palladio hoped to take in the *Commentari* for the 1556 edition in an autograph addition to MS Italian 5106:

And in our times, we do not have the remains of such a temple [as Vitruvius had described], but with the reasons imparted by Vitruvius, we will show the forms mentioned, with the figures of the plan [*pianta*] and elevation [*inpie*], sometimes also providing the profiles [*profili*] and the sides [*lati*] so that the whole may be understood; we will abandon shading, and, working only with lines, we will give examples, adorning some parts with the different styles of carvings [*tagli*], so that one will know which ornament fits which part and member.[65]

One can therefore deduce that these images were to be devoid of shading and perspective. The details were described later in the same autograph addition as resembling large measurable templates (*sagome*), like those used in the construction of buildings and prepared by the master mason or architect.[66] Palladio was an obvious source for this way of thinking, as he refers in his professional account books to the 'sagome', or cut-outs of details he provided for the builders on site.[67] By way of contrast, in the *folio* 1567 Latin edition of Barbaro's *Vitruvius*, which was probably directed more generally to the gentleman scholar, two of the reduced versions of these details, the Attic base and Ionic volute, were replaced by more highly detailed and shaded illustrations that would be of more interest to that readership.[68] Palladio also distinguishes between the likely recipients of his carefully selected images in the foreword to Book III of the *Quattro libri*.[69] Those of his readers 'interested in antiquities' would 'delight' in some of his drawings, while 'the devotees of architecture' would find other designs 'extremely useful'.[70]

Representing buildings as layered and symmetrical bodies

In the opening chapter of his Book III, before classifying the temple types, Vitruvius relates the perfect dimensions of the ideal male form to the proportions and symmetry of temples. Consequently, in his commentary Barbaro, like Vitruvius, refers metaphorically to temples as 'bodies' and their constituent elements as 'members', and describing these temples within an Aristotelian frame he invokes the 'order of human cognition'. Barbaro explains that when viewing an object from a distance 'human cognition' enables us: 'first [to] form a confused notion of it, then, coming closer, we see through its movement some of its parts, and thus we see that it is an animal. But passing closer, we know it as a man', until, from its details, the figure is recognizable as a friend.[71] Barbaro wrote his commentary on Vitruvius guided by a similar principle. He enabled his reader to construct a complete impression of an ancient building, little by little, through words and images, that lead from the general to ornamental details, as if – to maintain the body analogy prompted by Vitruvius – each elevation were an upright man.[72]

The bodily symmetry of a building *all'antica* obviates the need to draw both halves of an elevation or section, the missing half usually being the mirror reflection of that which is illustrated. Indeed, one may assume that in some cases a mirror may have been used to reveal a façade or interior in its entirety by placing one of its edges at right angles to the axis of symmetry.

The treatment of a building as if it were a rational body that could be subjected to analysis in order to determine facts and quantities, as well as qualities, had its parallel in the appraisal of the human body through anatomical studies. The sections through the body of a building that Palladio presents with such precision, clarity and detachment in the *Quattro libri* resemble the extraordinary anatomical drawings designed for the *De humani corporis fabrica* by Andreas Vesalius (1514–64), published in Basle in 1543.[73] Vesalius had been appointed professor of anatomy at the University of Padua in 1537, aged only 23, and he was a great success there, his lectures attracting large audiences. His approach, as he wrote in the preface to the *Fabrica*, emphasizes 'the rehabilitation of anatomy as a practical discipline and the introduction of visual material as a necessary instrument in its teaching'.[74] As Daniele Barbaro graduated from Padua University in 1540, he was probably familiar with Vesalius's approach. Indeed, Barbaro specifically urged architects to use *sciographia* to describe their drawings because this type of drawing had been put to such good use by the 'medics' in their anatomical studies.[75] Much as Vesalius presented the human form, in his presentation of Vitruvius Barbaro is concerned with the essential rather than the superficial, with representing architecture through its structure and detail, and as a complete body.

The twin concerns of practicality and the provision of clear drawings similarly influenced the composition and design of Palladio's *Quattro libri*. That Palladio carefully designed his treatise to succeed in this way is underlined by Barbaro in his 1556 *Vitruvius*, when he describes Palladio's forthcoming book on private houses as having been 'composto, & d[i]segnato dal Palladio'.[76] Barbaro had himself been made keenly aware of the benefit of composing his *Vitruvius* in such a way that information is conveyed as economically as possible, as Vitruvius recommends. Consequently, the reader is referred back several times in the text to a complete image of a building, as different aspects of its form, construction or detail are described.[77] It is likely that Barbaro saw his *Vitruvius* as a 'construction' of his own, a design of which he was the 'architect'. After the commentary to Book III, chapter 1, in which Vitruvius is concerned with relating the composition and compartmentation of temples with the proportions of the human body, Barbaro goes on to compare the art of building with oratory, and talks specifically about 'Architects of oratory'.[78] Perhaps this is how he regarded himself. He had received, or provided himself with, an education in many of the disciplines that Vitruvius had considered essential for the architect (in Book I, chapter 1 of *De architectura*), and although he did not design buildings as Palladio – or even Alberti – had done, his *Vitruvius* was a tangible architectural expression of his own thinking. Indeed, D'Evelyn has shown that as a humanist steeped in Vitruvius's writings, Barbaro applied architectural principles metaphorically 'to the construction of meaningful relationships between the words and images in the book'.[79] Barbaro and Palladio composed and designed their respective treatises along similar lines. Slight differences in their approaches to architecture are summarized pictorially in the opening motifs they adopted, which are derived from Roman triumphal arches.

The triumph of architecture *all'antica*

The frontispiece of each edition of Barbaro's *Vitruvius* depicts an elevation of the Arch of Trajan at Ancona framing an allegorical figure of 'Architecture' (see Figure 4.5). Allegorical figures representing the Quadrivium – Arithmetic, Geometry, Music and Astronomy – make explicit the context in which Barbaro wished architecture to be interpreted. The arch itself is an example of a fine Roman building that was built a century after the age of Augustus, in which Vitruvius was writing.[80] However, Barbaro's selection of that particular building type had a broader significance for his time. When applied to church façades by architects from Alberti onwards, the triumphal arch stood for the 'triumph' of eternal life over death and damnation.[81] Thus, as a frontispiece to a treatise on architecture, it may also be read as a symbol of the enduring qualities of the Aristotelian definition of the Quadrivium and of architecture *all'antica*, which had survived the barbarism of the post-Roman 'Gothic' era.

Raphael had spoken of this barbaric interlude in his letter to Pope Leo X.[82] Serlio wrote about the damage inflicted on ancient statues by 'the passing of time and the wickedness of men' and of the need to return to 'the grandeur of the Romans and their fine judgement in building'.[83] Renaissance humanists were concerned to erase the influence of barbarian or foreign culture and artefacts from Italy, and to reinstate Roman classicism. The Barbaro family name directly reflects this tradition, their name being inspired by a naval victory against the 'barbarians' during a twelfth-century crusade, in which one of Daniele's ancestors took a leading role.[84] Andrea had probably also acquired his new name Palladio (he had been baptised Andrea della Gondola) to signify the architectural lead he was taking to reinstate the forms of classical antiquity in northern Italy. His renaming was most likely stimulated by his earlier mentor, Giangiorgio Trissino, Trissino having written an epic poem, *L'Italia liberata dai Gotthi* ('Italy freed from the Goths', published in Rome in 1547, well after it was written). In the poem there appears a fictional archangel called Palladio who is characterized as an expert on architecture, and as one who is also instrumental in expelling the Goths from Italy. Both Barbaro and Palladio lived up to their names.[85]

The frontispiece to Palladio's *Quattro libri* is a freer adaptation of a triumphal arch (see Figure 4.6). It resembles some aspects of this type, with its paired columns and trumpet-blowing figures, but the segmentally arched half-pediments under these figures are more like the triangular half-pediments flanking the central façades of his Venetian churches, which are themselves undoubtedly inspired by the triumphal arch.[86] Also, instead of personifying Architecture at the centre of the arch, as Barbaro had done, Palladio sets the *Regina Virtus* (Queen Virtue) above figures representing only the principal disciplines that relate to architecture, 'geometry' and 'measure'; the remaining parts of the Quadrivium, Music and Astronomy, are absent.

Palladio's dedication of Book I to Count Giacomo Angarano, which follows his frontispiece, demonstrates powerfully the 'triumph' of classical values over the corruption of the barbarians. There Palladio emphasizes 'the virtue and greatness of the Romans', his own 'profound studies of virtue' and the 'most exalted virtue' of Angarano himself.[87] Presumably, Palladio intended to reinforce Alberti's requirement that architects should be complete individuals, and therefore virtuous, if they were to be worthy of their calling.[88] Barbaro makes clear with his frontispiece that virtue is acquired through disciplined study leading to a working knowledge of all the liberal arts. As Barbaro then goes on to explain, more than from academic rigour alone, virtue derived from individual action aimed at the benefit and enhancement of civic life.[89]

Palladio also highlighted this vision of the well-rounded architect in pursuit of excellence in the *Quattro libri* by depicting the 'triumphant' Queen Virtue on the frontispieces to each of his four Books. There she sits as mother of the arts, presiding over the thought and actions that shaped Palladio's approach to architecture, as a constant reminder of the essential force that should determine the architecture of the future. As Palladio himself declared within his books, through careful study and application the greatness of the architecture of antiquity could be understood and reinterpreted convincingly for the benefit of society.

Conclusion: the virtues of brevity and clarity

Palladio's approach to architecture reaches from the lofty heights of societal idealism to a basic concern for practicality. His practicality stems in part from Barbaro's interpretation of the relationship of the Aristotelian *artes* to architecture, which he expressed in Book I of his commentary. Palladio's approach, on the other hand, was also shaped by his early experiences as an apprentice stonemason. Then he would have been concerned to receive direct information about what was required for a building project, using precise measurements and two-dimensional templates in order to realise three-dimensional forms. Similarly, as an accomplished practising architect *all'antica*, he was concerned to communicate to those on the building site how the parts should relate harmoniously to the whole:[90] the finished building being the principal concern, of course, of the patron who commissioned the work. It is with good reason, therefore, that the drawings in his treatise are invariably represented to scale, and indicate the main external elevations of buildings as vertical, orthogonal and measurable planes. Furthermore, these drawings record key dimensions of a building's rooms, and in Book IV they demonstrate the positions and relative sizes of its ornament, which he had measured among the antiquities. Details are drawn to a scale larger than the main 'body' of the building, and carefully arranged, often being presented on separate sheets. In this way Palladio demonstrated the beauty and ornament of the ancient buildings, as he understood or imagined them to have been, having meticulously measured the *segni*, or details, proposing what was missing on the basis of his knowledge of both the antiquities and Vitruvius. His drawings are accordingly both delightful and informative.

Palladio's concern was for a speedy means of communication through a 'brief text',[91] accompanied by the appropriate architectural (non-scenographic) representation. He sets out his reasoning in the foreword to Book III of the *Quattro libri*, which is concerned with public buildings:

one learns much more rapidly from well-chosen examples, when measuring and observing whole buildings and all their details on one small sheet of paper, than one does in a long time from words, from which reliable and precise information can only be extracted slowly and with a considerable mental effort by the reader from what he is reading and can only be put into practice with great difficulty.[92]

This is a direct response to Vitruvius's foreword to Book V, where he states that he had written his treatise with brevity as a primary concern: 'since I have observed that our citizens are distracted with public affairs and private business, I have thought it best to write briefly, so that my readers, whose intervals of leisure are small, may be able to comprehend in a short time'.[93] For such reasons Vitruvius composed his treatise in 'short books'.[94]

Barbaro in turn applauds the ancient writer for his 'brevity and clarity', and says that similar terms – 'brevity without obscurity' – had been used by the poet Horace, a contemporary of Vitruvius.[95] This phrase rang in the ears of all the architectural writers who admired Vitruvius. It is evident in Barbaro's approach to his influential editions of Vitruvius, and is implemented even more successfully by Palladio, which is why his *I quattro libri dell'architettura* was received so well by successive generations of architects and their patrons.

Acknowledgements

I am indebted to Dr Margaret D'Evelyn for reading drafts of this chapter, and for her subsequent permission to refer extensively in this chapter to material in her doctoral dissertation, M. M. D'Evelyn, 'Word and Image in Architectural Treatises of the Italian Renaissance', PhD thesis, Princeton University 1994 (UMI Microfilm no. 94–29175), pp. 545 and 574–5, n. 27–8, and passim for references to the phrase used in this title. A more developed treatment of related themes by D'Evelyn is to be found in 'Venice as Vitruvius's City in Daniele Barbaro's *Commentaries*', in *Studi Veneziani*, N.S. XXXII (1996), 1997, pp. 83–104; and '*Varietà* and the Caryatid Portico in Daniele Barbaro's *Commentaries* on Vitruvius', in *Annali di architettura*, X–XI, 1998–99, pp. 157–74, which are also referred to in the notes below. I am also grateful to Dr Deborah Howard for her comments on the penultimate version of this chapter, and for directing me to L. Cellauro, 'Daniele Barbaro and his Venetian Editions of Vitruvius of 1556 and 1567', *Studi Veneziani*, N.S. XL, 2000, pp. 87–134, published after this chapter was submitted. It complements many of the views presented here.

Notes

1.   Leon Battista Alberti, *On the Art of Building in Ten Books*, transl. J. Rykwert, N. Leach and R. Tavernor, Cambridge, MA and London 1988; and R. Tavernor, *On Alberti and the Art of Building*, New Haven and London 1998.

2.   Vitruvius, *The Ten Books on Architecture*, transl. M. H. Morgan, New York 1960; *Vitruvius on Architecture* (Loeb Classical Library, 251), 2 vols, transl. F. Granger, Cambridge MA and London 1998 (repr. with corrections of the 1931 edn); Vitruvius, *Ten Books on Architecture*, transl. I. D. Rowland and T. N. Howard, Cambridge, New York and Melbourne 1999.

3.   Tavernor (as in n. 1), pp. 15–23.

4.   Ibid.

5.   Ibid., p. 16.

6.   *M. Vitruvius per Iocundum solito castigatior factus cum figuris et tabula ut iam legi et intelligi possit*, Venice 1511. See L. A. Ciapponi, 'Fra Giocondo da Verona and his Edition of Vitruvius', *Journal of the Warburg and Courtauld Institutes*, XLVII, 1984, pp. 72–90.

7.   Vitruvius, *Di Lucio Vitruvio Pollione De Architectura Libri Dece traducti del Latino in vulgare affigurati*, ed. Cesare Cesariano, Como 1521 (facsimile edn A. Bruschi, Milan 1981).

8.   *Gulielmi Philandri Castilionii Galli Civis Ro. In decem libros M. Vitruvii Pollionis de Architectura Annotationes*, Rome 1544. In the 1544 *octavo* edition Philandrier's *Annotationes* are published without Vitruvius's text. In a later 1552 *quarto* version Philandrier enlarges upon the 1544 notes and publishes Vitruvius's complete text for the first time. On the differences between the 1544 and 1552 editions, and on the manuscript underlying this version of Vitruvius's text, see *Les Annotationes de Guillaume Philandrier sur le De Architectura de Vitruve, Livres I à IV, Introduction, traduction et commentaire par Frédérique Lemerle, Facsimilé de l'édition de 1552*, Paris 2000, pp. 15, 23–9. For extensive references to these and other editions of Vitruvius see L. Cellauro, 'Danielo Barbaro and his Venetian Editions of Vitruvius of 1556 and 1567', *Studi veneziani*, n.s. XL, 2000, pp. 104–5 n. 98.

9.   For a full listing of the various printed editions of Alberti's *De re aedificatoria*, see Alberti (as in n. 1), pp. xxi–xxiii.

10.   For the most recent English translation of Serlio, see *Sebastiano Serlio on Architecture*, I [Books I-V of *Tutte l'opere d'architettura et prospettiva*], transl. V. Hart and P. Hicks, New Haven and London 1996.

11.   R. Tavernor, *Palladio and Palladianism*, London 1991, pp. 16–18; B. Boucher, *Andrea Palladio: The Architect in His Time*, New York and London 1994, pp. 22–4.

12.   Tavernor (as in n. 11).

13.   Andrea Palladio, *I quattro libri dell'architettura*, ed. L. Magagnato and P. Marini, Milan 1980, p. 9: 'mi proposi per maestro e guida Vitruvio'.

14.   M. Azzi Visentini, *L'Orto Botanico di Padova e il giardino del Rinascimento*, Milan 1984; B. Mitrovic, 'The Theory of Proportions in Daniele Barbaro's Commentary on Vitruvius' De Architectura', Ph.D. thesis, University of Pennsylvania 1996 (UMI Microfilm no. 96–27967), p. 19. For a detailed account of Barbaro's education, scholarship and design activities see Cellauro (as in n. 8), pp. 87–104.

15.   F. Sansovino, *Delle cose notabili che sono in Venetia, libri due*, Venice 1562, fol. 28v; see Cellauro (as in n. 8), p. 101 n. 83. Although Barbaro's own education in most of the various disciplines mentioned by Vitruvius far exceeded what Vitruvius expected of the busy architect (see Vitruvius, end of I.I, re: Pythius), the manner in which he addresses and exhorts practising architects in the *Commentari* suggests that he did not consider himself to be one. Rather, he probably regarded himself as a scholar-architect. See M. D'Evelyn, '*Varietà* and the Caryatid Portico in Daniele Barbaro's *Commentaries* on Vitruvius', *Annali di* Architettura, X–XI, 1998–99, esp. p. 160, 'The Ten Books as a Work of Architecture'.

16.   Alberti (as in n. 1), p. 154.

17.   'Noi vedemo chiaramente, che Vitr. … si ha proposto nell'animo di esplicare il tutto con bella, et artificiosa maniera, et con modo al trattamento d'un' arte convenevole, chi non ha veduto … l'ordine meraviglioso de i suoi precetti? chi non ammira la scelta delle belle cose? quale divisione, ò parte ci manca, che al suo luogo non sia collocata? chi levera, ò aggiugnera, che bene stia alcun suo documento?'; D. Barbaro, *I dieci libri dell'architettura di M. Vitruvio. Tradutti et*

commentati da Monsignor Barbaro, Venice: Francesco Marcolini 1556, V, p. 127; cf. D. Barbaro, *Vitruvio, I Dieci Libri dell'Architettura. Tradotti e Commentati da Daniele Barbaro*, Venice 1567 (repr. Milan 1987), p. 203. This quotation from the 1556 edition is taken from M. M. D'Evelyn, 'Word and Image in Architectural Treatises of the Italian Renaissance', Ph.D. thesis, Princeton University 1994, pp. 227–8 and 234–5 n. 4; subsequent quotations from the 1556 edition are from the same source.

18. G. Poleni, *M. Vitruvii Pollionis Architectura textu ex recensione codicum emendato cum exercitationibus notisque novissimis, Joannis Poleni et Commentariis variorum additis nunc primum studiis Simonis Stratico*, 4 vols (all in 2 pts), Udine 1825–29, I, pt I, pp. 79–81.

19. Barbaro 1556 (as in n. 17), pp. 162, 289; D'Evelyn 1994 (as in n. 17), pp. 300, 326 n. 31; Cellauro (as in n. 8), pp. 105–8.

20. Barbaro 1567 (as in n. 17), publisher's preface, n.p.

21. See M. Morresi, 'Le due edizioni dei Commentari di Daniele Barbaro', in Barbaro 1567 (as in n. 17), pp. xli–lviii; and D'Evelyn 1994 (as in n. 17), pp. 248ff., for tables comparing the illustrations in each edition, those attributed to Palladio being highlighted; and L. Cellauro, 'Palladio e le illustrazioni delle edizioni del 1556 e del 1567 di Vitruvio', in *Saggi e memorie di storia dell'arte*, XXII, 1998, pp. 55–128, which catalogues the images and provides their textual and archaeological sources. See also H. Zerner, 'Du Mot à l'image: le rôle de la gravure sur cuivre', in *Les Traités d'architecture de la Renaissance*, ed. J. Guillaume, Paris 1988, pp. 281–94. On Giovanni Chrieger see Cellauro (as in n. 8), pp. 128–9.

22. V. Hart, 'Serlio and the Representation of Architecture', in *Paper Palaces: The Rise of the Renaissance Architectural Treatise*, ed. V. Hart and P. Hicks, New Haven and London 1998, pp. 170–85.

23. Barbaro 1567 (as in n. 17), pp. 1–5.

24. See Alberti (as in n. 1), esp. p. 426, the Glossary entry on 'virtue/*virtus*'.

25. Barbaro 1567 (as in n. 17), p. 141: ' … & satisfaremo anche a quelli, che non si curano di tanta Filosofia, & che ci sanno oppositione di troppo alti concetti, & discorsi, con i quali io non voglio scusarmi, perche dubiterei di non gli credere, et non di dare ad intendere a me fusse vero, che o fusse piu Theorico, che pratico'; from D'Evelyn 1994 (as in n. 17), pp. 357, 393 n. 12; and D'Evelyn 1998–99 (as in n. 15), pp. 162, 172 n. 44.

26. Barbaro 1567 (as in n. 17), publisher's preface, n.p. From D'Evelyn 1994 (as in n. 17), pp. 357, 393 n. 13; and D'Evelyn 1998–99 (as in n. 15), pp. 162, 172 n. 43.

27. L. Puppi, *Andrea Palladio, Scritti sull'architettura (1554–1579)*, Vicenza 1988, pp. 11–36. For an English translation of Palladio's 1554 guide, see E. Howe, *The Churches of Rome*, Binghamton NY 1991.

28. Puppi (as in n. 27 above), pp. 37–56.

29. See n. 21 above. See also Cellauro (as in n. 21), pp. 55–128, on Palladio's fidelity to Vitruvius's text in making the reconstruction drawings for these woodcuts; and D'Evelyn 1998–99 (as in n. 15), p. 169, on the creative manner in which Barbaro and Palladio, following the principles of Francesco di Giorgio Martini, intended these woodcut images to be read.

30. Barbaro 1556 (as in n. 17), I.6, p. 40[a]: 'acquistato la vera Architettura non solo intendendo le belle, e sottili ragioni di essa, ma anco ponendola in opera … Et quanto appartiene a Vitr. l'artificio de i Theatri, de i Tempi de le Basiliche & di quelle cose, che hanno piu belle, & piu secrete ragioni di compartimenti tutte sono state da quello [di Palladio] con prontezza d'animo, & di mano esplicate, e seco consigliate, come da quello che di tutta Italia con giudici ha scielto le piu belle maniere de gli antichi … '; from D'Evelyn 1994 (as in n. 17), pp. 299, 325 nn. 28–9.

31. Puppi (as in n. 27), pp. 71–105.

32. Barbaro 1556 (as in n. 17), p. 179, and Barbaro 1567 (as in n. 17), p. 303; Puppi (as in n. 27), p. 62 and n. 18.

33. See E. Forssman, 'Palladio e Vitruvio', *Bollettino del centro internazionale di studi di architettura Andrea Palladio*, IV, 1962, pp. 31–42, esp. p. 34: 'Tuttavia i Quattro Libri e il Vitruvio del Barbaro vanno studiati parallelamente; al che si è indotti dagli stessi autori per i ripetuti rinvii ai rispettivi libri.'

34. Puppi (as in n. 27), p. 73, referring to Vitruvius's and Barbaro's accounts of the nature of stone in Book II, chapters 7 and 8.

35. Andrea Palladio, *The Four Books on Architecture*, transl. R. Tavernor and R. Schofield, Cambridge MA and London 1997, p. 61: 'Come si debbano fare gli ornamenti delle porte principali delle fabriche, si può facilmente conoscere da quello che c'insegna Vitruvio al capitolo VI del IV libro, aggiungendovi quel tanto che in quel luogo ne dice e mostra in disegno il reverendissimo Barbaro, e da quello ch'io ho detto e disegnato di sopra in tutti i cinque ordini'; Palladio (as in n. 13), p. 76.

36. Palladio (as in n. 35), p. 200; Palladio (as in n. 13), p. 235: 'io ne porrei qui i disegni se dal reverendissimo Barbaro nel suo *Vitruvio* non fossero stati fatti con somma diligenza'.

37. Palladio (as in n. 35), p. 217; Palladio (as in n. 13), p. 255: ' ... essendo di ciascuno di questi aspetti figurata la pianta e'l suo diritto nel *Vitruvio* commentato da monsignor reverendissimo Barbaro'.

38. Palladio makes five references to his 'book on antiquities', three to that on 'temples', one to 'baths', and two to 'amphitheatres'. In his dedication of Books III and IV to Emanuele Filiberto, Duke of Savoy (Books I and II having been dedicated to Count Giacomo Angarano), Palladio asks the Duke 'to receive this part of my work on architecture with your usual generosity so that [...] I can more readily prepare myself to publish the work that I have begun, in which theatres, amphitheatres, and other magnificent ancient piles will be dealt with'; Palladio (as in n. 35), p. 161. For other citations see ibid., p. 348 n. 25; see also Puppi (as in n. 27), pp. 57–69, and L. Puppi, *Palladio Drawings*, New York 1990, pp. 11–27, esp. p. 13.

39. G. G. Zorzi ed., 'La Vita di Andrea Palladio', *Saggi e memorie di storia dell'arte*, II, 1958–59, pp. 91–104; D. Lewis, *The Drawings of Andrea Palladio*, Washington DC 1981, p. 3; and Puppi (as in n. 27), p. 61.

40. Lewis (as in n. 39), p. 10 n. 16.

41. Palladio (as in n. 35), p. 18. For an edition of Cataneo's work see P. Cataneo, 'L'architettura', ed. E. Bassi and P. Marini, in Pietro Cataneo and Giacomo Barozzi da Vignola, *Trattati*, ed. E. Bassi et al., Milan 1985, pp. 163–498.

42. G. Barozzi da Vignola, 'Regola delli cinque ordini d'architettura', ed. M. Walcher Casotti, in *Trattati* (as in n. 41), pp. 499–577.

43. Cf. Vignola (as in n. 41), fol. xxvi, and Palladio (as in n. 35), p. 47.

44. Vitruvius 1999 (as in n. 2), p. 25. Vitruvius 1998 (as in n. 2), p. 26: 'Item scaenographia est frontis et laterum abscedentium adumbratio ad circinique centrum omnium linearum responsus.' This is rendered in Vitruvius 1960 (as in n. 2), p. 14, as: 'Perspective is the method of sketching a front with the sides withdrawing into the background, the lines all meeting in the centre of a circle.' Indeed, it was interpreted variously during the sixteenth century (and subsequently), as is outlined below.

45. Vitrurius, ed. Cesariano (as in n. 7), fol. xiiiiv.

46. Hart (as in n. 22), pp. 171–3.

47. Barbaro, MS Italian 5133 in the Biblioteca Nazionale Marciana, Venice, IV, 37; D'Evelyn 1994 (as in n. 17), p. 298. See also the discussion in Cellauro (as in n. 8), pp. 114–16.

48. See Morresi (as in n. 21), pp. xlii–xliii; and Mitrovic (as in n. 14), pp. 60–1. See also D'Evelyn 1994 (as in n. 17), pp. 298, 322 n. 26, on *scenographia* and Palladio's three-part drawings, with bibliography on the significance of these terms in antiquity; and Cellauro (as in n. 8), pp. 119–26.

49. Barbaro 1567 (as in n. 17), pp. 29–30: '[...] perche se bene la scenografia che è descrittione delle scene, & prospettiva, è necessaria nelle cose de i Theatri [...]'.

50. Ibid., pp. 31–2.

51. R. Bonelli ed., 'Lettera a Leone X', in *Scritti rinascimentali di architettura*, ed. A. Bruschi et al., Milan 1978, pp. 459–84, esp. p. 480 and passim; see also Hart (as in n. 22), p. 179.

52. Alberti (as in n. 1), p. 34. L. B. Alberti, *De re aedificatoria*, Florence 1484, sig. [ciiiii]r: '[...] picturae lenociniis falleratos producere non eius est architecti, qui rem docere studeat, sed eius est ambitiosi, qui spectantis oculos illicere et occupare animumque ab recta disquisitione partium pensandarum amovere ad se admirandum conetur. [...] Inter pictoris atque architecti perscriptionem hoc interest, quod ille prominentias ex tabula monstrare umbris et lineis et angulis comminutis elaborat, architectus spretis umbris prominentias istic ex fundamenti descriptione ponit, spatia vero et figuras frontis cuiusque et laterum alibi constantibus lineis atque veris angulis docet, uti qui sua velit non apparentibus putari visis, sed certis ratisque dimensionibus annotari.'

53.   E. Barbaro, *Castigationes Plinianae Hermolai Barbari Aquileiensis Pontificis*, Rome 1492–93, sig. [fiiiii]v.

54.   Barbaro 1567 (as in n. 17), p. 30.

55.   Mitrovic (as in n. 14), pp. 63–71.

56.   L. Puppi ed., *Palladio Drawings*, New York 1989, pp. 21–2; and see, for example, RIBA: Palladio XII/14, illustrated in Lewis (as in n. 39), p. 33.

57.   Hart (as in n. 22), p. 179.

58.   D'Evelyn (as in n. 17), pp. 248–66.

59.   These are illustrated on pp. 139, 250 and 281, respectively, in Barbaro 1567 (as in n. 17). See D'Evelyn 1998–99 (as in n. 15), p. 98, for observations regarding the difference between Barbaro's humanist and Palladio's architectural imagination. While Palladio could envision ruined buildings as if they were whole, Barbaro did not possess this capacity, nor had he cultivated it, and consequently he never developed a taste for ruins *per se*. Like Cesariano (and Vitruvius himself), Barbaro was concerned to prevent buildings from being ruined, then and in the future.

60.   *M. Vitruvii Pollionis de Architectura Libri decem ad Caesarem Augustum, omnibus omnium editionibus longe emendatiores, collatis veteribus exemplis. Accesserunt, Gulielmi Philandri Castilionii, civis Romani, annotationes castigatiores & plus tertia parte locupletiores*, Geneva 1552, p. 163.

61.   D'Evelyn 1994 (as in n. 17), pp. 257, 265.

62.   Though some of the illustrations Barbaro uses are by unknown artists. See his sequence of six engravings of pumps and mills: G. Scaglia, *Francesco di Giorgio: Checklist and History of Manuscripts and Drawings in Autographs and Copies from ca. 1470 to 1687 and Renewed Copies (1764–1839)*, Bethlehem, London and Toronto 1992, p. 117.

63.   Margaret D'Evelyn has noted that when, in an autograph addition to MS Italian 5106, Barbaro makes a quick note, 'segni', in a margin adjacent to his own comments on spaces between ancient pedestals, he may have been considering a second type of drawing by Palladio (beyond the reconstructions from Vitruvius's text). This type would represent purely archaeological evidence, or 'signs', a term used by Francesco di Giorgio (after Vitruvius I.I) when matching ancient sculptural details with Vitruvius's terms for them. By 1556, these two types of drawings would be fused in Palladio's reconstruction drawings of the temples, based as they are on both Vitruvius and the antiquities. See D'Evelyn 1994 (as n. 17), pp. 267–72, 296–8. See also D'Evelyn 1998–99 (as n. 15), esp. pp. 169–70.

64.   Palladio (as in n. 35), p. 213; see also Palladio (as in n. 13), p. 250: 'Et in questo mi è stato di grandissimo aiuto Vitruvio, perciochè, incontrando quello ch'io vedeva con quello ch'egli ci insegna, non mi è stato molto difficile venire in cognizione e degli aspetti e delle forme loro. Ma, quanto agli ornamenti, cioè base, colonne, capitelli, cornici e cose simili, non vi ho posto alcuna cosa del mio, ma sono stati misurati da me con somma considerazione da diversi fragmenti ritrovati ne' luoghi ove erano essi tempii.'

65.   Barbaro, MS Italian 5106 in the Biblioteca Nazionale Marciana, Venice, III.1, fol. 95v, autograph addition: 'Et [à] nostri giorni non hauemo reliquia di simil tempio per[ò] con le dritte ragioni imparate da Vit[ruuio] con le figure della pianta, et dello inpie dimostreremo le forme predette. [p]onendoui alcuna uolte anche i profili, et i lati accioche il tutto se intenda, lasciaremo le ombre, solamente con le linie operando preponeremo gli esempi adornando ne qualche parte con diuerse maniere di tagli, accioche si sappia qual'ornamento à qual parte è membro conuenga'; from D'Evelyn 1994 (as in n. 17), p. 321 n. 24; English translation ibid., p. 297 (with recent corrections by D'Evelyn communicated to the author). See the longer version of the passage in D'Evelyn 1998–99 (as in n. 15), p. 161, which includes the reference to the details as 'sagome', cited below.

66.   Indeed, as Barbaro goes on to say, the drawings will not make use of perspective or shading because he wished to demonstrate facts, not teach painting; from D'Evelyn 1994 (as in n. 17), pp. 324 n. 24, 360–63; and D'Evelyn 1998–99 (as in n. 15), p. 161.

67.   H. Burns, 'Building and Construction in Palladio's Vicenza', in *Les Chantiers de la Renaissance* (Actes des colloques tenus à Tours en 1983–1984), ed. J. Guillaume, Paris 1991, pp. 191–226, esp. p. 207.

68.   D'Evelyn 1994 (as in n. 17), p. 321 n. 24; and D'Evelyn 1998–99 (as in n. 15), p. 172 n. 20 and n. 39, without further bibliography.

69.   Palladio (as in n. 35), pp. 163–4.

70. Ibid., p. 163. Palladio (as in n. 13), p. 189: ' ... io ho redutto quei fragmenti che ne sono rimasi degli antichi edifici a forma tale che gli osservatori dell'antichità ne siano (come spero) per pigliar diletto e gli studiosi dell'architettura possano riceverne utilità grandissima ... '.

71. Barbaro 1556 (as in n. 17), III.2, p. 74: ' ... solo ne darò un'essempio della cognitione de i sensi. Vedendo noi di lontano alcuna cosa, ci formiamo prima una cognitione confusa dipoi avvicinandosi quella, vedemo, che col movimento ella si porta in alcuna parte, et però dicemo esser animale, ma piu oltre passando conoscemo esser un' huomo, et avicinandosi anchor piu, trovamo esser un' amico, et raffigurandolo piu d'appresso ogni parte di lui distintamente consideramo, et cosi dallo esser, che è universalissima cosa, al movimento venimo, et dal movimento ci restrignemo all'animale, et à piu distinta cognitione pervenuti conoscemo l'huomo, riconoscemo l'amico, distinguemo ogni sua parte'; cf. Barbaro 1567 (as in n. 17), p. 124, and cf. D'Evelyn 1994 (as in n. 17), pp. 291–3, and pp. 318–19 n. 10–15, esp. n. 13 for the passage from which this quote is taken.

72. D'Evelyn 1994 (as in n. 17), pp. 291–3, 300–301.

73. The names of the artists who made these designs in the *Fabrica* are not recorded. Traditionally they have been attributed to Titian, though more probably his pupils, including Jan Steven van Calcar, drew them. See J. B. Sanders and C. D. O'Malley, *The Illustrations from the Works of Andreas Vesalius*, Cleveland and New York 1950 (repr. 1973); and for a comparison with Palladio's representation of buildings, see R. Tavernor, 'Palladio's "Corpus": I Quattro Libri dell'Architettura', in Hart and Hicks (as in n. 22), pp. 232–46. Paradoxically, while Palladio's buildings may read as bodies laid bare, Palladio's ability to represent the human form – as sculptures on his buildings – was limited. It has been suggested that for his most important drawings he employed the drafting skills of artists who worked on decorating his buildings, such as Federico Zuccari and Bernardino India; see Puppi 1990 (as in n. 38), p. 23.

74. A. Carlino, 'The Book, the Body, the Scalpel: Six Engraved Title Pages for Anatomical Treatises of the First Half of the Sixteenth Century', *Res*, XVI, 1988, pp. 32–50, esp. p. 39.

75. Barbaro 1567 (as in n. 17), p. 30: ' ... & in questo l'Architetto come medico dimostra tutte le parti interiori, & esteriori delle opere ... '; see also his commentary to Book I, on p. 11.

76. Barbaro 1556 (as in n. 17), p. 179; and Barbaro 1567 (as in n. 17), p. 303; D'Evelyn 1994 (as in n. 17), p. 237 n. 13.

77. According to D'Evelyn, Cesariano had also combined words and images in this way; see D'Evelyn 1994 (as in n. 17), pp. 277–8.

78. Barbaro 1567 (as in n. 17), p. 115: ' ... Architetti dell'oratione'. See also D'Evelyn 1994 (as in n. 17), pp. 308, 326 n. 10. The passage it relates to runs as follows (translation by author and Kim Williams): 'as oration takes different forms and ideas in order to satisfy the ear, thus does Architecture take on its aspects and forms to satisfy the eye. [...] Different rationales for sentences, artifices, words, figures, parts, numbers and terms are used when the orator wants to be clear, pure and elegant in his expressions. Others are used to be grand, vehement, sharp, and severe; others again require pleasantness; still others, beauty and ornateness in speaking. Similarly, with the idea of building, we require different ratios, dispositions, orders, and partitionings when beauty, delicacy, simplicity is wanted, because the nature of the things that go into the formation of one idea causes this to be worthy of being placed next to another, which then forms yet another idea. Thus, the great may be found in purity; in greatness, beauty; in beauty, simplicity, and in the simple, the splendid. Indeed, this is the highest praise for the orator, and is earned by mixing the conditions of one form with the conditions of another, as is made manifest by the true Architects of oratory.' See also A. A. Payne, 'Architects and Academies', pp. 118–33, esp. p. 128, and P. Davies and D. Hemsoll, 'Sanmicheli's Architecture and Literary Theory', pp. 102–17, esp. p. 116, in *Architecture and Language: Constructing Identity in European Architecture, c. 1000 – c. 1650*, ed. G. Clarke and P. Crossley, Cambridge 2000.

79. See D'Evelyn 1994 (as in n. 17), pp. 290, 495 and passim.

80. For D'Evelyn (1994, as in n. 17, pp. 217, 312 n. 10) the use of the triumphal arch signifies that 'more than in any other edition of Vitruvius to date, the surviving antiquities would play a major role as Palladio brought his wide knowledge of ancient architecture to the often obscure text [...]'. Cellauro (as in n. 21), p. 66, identifies this arch as a modified version of the Arco dei Gavii in Verona, which is attributed to 'C. da Lucius Vitruvius Cerdo', who was confused with Vitruvius the author of *De architectura* in the Renaissance.

81. Tavernor (as in n. 1), pp. 178–87.

82. Bonelli (as in n. 51), pp. 461–84, esp. p. 473.

83. Serlio (as in n. 10), pp. 97–8.

84. P. Gothein, *Francesco Barbaro: Früh-Humanismus und Staatskunst in Venedig*, Berlin 1932, pp. 11–12, 346 n. 3; see also Mitrovic (as in n. 14), p. 10.

85. Tavernor (as in n. 11), pp. 16–24; Boucher (as in n. 11), p. 21.

86. Tavernor (as in n. 11), pp. 57–75. See also Tavernor (as in n. 1), pp. 178–87.

87. Palladio (as in n. 13), pp. 7–8: 'della virtù e della grandezza romana', 'negli ottimi studi di questa qualità di virtù' and 'per splendore e fama di nobilissime virtù'.

88. Alberti (as in n. 1), pp. 3, 315.

89. Barbaro 1567 (as in n. 17), pp. 1–5.

90. See L. March, *Architectonics of Humanism: Essays on Number in Architecture*, Chichester 1998, on Palladio's approach to the harmonic proportion of buildings.

91. Palladio (as in n. 13), p. 188: 'quel poco che si dirà', literally, 'the little that will be said'; cf. Palladio (as in n. 35), p. 163.

92. Palladio (as in n. 35), p. 163. Palladio (as in n. 13), p. 189: ' ... essendo che molto più s'impari dai buoni esempi in poco tempo, col misurarli e col veder sopra una picciola carta gli edifici intieri e tutte le parti loro, che in lungo tempo dalle parole, per le quali solo con la mente e con qualche difficoltà può il lettore venir in ferma e certa notizia di quel ch'egli legge e con molta fatica poi praticarlo'.

93. Vitruvius 1960 (as in n. 2), p. 130; Vitruvius 1998 (as in n. 2), p. 252: 'Non minus cum animadvertissem distentam occupationibus civitatem publicis et privatis negotiis, paucis iudicavi scribendum, uti angusto spatio vacuitatis ea legentes breviter percipere possent.'

94. Ibid.

95. Barbaro, MS Italian 5106, fol. 156r. From D'Evelyn 1994 (as in n. 17), pp. 545, 574–5 nn. 27–8; and D'Evelyn 1998–99 (as in n. 15), p. 173 n. 86. 'Brevity without obscurity' is a phrase popularized by the Augustan poet Horace, in his *Ars Poetica*, and echoed by Barbaro. In fact, in the passage from Horace to which Barbaro alludes, 'breuis esse laboro/obscurus fio' (Horace, *Epistles, Book Two, and Epistle to the Pisones*, 'Ars Poetica', ed. N. Rudd, Cambridge 1989, p. 59, v. 25–6), the ancient poet is warning about the danger of extreme brevity. However, at the end of the poem Horace writes, 'Instruction must be brief if it is to be retained by the reader' (C. O. Brink, *Horace on Poetry: Prolegomena to the Literary Epistles*, Cambridge 1963, p. 262; in Rudd ed., v. 335, 'quidquid praecipies esto brevis'). It is this latter passage that Barbaro translates and quotes for his edition of Vitruvius. See also Cellauro (as in n. 8), pp. 114–15.

ftali? che uengono in fuori , & non uanno continuando , ma rompeno la drittura del poggio : &

Lato del Tempio fatto col poggio.

4.1   Daniele Barbaro, *Vitruvio*, 1567, side elevation of an Ionic temple portico, woodcut

QVINTO. 250

4.2   Daniele Barbaro, *Vitruvio*, 1567, part exterior elevation of a Greek theatre,
woodcut

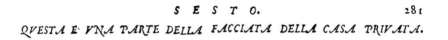

4.3   Daniele Barbaro, *Vitruvio*, 1567, part elevation of the portico and front window wall of the 'House of the Ancients', woodcut

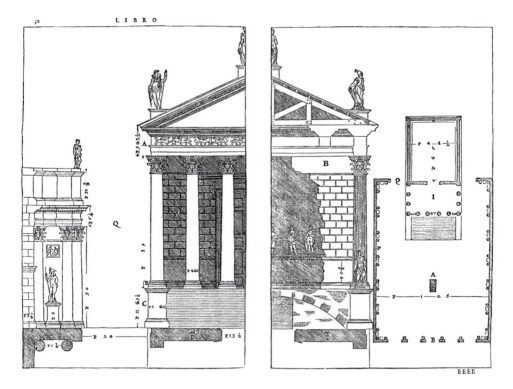

4.4   Andrea Palladio, *I quattro libri dell'architettura*, 1570, double-page spread, *The Temple of Antoninus and Faustina in Rome*. Left-hand side: elevation and part plan of half the portico and part of the enclosing wall; right-hand side: cross section and part plan of half the portico alongside the plan of the temple and its enclosure

4.5   Daniele Barbaro, *Vitruvio*, 1567, woodcut frontispiece

4.6   Andrea Palladio, *I quattro libri dell'architettura*, 1570, woodcut frontispiece to Book I

5

'The beauty and majesty of the images': Pietro da Cortona's Barberini ceiling in Teti's *Aedes Barberinae*

Thomas Frangenberg

The fresco painted by Pietro da Cortona (1597–1669) in the Salone of the Barberini Palace in Rome (1632–39) is celebrated in two chapters of one of the most lavish books to have been published in Rome during the seventeenth century, Girolamo Teti's *Aedes Barberinae ad Quirinalem … descriptae* of 1642.[1] In this article I will study the interrelation of text and plates through which the reader of the *Aedes Barberinae* is given access to Cortona's work.

To assist comprehension of Teti's treatment of the Barberini ceiling, a concise summary of its iconography may be useful. The central section of the fresco depicts Divine Providence decreeing that Immortality be bestowed on Pope Urban VIII (see Figure 5.5). This central subject is surrounded by four scenes in the coves, representing Minerva fighting the giants (see Figure 5.4), Hercules casting out the Harpies (see Figure 5.7), Knowledge assisted by Divine Help, Chastity overcoming Lust and Piety triumphing over a Bacchic group standing for Gluttony (see Figure 5.6) and Power guaranteeing Peace in preparing for war.[2]

The fresco is unprecedented in a variety of ways: it is the first ceiling fresco that freely combines mythological scenes and personifications and that is intended to convey a second level of meaning in the form of allusions to Pope Urban VIII Barberini (reigned 1623–44) and members of his family.[3] The Barberini deployed ceiling frescoes as one of the principal, arguably *the* principal, means of communicating their political ambitions to wider audiences.

Such use of ceiling painting is given additional weight by the suggestion of one author active in the circle of the Barberini that ceiling painting is in fact the most prominent form of painting. Giovanni Battista Ferrari's *Hesperides sive de malorum aureorum cultura et usu* of 1646 is lavishly adorned with plates; these depict a number of ancient sculptures of Hercules with the golden apples of the Hesperides, and numerous varieties of citrus fruits and the garden buildings and tools their cultivation requires. A series of engravings after works by the foremost painters active in Rome during the first half of the seventeenth century visualize the mythological narratives that enliven Ferrari's text. The author takes these last plates as an opportunity to highlight not only the quality of the illustrations, but also the respective painters' artistic merits. In these comments, the main emphasis is placed on ceiling painting wherever the painter's output lends itself to such treatment. The first of the mythological plates reproduces a work of Pietro da Cortona, and in his discussion of this painter's art, Ferrari focuses on the Barberni ceiling.[4] Likewise, in his praise of Andrea Sacchi the author mainly discusses a ceiling, the *Divine Wisdom* fresco in the Barberini Palace.[5] In his discussions of the work of other painters Ferrari places similar emphasis on ceiling frescoes even though they were not painted for the Barberini, leaving little doubt that in his estimation ceiling frescoes are the culmination of the art of painting.[6]

The political effectiveness of the Barberini ceiling was assisted by several descriptions, a short explanatory pamphlet written by the caretaker of the palace, Mattia Rosichino, published in 1640,[7] and an extremely detailed description and exegesis of the ceiling in Teti's *Aedes Barberinae*, a work devoted principally to the contemporary ceiling paintings decorating the Barberini Palace.[8] A further text, written by the court poet Francesco Bracciolini, remained in manuscript.[9]

Long before its completion Cortona's ceiling had already attracted the interest of foreign visitors. After its unveiling, the fresco was shown to high-ranking guests, but also attracted a steady stream of less illustrious visitors.[10] Access to the fresco was not problematic; the Salone was a semi-public part of the palace.[11] As Rosichino states in his introduction, his short text was written for the benefit of visitors to the palace;[12] the concise explanation offered by the pamphlet could thus be perused whilst viewing the fresco.

Girolamo Teti's lavish *Aedes Barberinae* is written for a very different audience. Teti was a member of the household of Cardinal Antonio Barberini. Barberini papers refer to him as 'prelate and gentleman'.[13] His book aims to impress; unlike Rosichino's brochure, it is adorned with high-quality engravings. Four engravers signed (at least some of) their plates: we find Cornelis Bloemaert (c. 1603–92), Michael Natalis (1606/10–1668/70) and Johann Friedrich Greuter (c. 1590/3–1662), three of the most prominent northern engravers who had successful careers in Rome during the seventeenth century, and the Italian Camillo Cungi (Camillus Cungius) (1570/80–1649). The renown of the engravers and the predominance of northern artists among them were certainly intended to enhance the international prestige of the publication.

Given the scale and weight of the book, it does not lend itself for perusal by a reader standing with the unsupported volume in hand. The large fold-out plates require a library table for comfortable study. We can therefore be certain that the text was not written to be read during a visit to the palace. The volume was to stand in for such a visit, and it fulfils this function by means of descriptive and explanatory texts and detailed illustrations.

The book aims to extend the propagandistic reach of the fresco decorations and other art treasures housed in the Barberini Palace beyond the confines of the palace itself; it presents to readers outside Rome the greatness of Barberini rule and the lavishness of their art patronage, and it does so hardly less effectively than the palace itself. We know that the volume was used as a diplomatic gift; the red leather binding of a copy in the British Library is adorned with the coat-of-arms of the 'Grand Dauphin', son of Louis XIV.[14] As late as 1670 Cardinal Francesco Barberini bought two copies of this work, one for his own library and one for the Spanish ambassador,[15] which reveals that the ceiling paintings in the Barberini Palace as portrayed in Teti's book remained crucial in the promulgation of the fame of the family long after the pontificate of Urban VIII had come to an end in 1644.

No documentation has yet come to light regarding the funding of the first edition of Teti's book. The second edition of this work, published in 1647 after Teti's death in an obviously not entirely completed form, was, as the title page indicates, funded by the typographer Filippo de Rossi. De Rossi points out that the considerable sum of 2,000 *aurei* was expended on the first edition,[16] but does not comment on the source of these funds.

The major additions to the 1647 edition are an address to the reader, dated 1644, a new dedication and fifteen engraved plates displaying poems in praise of the Barberini Palace, its decoration or Teti's book and portraits of the poems' authors, all set in elegant architectural settings.[17] The collection is named 'Purpurei cycni' (Purple Swans) after a group of cardinals and other men of letters who met in an oval room adjacent to the Salone to devote themselves to poetry.[18] Among the 'Purple Swans' Cardinal Antonio Barberini held the leading position, and his is the poem on the first sheet.[19]

In their individual ways, several of the poems underline the functions of Teti's tome. Many authors dwell on its propagandistic effectiveness. Cardinal Giovanni Battista Altieri maintains that earthly things are transient, but Teti's efforts will last unchanged for ever.[20] Paolo Giordano Orsini, Duke of Bracciano, introduces a similar notion when he maintains that the Barberini Palace is singular, whereas Teti's engraved sheets are spread over the world in hundreds of copies.[21] Several of the poems, such as Cardinal Carlo Rossetti's epigram,[22] address the building's pictorial decoration, and its place in Teti's book. One of the poems, written by Cardinal Juan de Lugo, focuses on Cortona's fresco, revealing that the author considered it as the key work to be discussed in the *Aedes Barberinae*.[23]

The effectiveness of Teti's book depends to a large measure on its illustrations. As much as the Barberini's deployment of ceiling painting for family propaganda, Teti's focus on ceiling painting, and his use of plates, were innovatory. Most discussions of painting or sculpture during the sixteenth century and the first half of the seventeenth were not illustrated, with rare exceptions such as the artists' portraits in the second edition of Vasari's *Lives*,[24] and the three woodcuts adorning a collection of poems in praise of Giambologna's *Rape of the Sabine Woman*.[25] Illustrations of works of art or architecture were, however, not uncommon in some literary genres such as technical treatises, in particular those on architecture,[26] in guidebooks and works on archaeological subject matter[27] and in descriptions of the ephemeral decorations of festivals.[28] Engraved reproductions after pictorial works, published in the form of individual sheets or in folders,[29] were well established by the seventeenth century, but were accompanied by only very minimal textual information that could be provided in captions on the engravings themselves or on the frontispieces of collections.[30] In combining textual exegesis and illustrations, Teti opens a new chapter in the history of the art book.

Better to understand the peculiarities of the plates devoted to Cortona's ceiling, the subtle interrelation of words and images in Teti's work deserves some consideration. Teti's volume in its entirety is dedicated to Cardinal Antonio Barberini the Younger (1607–71), Teti's patron and from 1635 the principal resident of the palace.[31] In the dedication Teti claims that his description functions 'as a second building, a domicile of the soul' which he 'attempted to construct with the intellect'.[32] Teti does not define what kind of use an inhabitant of the palace will make of his work. In his dedication of a section of the book to Lodovico Cantagalli, on the other hand, Teti addresses the requirements of readers who have not seen the palace. As Teti writes, Cantagalli had hoped to see the Barberini Palace during his stay in Rome, but circumstances had prevented him from doing so. Teti's book now takes Cantagalli – who had since left Rome – effortlessly into the palace where eyes and ears are made to 'see'.[33] The reference to the two senses of sight and hearing may be intended to refer to the interrelation of images and text in Teti's book; when imagined read aloud, the text might be construed as principally addressing hearing. If such a distinction between the senses was intended here, other sections of the book suggest that Teti did not advocate an exclusive link between images and sight on the one hand and text and hearing on the other. In his dedication to the Barberini Princes Carlo, Maffeo and Niccolò, the author asserts that his *text* makes the Barberini Palace available to everybody's eyes.[34] That Teti refers to the readers' corporeal eyes is intimated in another chapter devoted to the deeper levels of meaning of Cortona's ceiling; here the author distinguishes between the readers' eyes and their 'eyes of the mind'; the latter are addressed in the chapter devoted to iconographic analyses.[35] Teti seems to suggest that the reading of his descriptions – when they are not exclusively concerned with content – will generate visual images comparable with visual impressions gleaned from the fresco itself. In the dedication to the Barberini Princes he adds, however, that his text is greatly helped by the tome's illustrations. Whatever boredom his 'inert text' might bring will be 'dispelled by the beauty and majesty of the images'.[36]

Teti's volume is subdivided into six sections, all accompanied by one or more illustrations. An engraving also accompanies the dedication to the three Barberini Princes. The first section[37] introduces the reader to the architecture of the palace, briefly describing the façades and the main rooms. Two plates pertain to this section: the frontispiece shows the entrance façade of the palace and the garden façade is illustrated on another plate.[38] That the book is not principally addressed to readers with architectural interests, however, is suggested by the absence of a ground plan. The remainder of this section focuses on the picture collection, much of which was kept in quiet rooms on the ground floor,[39] the library, a museum of mostly small-scale antiques, the armoury and the theatre. The second and third sections[40] are both devoted to different aspects of Pietro da Cortona's fresco. No less than nine engravings on substantial double-page or fold-out plates inserted into the text of the second section illustrate Cortona's ceiling (see Figures 5.2–5.7). The explanation of Cortona's fresco is furthermore accompanied by portraits of four members of the Barberini family to which we shall return.[41] The fourth part[42] describes the *Divine Wisdom* ceiling, painted by Andrea Sacchi (c. 1599–1661) in 1629–30. The central section of Sacchi's fresco is illustrated on a large fold-out plate engraved by Michael Natalis (Figure 5.1) that focuses on the figures and eliminates significant amounts of the celestial background and of the terrestrial globe floating beneath the personifications.

Teti's Section Five[43] is devoted to Andrea Camassei's ceiling fresco *Creation of the Angels* (1630). The last part[44] describes Camassei's *Parnassus* ceiling (1630, destroyed), and then uses this fresco as a starting point for a discussion of the Barberini Parnassus. Teti comments on the poets active in the Barberini circle, on painters represented in their collection and their respective merits and on the sculptures displayed in the Barberini Palace.

Camassei's frescoes, unlike Sacchi's, fill only the centres of their respective ceilings, and in the engravings they are reproduced in their entirety. We shall find that the engravings devoted to Cortona's ceiling refuse even more conspicuously than the Sacchi illustration to give an impression of the totality of the Salone fresco.

Whereas the engravings reproducing the ceiling paintings are bound among the text pages, thus emphasizing that the frescoes are the principal subject of the book, numerous sculptures are illustrated at the end of the volume, both busts and full-length figures; all these works are ancient with the exception of a bust of Carlo Barberini (1562–1630), brother of Pope Urban VIII and father of Taddeo, Francesco and Antonio the Younger. The merit of the sitter and the quality of the bust carved by Francesco Mochi (1580–1654) warrant its inclusion among the ancient works.[45]

The importance of the ancient sculptures in the context of Teti's book is confirmed also by the fact that only the plates devoted to sculpture are cross-referenced with the text by means of letters. In Teti's view, the plates translate the qualities of the sculptures most successfully.[46] Teti's comments on individual busts focus mainly on the importance of the persons represented and on their character rather than on the artistic worth of the sculptures. In the descriptions of other kinds of sculpture, on the other hand, evaluation of artistic achievement and other comments are more closely intertwined. A relief depicting hunters is amply described;[47] Teti states that it is displayed near the busts of rulers because the hunt trains princes for war. A long digression on the ability of Cardinal Antonio Barberini the Younger as a huntsman demonstrates a more specific pertinence of the ancient work to the Barberini.[48] The appearance and psychological nuances of the Barberini *Faun* are analysed with great subtlety; this sculpture, Teti suggests, was displayed in antiquity like a trophy to mark the victory over base passion; such a reading gives moral connotations also to the display of the work in a contemporary context.[49] The emphasis on historical importance and on moral or cultural lessons in Teti's literary treatment of the sculptures strongly suggests that, in associating themselves with ancient achievement, the Barberini wished to document their own merit. Like all other elements of the *Aedes Barberinae*, the ancient works discussed and illustrated contribute to the propagandistic function of the book.

Given the number of plates devoted to sculpture and to ceiling painting, it is conspicuous that no illustration is devoted to any of the easel paintings mentioned in the volume.

The relatively straightforward illustrations of the architecture of the palace, of Sacchi's and Camassei's ceiling paintings and of ancient works, are overshadowed by the profusion of images devoted to Cortona's fresco. Four illustrations of the four corner piers (see Figures 5.2 and 5.3) are followed by five others depicting the figurative scenes (see Figures 5.4–5.7). This quantity of images cannot detract from the fact that the reader is in this instance, and only in this instance, not given the benefit of an overall view of the ceiling, even though representational techniques were available to provide two-dimensional renderings of frescoes on coved ceilings: the foreshortening of figures on steep coves could be obviated by introducing diagonal cuts in the corners that allow the sides to flatten out. This solution was adopted by the author of the anonymous oil-on-canvas copy of the Barberini ceiling in the collection of the Galleria Nazionale d'Arte Antica, Rome.[50]

Assembling knowledge of the visual appearance of Cortona's Barberini ceiling from the plates is a piecemeal affair, and retention of an overall image in the observer's memory must have seemed to Teti to be unlikely, given the fresco's profusion of figures.

Before studying the plates further, it is interesting to note that Teti's text presents a comparably fragmented picture of Cortona's ceiling fresco. Teti shares the assumption held by the authors of the two other contemporary accounts of Cortona's ceiling, Bracciolini[51] and Rosichino,[52] that the perception of the ceiling fresco can be subdivided into two distinct stages, a first one devoted to the visual appearance of the work and a second one concerned with its iconography and its deeper meaning.[53] Unlike Bracciolini and Rosichino, however, Teti cannot assume that the appreciation of the ceiling's visual characteristics can be left largely to the reader as he writes for an audience that cannot be assumed to have seen the ceiling. Furthermore, Teti repeatedly enlivens his text by pointing out that viewers change the direction of their glance as they turn their attention from one section of the fresco to the next.[54]

The first of the two chapters devoted to Cortona's fresco addresses the ceiling's general compositional characteristics, and, as the author states, 'the outward images of things';[55] it is based, so the author maintains, on no more than a brief inspection of the work.[56] Throughout this chapter, Teti provides a fictional account of what a viewer of reasonable learning, but without any specific information regarding the fresco's iconography, might perceive. Teti first turns the reader's attention to the subdivision of the ceiling into five pictorial fields by means of fictitious architecture. In the areas defined by this framework some figures are supported on clouds, while others appear in terrestrial settings.[57] These general introductory remarks provide an impression of the characteristics of the fresco in its entirety, standing in for an overall illustration of the ceiling fresco and allowing the user of the volume to comprehend the interrelation of the details, be they discussed in Teti's highly particularized descriptions or represented in the illustrations. Throughout the first description, Teti withholds the names of almost all the figures; he characterizes them by naming their attributes, or by obliquely pointing to aspects of their significance. Rome, for example, 'shows that she is Queen of the World',[58] the likewise here unnamed personification of Eternity 'carries the starry eternal crown'.[59]

In the second description of Cortona's fresco Teti moves from the 'external images of things' to meaning 'hidden inside, beneath the colours', accessible to 'the eyes of the mind'.[60] In this chapter, the fiction of a principally visual response to the fresco is given up; the author in fact seems to assume that

more of the iconography had been understood whilst reading the first
description than the text made explicit. For example, comments on the cove
over the left wall are introduced with the suggestion: 'Let us now look again
at the Forge of Vulcan'[61] which, Teti no doubt assumes, the reader readily
identified when it was described in the previous chapter, and equally easily
found among the plates.

The meaning hidden 'beneath the colours' does not exhaust itself in the
names of the depicted figures which are given throughout the second
description; more importantly, the second description suggests to the readers
how their ingenuity may uncover or devise references to the virtues of
members of the Barberini family by subjecting the entire ceiling to a reading
focusing on the Barberini. To give but two examples: the arms in the Forge of
Vulcan allude to Urban's providence in assembling armouries and the Temple
of Janus depicted in the same cove refers to Urban's building of fortifications.[62]
Other members of the Barberini family referred to in individual scenes are
Cardinals Antonio the Elder and the Younger, Francesco Barberini and Taddeo
Barberini, the Prefect of Rome. The presence of the Barberini family in Teti's
account of the fresco's iconography is underlined by the inclusion in this
section of the text of engraved portraits of these four relatives of Urban
VIII.[63]

Drawings for the engravings after Cortona's fresco were produced at Teti's
instigation, and were submitted to the painter for information and perhaps
for his approval.[64] Three highly detailed drawings, two of piers and one of
the south-eastern long cove, are extant today.[65] The drawings were then
passed on to engravers of Teti's choosing. Of the plates devoted to Cortona's
ceiling, only three are signed: Cungi engraved the plate after the Minerva
cove, Bloemaert those depicting the long coves. The artist(s?) producing the
drawings no less than the engravers had to address the question of how to
subdivide the ceiling into units that could conveniently be reproduced. All
of the plates emphasize their fragmentary character by referring to the larger
whole; adjacent scenes, clouds or architectural elements leave traces at the
edges of most engravings in the form of concave indentations (see the top of
Figure 5.2). Such negative presences, such emptiness of white paper,
constantly remind the viewer that each detail needs to be understood in
terms of its neighbour in the context of the fresco. To find these neighbours
among the illustrations, however, is not a task that the book makes easy. As
there is no overall illustration and the plates with the four piers and the five
figurative scenes are grouped together, rather than alternating with each
other, it requires considerable powers of recollection to recognize individual
plates as depicting adjacent areas of the fresco.

No straightforward solution presented itself regarding the question of
how to allocate figures and other details to individual plates, given that in

the fresco numerous figures that form part of the narrative scenes overlap the architectural framework. More than any other, the Minerva cove spills over into the area of the piers, and the engraving after that cove (Figure 5.4) therefore includes the lower sections of the halves of the piers adjacent to the narrative. Thus there exists some duplication between the engraving of the Minerva scene and those depicting the piers, and not only concerning the feigned architecture. The plate depicting the pier with the unicorn (Figure 5.2) includes the figure of a giant falling backwards behind a large boulder in the Minerva cove. The posture and the partial occlusion of the giant by the boulder furthermore necessitated indications in outline of the position of the boulder in the plate depicting the pier. The reach of this engraving thus extends almost to the centre of the area covered by the illustration depicting the Minerva cove.

A comparison between the drawings and the engravings suggests that several decisions were arrived at in stages. The drawing of the long cove depicting Knowledge assisted by Divine Help includes the leg of a putto seated in the vicinity of the Fates in the central section of the fresco (compare the lower right of Figure 5.5). The engravings, on the other hand, consistently aim to avoid fragmentation of figures. The putto's leg is therefore missing in the plate engraved by Bloemaert (top left of Figure 5.6). There are furthermore a variety of indications to suggest that the engravers attempted to avoid overly complicated outlines for the engraved areas. For this reason the putto's missing leg does not leave an indentation in the cornice.

Fragmentation was perceived as problematic also regarding the architecture, but in this instance appears to have been, at least in most instances, acceptable to the engravers. The drawing of the pier with the lion presents this pier in ideal completeness, with a mask, scrolls and foliage above the octagon, even though in the fresco these crowning elements are occluded by clouds. Unlike the drawing, the engraving takes this occlusion into consideration (see Figure 5.3), representing the clouds in a medium grey. That different engravers contributed to the making of the plates is suggested, even without considering the signatures appearing on three of the engravings, by different approaches to individual problems. All of the plates other than that depicting the pier with the lion register the clouds by means of the whiteness of the paper penetrating the engraved areas in accordance with the clouds' outlines (compare Figure 5.2).

A feature found on only one of the plates depicting the coves is the indication, in outlines, of a triton, scroll and festoon, parts of the sculptural decoration of the pier on the right of the Hercules cove (Figure 5.7). More than the others this engraving displays a knowing deployment of graphic techniques to distinguish from each other those components that constitute the principal subject of the illustration from others that, greatly reduced in their three-dimensional appearance, principally serve to provide a context for the main scene. The idiosyncrasy of this plate is underlined by the fact that the engraver amended the fragmentation of the architectural framework: he presented the frame on the right of this scene in its entirety even though in the fresco it is intersected by a broken pediment decorated with a drapery, among other adornment.

All of the plates offer solutions to the requirement of presenting a satisfactory configuration even though they clearly depict only parts of a larger whole; all profess allegiance to their own objects of representation, be it the respective scene or pier or elements that significantly penetrate into the area covered by the plate. The engravings in their totality do not aim to provide an inventory without duplication; they do not function like a jigsaw puzzle in which cut-outs would fit without overlaps.

The plates illustrating Cortona's ceiling do not translate the experience of the decoration enveloping the viewer in all directions. Glimpses of a comprehensive visual experience are found less in the plates than in the few concise introductory comments in Teti's text. In like manner, the simultaneous intellectual availability of the fresco is hinted at only in short opening statements. The remainder of Teti's description of Cortona's ceiling as much as all the plates focuses on details of the ceiling which the user of the book encounters consecutively. Simultaneous accessibility of Cortona's work in Teti's book is granted more by the readers' mental collaboration than by what the book provides.

Teti's fragmented portrayal of Cortona's ceiling suggests to the user of the book to engage with the fresco's details and their potential meanings in turn; the successive experience of individual sections of the ceiling is echoed in the unfolding of the plates. The readers' necessarily consecutive engagement with the numerous subjects portrayed on the ceiling would not have been helped by an overall illustration of the fresco. The plates allow viewers to create their own syntheses of their observations and conclusions, culminating in what is certainly the most important objective of Teti's book – a comprehension of the multifaceted achievements and the divinely ordained nature of Barberini rule.

Given the ambition of both the decorations of the Barberni Palace and of Teti's project, it is unsurprising that this book was not immediately influential. No later-seventeenth-century ruling family in Italy deployed ceiling painting in so deliberately propagandistic and public a manner, and no family therefore saw the need to divulge the frescoes they commissioned in illustrated publications.

This is not to say that Teti's synthesis of text and image remained without successors. In 1661, Borboni published his *Delle statue*, containing twelve plates of classical and contemporary sculptures in Rome.[66] In the later seventeenth and eighteenth centuries, a number of European patrons of art or architecture were celebrated in collections of engravings, some of which were accompanied by text.[67] By the late seventeenth century the illustrated book could function also as a sophisticated art historical tool. Teti, in spite of his concern to convey the visual appearance of Cortona's fresco in the second section of his work, does not dwell at any length on issues of pictorial style. Malvasia's *Il Claustro di S. Michele in Bosco di Bologna* of 1694,[68] on the other hand, is primarily given over to stylistic analyses of Ludovico Carracci's works; the author's discussion is assisted by engravings that make lengthy descriptions unnecessary.

Not until the mid-eighteenth century were further illustrated books devoted to ceiling painting published in Italy. D. M. Manni's *Azioni gloriose degli uomini illustri fiorentini espresse co' loro ritratti nelle volte della Real Galleria di Toscana*[69] is exclusively devoted to the ceiling paintings in the western and southern corridors of the Uffizi, frescoes that in terms of their accessibility[70] and propagandistic ambition are comparable with Pietro da Cortona's Barberini ceiling. In this book, the plates are accompanied by a detailed iconographic explanation of the frescoes. In 1753, a learned and richly annotated iconographic commentary was written by L. Philarchaeus to accompany Cesio's engravings after the Farnese ceiling, thus establishing an equilibrium between text and image in a publication that in the seventeenth century had been envisaged as a collection of engravings with only a short introduction.[71] By the middle of the eighteenth century richly illustrated art books, a genre of publication inaugurated by Teti's *Aedes Barberinae*, were no longer unusual.[72]

Notes

1. G. Teti (H. Tetius), *Aedes Barberinae ad Quirinalem … descriptae*, Rome: Mascardi 1642. On this work see F. Haskell, *Patrons and Painters: A Study in the Relations Between Italian Art and Society in the Age of the Baroque* (1st edn 1963) New Haven 1980, p. 56; M. Fumaroli, *L'Age de l'éloquence: rhétorique et 'res literaria' de la Renaissance au seuil de l'époque classique*, Geneva 1980, pp. 205–13, and, 'Rome 1630: entrée en scène du spectateur', in *Roma 1630: il trionfo del pennello*, Milan 1994, pp. 53–82, esp. pp. 74–5; and F. Haskell, *The Painful Birth of the Art Book*, London 1987, p. 8. On Pietro da Cortona see G. Briganti, *Pietro da Cortona o della pittura barocca*, Florence 1962 and, with recent bibliographies, J. M. Merz, *Pietro da Cortona: der Aufstieg zum führenden Maler im barocken Rom*, Tübingen 1991; *Pietro da Cortona e il disegno*, ed. S. Prosperi Valenti Rodinò, Milan 1997; *Pietro da Cortona 1597–1669*, ed. A. Lo Bianco, Milan 1997. On Cortona's Barberini ceiling see H. Posse, 'Das Deckenfresko des Pietro da Cortona im Palazzo Barberini und die Deckenmalerei in Rom', *Jahrbuch der Preussischen Kunstsammlungen*, XL, 1919, pp. 93–118, 126–73; D. Bernini, Introduction, *Il voltone di Pietro da Cortona in Palazzo Barberini* (Quaderni di Palazzo Venezia, 2), Rome 1983; J. B. Scott, *Images of Nepotism: The Painted Ceilings of Palazzo Barberini*, Princeton NJ 1991, pp. 123–97; M. A. Lee, '"Hic Domus": The Decorative Programme of the Sala Barberina in Rome', Ph.D. thesis, Ann Arbor 1993; and H. Locher, 'Das Staunen des Betrachters: Pietro da Cortonas Deckenfresko im Palazzo Barberini', in *Werners Kunstgeschichte 1990*, ed. H. J. Kunst, A. B. Rave and W. Schenkluhn, Worms 1990, pp. 1–46; see also G. Magnanimi, *Palazzo Barberini*, Rome 1983.

2. The three accounts of the iconography of the ceiling written by contemporaries – by Teti, Rosichino and Bracciolini (on the last two see notes 7 and 9 below) – do not agree on the

identification of all the figures; for reasons that I will present in a discussion of Bracciolini's text (in press) I have chosen among the titles given by Rosichino and Teti.

3. This latter point was driven home not only by contemporary descriptions of the ceiling, but was also divulged in a more general art historical work which documents how specific references to the Barberini were envisaged even before the commission was awarded to Pietro da Cortona. In his life of Andrea Camassei (1602–49) who initially was to paint the Salone ceiling, Passeri states: ' ... alcuni concetti poetichi, con allusioni alle imprese, et heroiche azioni del Pontefice Urbano, espressi con la penna gloriosa del Signor Francesco Bracciolini dell'Api. Questa volta poi per mutazione di parere, o di Fortuna, fù dal medesimo Pontefice collocata al Signor Pietro da Cortona; et egli nello spazio di quattordeci anni la ridusse à quella bellezza, che hoggi si vede, con le medesime invenzioni'; in J. Hess ed., *Die Künstlerbiographien von Giovanni Battista Passeri*, Leipzig and Vienna 1934, pp. 169–70. (Passeri greatly overestimates the time Pietro da Cortona spent on this fresco.) As with the identification of individual figures, the three contemporary descriptions differ in their readings of the fresco's allusions to the Barberini family. Such differences in the interpretation of the fresco strongly suggest that the decoration was not intended to communicate a fixed canon of meanings, but affords all viewers the opportunity of establishing their own poetic readings; see J. Montagu, 'The Painted Enigma and French Seventeenth-Century Art', *Journal of the Warburg and Courtauld Institutes*, XXXI, 1968, pp. 307–35, esp. pp. 334–5, and Locher (as in n. 1), pp. 21–4, 34. Direct support for this suggestion is found in Teti's book (as in n. 1); in the dedication of one of the chapters to Rosato Torelli, who had seen the fresco, Teti writes (pp. 44–5): 'Barberinorum Principum virtutes ... variis hisce imaginibus expicta, hic tibi recensere supervacaneum censeo: tu ipse Pontificem Maximum, nostrosque Principes in iis, per argumenta non fallacis gloriae, undique intuere.'

4. ' ... Barberinorum aula Quirinalis: cuius concameratio efficaci Petri penicillo mutata in caelum est: quoniam inde caelestium chorus virtutum, fugato vitiorum agmine, cum aureo melleoque regnantium Apum saeculo in terras remigravit. Sic autem reduces inter virtutes pictura ipsa eminet, sic vivit, et insolito vigore spirat: ut cum iisdem caelo delapsa videatur'; in G. B. Ferrari, *Hesperides sive de malorum aureorum cultura et usu, libri quatuor*, Rome 1646, p. 2. On this work see Fumaroli 1994 (as in n. 1), pp. 75–81.

5. Ferrari (as in n. 4), pp. 91–2.

6. Ibid., pp. 53–4 (on Francesco Albani and his loggia ceiling in the Palazzo Verospi, Rome); pp. 345–6 (on Guido Reni and his *Aurora* fresco in the Casino Borghese, now Pallavicini-Rospigliosi); pp. 449–50 (on Giovanni Lanfranco and his dome in the Cappella del Tesoro, Naples Cathedral). No reference to ceiling painting is made in the relatively short comments on Nicolas Poussin (p. 99), and Giovanni Francesco Romanelli (p. 279) or, surprisingly, in Ferrari's praise of Domenichino (p. 421).

7. M. Rosichino, *Dichiaratione delle pitture della sala de' Signori Barberini*, Rome 1640.

8. Teti (as in n. 1).

9. F. Bracciolini, 'Il pellegrino, o vero la dichiaratione delle pitture della Sala Barberina', MS Biblioteca Apostolica Vaticana, Codice Barberini Latino 4335. For the correct attribution of this text see Magnanimi (as in n. 1), pp. 120–2, and Lee (as in n. 1), pp. 17–21; the most useful transcription is found in Lee, pp. 244–95. On Bracciolini (1566–1645) see L. Rossi, 'Bracciolini (Dell'Api), Francesco', in *Dizionario biografico degli Italiani*, XIII, Rome 1971, pp. 634–6.

10. See Scott (as in n. 1), pp. 193–4.

11. See P. Waddy, *Seventeenth-Century Roman Palaces: Use and the Art of the Plan*, Cambridge MA and London 1990, esp. pp. 4–5, 7.

12. Rosichino (as in n. 7), p. 3: 'Come l'huomo mira le pitture fatte dal Signor Pietro Berettini da Cortona nella volta della sala de'Signori Barberini; così comprende ch'elle sono quelle cose, che sopra tutte le altre dilettano gli occhi de'mortali. Ma perche tal diletto non si dilata, se non alla forma, e alla dispositione de'colori, e delle figure; i riguardanti rimanendo privi del godimento d'intenderne il significato, tutto il giorno si volgevano a me, che di continuo (così portando il mio carico) dimoro quì, e richiedevanmi che io gliel dichiarassi ... '.

Rosichino was employed as *scopatore* (sweeper), a position that entailed supervising the cleaning of the palace, and probably also the locking of the palace gates (Scott, as in n. 1, p. 137). His claim that he was frequently approached by visitors for the meaning of the Barberini ceiling is therefore a very plausible one. Rosichino is furthermore not the only employee of a palace to have published a description of it; see G. (I.) Manilli, *Villa Borghese fuori di Porta Pinciana. Descritta da Iacomo Manilli Romano guardarobba di detta villa*, Rome 1650.

13. Merz (as in n. 1), p. 240; Scott (as in n. 1), p. 138 and see also p. 102.

14. BL G1295.

15. F. Petrucci Nardelli, 'Il Card. Francesco Barberini Senior e la stampa a Roma', *Archivio della Società Romana di Storia Patria*, CVIII, 1985, pp. 133–98, esp. p. 162.

16. G. Teti (H. Tetius), *Aedes Barberinae ad Quirinalem … descriptae*, Rome (sumptibus Philippi de Rubeis) 1647, 'Lectori', n.p.

17. Several plates lack the poems, and in one instance both portrait and poem.

18. Scott (as in n. 1), pp. 194–5.

19. Teti 1647 (as in n. 16), 'Purpurei cycni', p. 5.

20. Ibid., p. 19.

21. Ibid., p. 33:
Dell'Ecc. Sig. Duca di Bracciano
Paolo Giordano Orsino
…
Il bel palagio a nullo altro secondo,
Di cui descrivi tu ciascuna parte,
Con imagini belle in stil facondo,
Èpur un solo e, ne l'impresse carte
Multiplicate, ne riceve il mondo
Date ben cento, e cento. Opra è del'arte.

22. Ibid., p. 17.

23. Ibid., p. 23:
Em. Cardinalis de Lugo

Epigramma

Petrus apelleâ, quas pinxerat arte figuras,
Haec brevis expressas pagina, lector, habet.
Exhibet appictas muris immobilis aula,
Ista volaturas charta sub astra dabit.
Trans anni, solisque vias levis ista feretur,
Augustamque domum littus in omne feret.
Ergo licet Petro aulam tantam urbs debeat una,
Debebit Teti mundus uterque tibi.

24. See the essay by S. Gregory in this volume.

25. M. Sermartelli ed., *Alcune composizioni di diversi autori in lode del ritratto della Sabina. Scolpito in marmo dall'eccellentissimo M. Giovanni Bologna, posto nella piazza del Serenissimo Gran Duca di Toscana*, Florence 1583.

26. See V. Hart and R. Tavernor in this volume.

27. For example P. Totti, *Ritratto di Roma antica, nel quale sono figurati i principali tempij … et altre cose notabili*, Rome 1627.

28. See, for example, the descriptions devoted to Florentine festivals: G. Gaeta Bertelà and A. Petrioli Tofani, *Feste e apparati medicei da Cosimo I a Cosimo II, mostra di disegni e incisioni* (Gabinetto Disegni e Stampe degli Uffizi, 31), Florence 1969.

29. See, for example, *Annibale Carracci e i suoi incisori*, ed. E. Borea and G. Mariani, Rome 1986.

30. An exception is G. P. Bellori's introduction accompanying Carlo Cesio's engravings after Annibale Carracci's Farnese ceiling, published in 1657; see *Art and its Images: An Exhibition of Printed Books Containing Engraved Illustrations after Italian Painting*, ed. C. H. Lloyd with T. Ledger, Oxford 1975, pp. 104–6.

31. Scott (as in n. 1), p. 59.

32. Teti (as in n. 1), p. 1: ' … Tui Aedium Descriptionem … quam ego veluti Aedificium alterum, atque animi domicilium … ingenio construere tentavi … '.

33. Ibid., p. 12: 'itaque rem tibi haud ingratam facturum me credidi, si te, vel absentem, in augustissimas Aedes introducerem, quod tamen absque incommodo tuo fiet. quamquam vereor, ne, quò Romae gratiùs, eò graviùs per me istic oculis, atque auribus videantur!'

34. Ibid., p. 7: 'Barberinas Aedes … à me descriptas, ut oculis omnium exponerem … '.

35. Ibid., p. 61: 'Iam satis puto narratione altera oculis datum; externasque rerum imagines satis lustravimus: nunc mentis oculos propiùs admoventes, quid intus sub coloribus hisce lateat seriò reputemus … '.

36. Ibid., p. 8: ' … quidquid fastidii oratio inanis afferret, Imaginum pulchritudine, & maiestate facillimè abstersum iri'.

37. Ibid., pp. 11–41.

38. The placing of the plates in individual copies of Teti's book is not consistent, suggesting that standardization was not yet perceived as essential; their positions will therefore not be discussed here.

39. Waddy (as in n. 11), p. 245.

40. Teti (as in n. 1), pp. 43–58, 59–82.

41. Ibid., pp. 67, 71, 73, 75.

42. Ibid., pp. 83–96.

43. Ibid., pp. 97–106.

44. Ibid., pp. 107–95.

45. Ibid., pp. 188–9, 221; Mochi's bust is now in the Museo di Roma (Palazzo Braschi); see M. De Luca Savelli, 'Le opere del Mochi', in *Francesco Mochi 1580–1654*, Florence 1981, pp. 35–85, esp. pp. 71–2.

46. Teti (as in n. 1, p. 173) writes about the busts: ' … quique in singulis marmoreis Imaginibus apparent animorum sensus, perturbationes, motus, mores, omnes in exemplis ipsis perspicias, penicilli industria: ora, oculos frontem, genas, capillos, quave singula membra pollent maiestate, decore, venustate, ab expressione decoloris lapidis, Pictura reddit tam ad vivum, ut *Sculpta putes, quae picta vides*.' (The last line is quoted after a poem by Maffeo Barberini, 'De picturis Guidonis Rheni in sacello exquilino S. D. N. Pauli V.'; see *Maphaei S. R. E. Card. Barberini postea Urbani PP. VIII. poemata*, Oxford 1726, pp. 132–3).

47. Now in the Wisbech Museum, Wisbech (Cambs.); see C. C. Vermeule, 'The Dal Pozzo-Albani Drawings of Classical Antiquities in the British Museum', *Transactions of the American Philosophical Society*, N.S. L, 5, 1960, p. 19 (fol. 133, no. 150). I owe this reference to Lucia Faedo.

48. Teti (as in n. 1), pp. 179–81, plate on p. 213.

49. Ibid., pp. 181–4, plate on p. 215; the sculpture is now in the Glyptothek, Munich.

50. Published as Cortona's *bozzetto* in E. Lavagnino, 'Il bozzetto di Pietro da Cortona per la volta della sala maggiore del Palazzo Barberini', *Bollettino d'Arte*, XXIX, 1935, pp. 82–9, but listed as workshop copy by Briganti (as in n. 1), p. 282. This representational technique was employed by Jacopo Strada in his drawing (Kunstmuseum, Düsseldorf) after Giulio Romano's ceiling in the Sala di Troia, Ducal Palace, Mantua (M. Campbell, *Pietro da Cortona at the Pitti Palace: A Study of the Planetary Rooms and Related Projects*, Princeton NJ 1977, fig. 168). This technique was not, however, widely adopted in graphic reproductions of coved ceilings and domes. In his engraving after Cortona's lost ceiling fresco in the now-destroyed Villa del Pigneto, Rome, Gherardo Audran transforms the short sides of his illustration into polygons so as to show the *quadri riportati* in the coves unforeshortened (Campbell, as above, fig. 141). Other engravers preferred to devote separate plates to individual sections of the respective fresco and not to provide an overall view; compare, for example, the engravings after Annibale Carracci's Farnese Ceiling (Borea and Mariani eds, as in n. 29, pp. 111–201), after Giovanni Lanfranco's dome in S. Andrea della Valle, Rome (N. Turner, 'Ferrante Carlo's "Descrittione della Cupola di S. Andrea della Valle depinta dal Cavalier Gio: Lanfranchi"; a Source for Bellori's Descriptive Method', *Storia dell'arte*, XII, 1971, pp. 297–325, see figs 3A–6B) and after Ciro Ferri's dome in S. Agnese in Agone, Rome (H. Trottmann, *Cosmas Damian Asam 1686–1739: Tradition und Invention im malerischen Werk*, Nuremberg 1986, figs 16, 19–21).

51. Bracciolini (as in n. 9), fols 2r–3r (Lee, as in n. 1, pp. 247–9) begins his description with general comments regarding the visual appearance of the work, and then goes on to engage with details of the iconography.

52. See n. 12, above.

53. Similar subdivisions of the viewing process into distinct phases, ultimately derived from medieval optics, are found both in earlier art literature and in perspective theory; see T. Frangenberg, 'The Image and the Moving Eye: Jean Pélerin (Viator) to Guidobaldo del Monte', *Journal of the Warburg and Courtauld Institutes*, XLIX, 1986, pp. 150–71, and *Der Betrachter: Studien zur florentinischen Kunstliteratur des 16. Jahrhunderts*, Berlin 1990, pp. 184–90.

54. E. g. Teti (as in n. 1), p. 47: 'At quoniam artificiosi huius Caeli partes, et cardines inspeximus, nunc ad singula partium ornamenta advertamus'; p. 51: 'Nunc verò ad meridiem aspice … '; p. 52: 'Verùm ab hac peste oculos, quaeso, ad nobile spectaculum convertamus.'

55. Ibid., p. 61; see n. 35.

56. Ibid., p. 57: 'Atque haec quidem sunt, quae de Cortonensis Petri Picturis pauca potui, ab unica tantum brevique inspectione, in abeuntem iam reducere memoriam, tibique inspicienda proferre.'

57. Ibid., p. 45: 'in quo quidem [caelo], seorsim ab alijs, Imagines aliquot contemplamur; quaedam enim nubibus imminentes, quasi proxima nobis sidera, liberè vagantur; reliquae suo quaeque loco fixae, suisque limitibus clausae conspiciuntur'.

58. Ibid., p. 47: 'Orbis se Reginam ostendit.'

59. Ibid.: 'sideream, aeternamque coronam sustinet'.

60. Ibid., p. 61; see n. 35.

61. Ibid., p. 62.

62. Ibid.

63. See n. 41.

64. In a letter to Cassiano dal Pozzo of 17 August 1641 Cortona writes: 'Il sig. Girolamo Tezio di già m'ha mandati alcuni disegni della sala del sig. cardinal Barberini, e, per quanto mi accenna, di già li fa intagliare. Ho inteso che uno ne fa il Greuter, il quale è buono. Gli altri non so come li abbia spartiti, acciò possa essere uniforme coll'opera tutta insieme'; G. Bottari and S. Ticozzi ed., *Raccolta di lettere sulla pittura, scultura ed architettura*, 8 vols, Milan 1822–25, I, p. 415; see also Briganti (as in n. 1), pp. 202–3, and *Il voltone* (as in n. 1), p. 85. As none of the plates devoted to the Barberini ceiling bears Greuter's signature, we do not know which engraving he produced.
   Baldinucci comments on Bloemaert's involvement in Teti's publication: 'Similmente intagliò … due storie della sala Barberina, pure del Cortona, in una delle quali sono favole di Bacco e Venere, nell'altra di Vulcano e del Furore, con alcuni ritratti di persone di casa Barberini: i quali tutti intagli vanno congiunti al bel libro in foglio, intitolato: *Ædes Barberinae*'; F. Baldinucci, *Notizie dei professori del disegno da Cimabue in qua*, ed. F. Ranalli, IV, Florence 1846, p. 599. Pascoli, freely quoting Baldinucci, gives the misleading impression that this artist engraved the entire ceiling; L. Pascoli, *Vite de' pittori, scultori, ed architetti moderni*, introduction A. Marabottini, Perugia 1992, p. 50. It is likely that Teti's choice of Bloemaert met no less with Cortona's approval than his choice of Greuter, even though Baldinucci (as above, pp. 600–1) reports that Cortona and Bloemaert had a difficult working relationship: 'Egli è ben vero, che quanto il Cortona desiderava Bloemaert per lo intagliare delle opere sue, altrettanto il Bloemaert in certo modo aborriva il servirlo, a cagione, no so se dobbiamo dire del gran buon gusto di quel pittore, o pure della di lui molta fastidiosaggine; perchè non mai si trovava pienamente contento della sua taglia, per altro maravigliosa, e talvolta de' dintorni, i quali volea veder fare in sua propria presenza: e spesse volte faceva rimutare dopo che eran fatti: e non ha dubbio, che se ciò non fosse occorso, assai più opere vedremmo del Cortona intagliate per mano di questo artefice, che non veggiamo'; paraphrased by Pascoli (as above).

65. *Il voltone* (as in n. 1), pp. 85–8. The two drawings after corner piers are in the Ashmolean Museum, Oxford; the drawing after the cove is in the Royal Library, Windsor Castle.

66. G. A. Borboni, *Delle statue*, Rome 1661.

67. See Lloyd and Ledger (as in n. 30), passim, Haskell 1987 (as in n. 1) and J. Greitschus, 'Theatres of Painting in Brussels and Vienna, 1650–1750', PhD thesis, University of Essex 1994.

68. C. C. Malvasia, engravings by G. Giovannini, *Il Claustro di S. Michele in Bosco di Bologna dipinto dal famoso Lodovico Carracci e da altri eccellenti maestri usciti dalla sua scola*, Bologna 1694.

69. D. M. Manni, *Azioni gloriose degli uomini illustri fiorentini espresse co' loro ritratti nelle volte della Real Galleria di Toscana*, I. Orsini introduction [Florence 1745].

70. See R. del Bruno, *Ristretto delle cose più notabili della Città di Firenze*, ed. I. Carlieri, Florence 1689, p. 76.

71. L. Philarchaeus, engravings by C. Cesio, *Aedium Farnesiarum tabulae ab Annibale Caraccio depictae*, Rome 1753; on the 1657 edition see n. 30, above.

72. See Lloyd and Ledger (as in n. 30), passim; Haskell 1987 (as in n. 1).

5.1 Michael Natalis, after Andrea Sacchi, *Divine Wisdom* ceiling, Palazzo Barberini, engraving in Teti's *Aedes Barberinae*, 1642

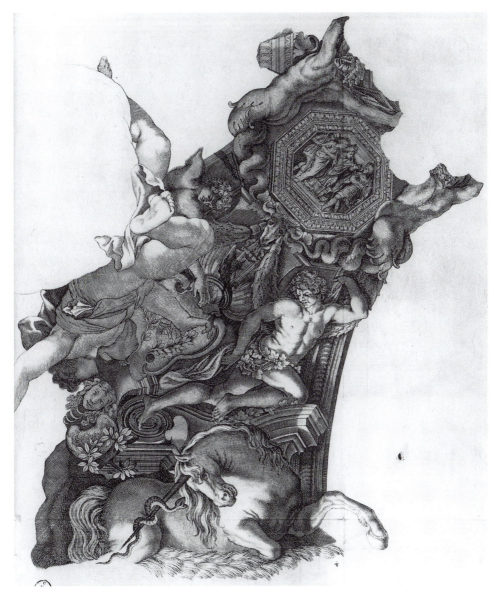

5.2   After Pietro da Cortona, Barberini ceiling, pier with unicorn, engraving in
Teti's *Aedes Barberinae*, 1642

5.3   After Pietro da Cortona, Barberini ceiling, pier with lion, engraving in Teti's, *Aedes Barberinae* 1642

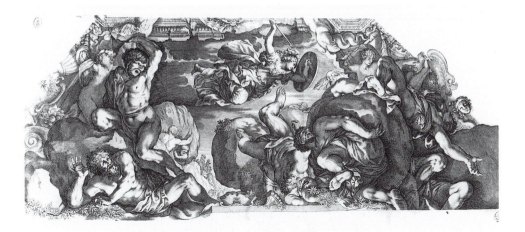

5.4   Camillo Cungi after Pietro da Cortona, Barberini ceiling, north-eastern cove,
Minerva casting down the Giants, engraving in Teti's *Aedes Barberinae*, 1642

5.5   After Pietro da Cortona, Barberini ceiling, central section, *Divine Providence and Barberini coat-of-arms*, engraving in Teti's *Aedes Barberinae*, 1642

5.6   Cornelis Bloemaert after Pietro da Cortona, Barberini ceiling, south-eastern cove, *Knowledge assisted by Divine Help, Chastity overcoming Lust, and Piety triumphing over Gluttony*, engraving in Teti's *Aedes Barberinae*, 1642

5.7   After Pietro da Cortona, Barberini ceiling, south-western cove, *Hercules casting out the Harpies*, engraving in Teti's *Aedes Barberinae*, 1642

6

'All is very plain, upon inspection of the figure': the visual method of Andrea Pozzo's *Perspectiva Pictorum et Architectorum*

Rodney Palmer

Introduction

The *Perspectiva pictorum et architectorum* by the Jesuit lay brother Andrea Pozzo marks the culminating moment in the tradition of illustrated books on perspective.[1] Although geometrical procedures for the depiction of three-dimensional settings were available to Graeco-Roman and to Oriental artists,[2] a mathematically coherent linear perspective was defined in early modern art and its texts. The first part of this essay will briefly consider the role of perspective in Renaissance artistic theory printed prior to the publication of Volume I of the first edition of the *Perspectiva pictorum et architectorum* in 1693; only the illustrating strategies that directly informed Pozzo will be taken into account. Perspective and related optical themes generated an extensive twentieth-century critical literature,[3] which is pertinent to the present enquiry only where it concerns the question of visual information. This study of figurative expositions of perspective will lead from and intermittently return to the relationship of theory to practice. Pozzo's essentially practical visual method was not without theoretical implications.

The second part of this essay focuses on the visual characteristics of the *Perspectiva*. The third and final part analyses the reception of Pozzo's book beyond Italy as measured both by published translations of the *Perspectiva* into other languages and by paintings and buildings informed by the engravings in Pozzo's book. While the intercontinental distribution of the *Perspectiva* was initially helped by the author's lay position in the Jesuit Order, its success was due above all to the usefulness of its image-and-text layout.

The Italian and Jesuit perspectival traditions prior to Pozzo

PERSPECTIVE IN RENAISSANCE ARTISTIC AND ARCHITECTURAL THEORY

Leonardo da Vinci wrote that 'Practice must always be built on sound theory, of which perspective is the signpost and gateway, and without this nothing can be done well in the matter of painting.'[4]

As Robert Zwijnenberg put it when discussing 'the epistemological power of linear perspective', 'the introduction of geometry as a resource the painter could use to depict a story meant that the watershed between the *artes mechanicae* and *artes liberales* had been overcome'.[5] Pozzo's image-led treatise demonstrated how to achieve good perspectival painting mechanically and with the minimum intellectual effort, and by so doing partially undid the breakthrough ascribed to fifteenth-century Tuscan artists. On the other hand Pozzo's book made linear perspective available to a wide, indeed worldwide, body of artists.

While perspective was considered a *sine qua non* for figurative painting by writers on art from Alberti in *De pictura* to the nineteenth century, the relationship of perspective to early modern architecture was much more contentious. Notwithstanding Vitruvius's view that the second basis of architecture, *dispositio* or arrangement, consisted of *ichnographia* (plan), *orthographia* (elevation) and *scaenographia* (scenography or perspective),[6] in Quattrocento architectural theory perspective was in the main distrusted. In his essay for this volume, Robert Tavernor has quoted Alberti in *De re aedificatoria* on the inappropriateness of painterly effects to architectural design. As Liliana Grassi pointed out in her introduction to Filarete's *Trattato di architettura*, Alberti's contention that perspective was harmful to architectural design, and that the façade and interiors of buildings should be represented frontally rather than by any perspectival means, influenced Filarate's approach.[7] In fact, as Tavernor has shown in the fourth essay in this volume, the Albertian rejection of perspective in architectural design continued to be accepted into the Cinquecento. As Vaughan Hart has demonstrated, Serlio illustrated his Books on architecture with eight types of projection, all of them, however, variations of the planar (ichnographic) or elevational (orthographic) view, excepting only the demonstration of linear perspective (*scenografia*), which Serlio confined to his Book II.[8] Even though Serlio's *Libro secondo* demonstrated through image-and-text how to use linear perspective to give visual form to designs in the mind of the architect, elsewhere he hardly used perspective as a graphic technique but rather represented architecture mainly within Albertian premises. As Tavernor discusses in his contribution to the present volume, Palladio always based his design ideas on the plan (*icnografia*) and elevation (*ortografia*), eschewing linear perspective (*scenografia*).

The layout of Giacomo De Franceschi's complete Serlio of 1619, which further rationalized earlier Serlian editions' spreads of imagery on the right and text on the left in parts of the *Libro secondo* and most of the *Libro settimo*,[9] supplied an important precedent for Pozzo's very measured equivalence of image-and-text. To specify, Pozzo's first volume is entirely composed of spreads of text on one side and imagery on the other (from spreads 1 to 35 and 53 to 100 the text is on the left and the imagery on the right, from spreads 36 to 52 *vice versa*), as is also the case for the greater part of volume II (on the first 83 spreads of which the text is on the left and the imagery on the right). The didactic text-and-image balance is then given up in the last 35 double-pages of Pozzo's work in which double-page spreads of engraved imagery are typically devoted to series of 'ideas' for designs of religious and then secular buildings.[10]

TREATISES ON PERSPECTIVE

Notwithstanding the importance of perspective in fifteenth-century Italian workshop practice and art theory, the first published illustrated book on perspective was printed in sixteenth-century France. The brief text of Viator's *De artificiali perspectiva* sandwiches a sequence of 36 woodcuts, the first two of which demonstrate the principles of double-sided distance-point construction.[11] Viator's illustrations of the distance-point method informed later sixteenth-century theorists including his compatriot Jean Cousin and Vignola. Pozzo included versions of Viator's distance-point construction at the beginning of his *Perspectiva* and, as will be revealed at the end of this chapter, Viator's graphic model retained its usefulness as far in distance and time as the adaptation of Pozzo and his precursors printed in Qing China.

Daniele Barbaro's *La pratica della perspettiva* of 1569 was openly indebted to Piero della Franscesca's *De prospectiva pingendi*.[12] The stylishly decorative wickerwork hoop, resembling a *mazzocchio*, or frame for a Renaissance head-dress, surrounding the information on the title-page, is perhaps intended to allude to this debt. The same imaginary object is then revolved through ninety degrees and viewed frontally as the header to the *Proemio*, from which position it begins an amusing sequence of variations on the theme. Relevant as these images are to Barbaro's book, for which they were clearly made, they are not in themselves instructive. It is not until the end of the third part, well over two-thirds of the way through Barbaro's treatise, that data helpful for the making of the designs just described are given. The vehicle of Barbaro's mathematical exposition – as of many such in the course of his treatise – is a woodcut, derived from Piero, of the *mazzocchio* itself.[13] Barbaro's *Perspectiva* also replicates a classic of Renaissance perspective theory,

Dürer's perspective frame – a further instance of visual information rather than verbal reasoning being a principal vehicle of artistic ideas.[14] The most important passage of Barbaro's treatise for the subsequent illustration of treatises on perspective is the fourth part, on scenography.[15] Barbaro here anticipates, albeit in text-led manner, some of the basics of the didactic method that would inform Pozzo. Barbaro describes and then illustrates Tuscan, Doric, Ionic and Corinthian bases, shafts, capitals and architraves, the woodcuts, however, often being unkeyed to and/or inconveniently positioned on a different spread from their corresponding text.[16]

Barbaro's research, proceeding from architectural design to its representation, was paralleled by that of Giacomo Barozzi da Vignola. In his *Five Rules of Architecture* (*Regola delli cinque ordini d'architettura*) of 1562 Vignola had announced his forthcoming book on the rules of perspective as a necessary corollary, relevant both to architecture and to painting.[17]

By the time of his death in 1573, Vignola considered his short text complete and had indeed commissioned engravings for it.[18] The authorship of the engravings in the posthumous *editio princeps* of Vignola's text, Egnatio Danti's hugely expanded edition printed in Rome in 1583, is a complex issue that need not detain us here. To attend to those aspects of Vignola–Danti that appear to have informed Pozzo's approach to illustration: Danti pointed out in his preface that 'craftsmen who enjoy working more than studying various rules, can, having left Vignola's first Rule behind, devote all their study to the second' rule which is correspondingly more densely illustrated, 'and take very great practical advantage from it'.[19] Pozzo seems to have followed Danti's advice, and concentrated exclusively on Vignola's second rule; indeed Pozzo took the last four chapters of Vignola's second rule as his point of departure. Pozzo's starting from the very end of Vignola–Danti marks the culmination in a reversal of priorities from an emphasis on the textual exposition of the principles of perspective to the more visual approach which Pozzo's engravings best embody; however, Vignola's and Danti's roles in effecting this reversal should not be underestimated.

In terms of illustration, the most important section of Vignola–Danti for illustrated treatises on perspective in general, and for Pozzo's image-led method in particular, is the latter part of the second rule. Vignola's closing chapters on *sagme* or templates for drawing bodies in perspective apply an image-led method to bases and capitals.[20] The layout of spreads with imagery on one page and text on the other characterizes our imminent object of enquiry, the *Perspective pratique* of Pozzo's Jesuit precursor Jean Dubreuil and Pozzo's *Perspectiva*.

Dubreuil's *Perspective pratique* is one seventeenth-century work that exemplifies the models inherited by Pozzo at the end of the century. Another is Pietro Accolti's *Lo inganno de gl'occhi*. Printed at Florence in 1625,[21] Accolti's three-part treatise is clearly indebted to parts of Piero della Francesca's, Barbaro's and Vignola's. The section of Accolti's treatise that was most influential on Pozzo's method is the second part, ultimately derived from Book II of Piero's *Libellus de quinque corporibus regularibus*, perhaps via Luca Pacioli's *De divina proportione* (Venice 1509),[22] on 'drawing bodies in perspective'. Accolti, with the benefit of woodcut diagrams in the text, describes how to design the 'Platonic polyhedra',[23] first the regular tetrahedron (because it is the object with the minimum number of sides), then the cube, octahedron, dodecahedron, icosahedron, from all of which, he posits, 'whatever body you like' can be inferred.[24] Despite Accolti's 'practical' intentions, his vehicle remained the purely mathematical 'Platonic polyhedra'. Pozzo's breakthrough would be to devise an incremental visual method, still based on a fifteenth-century model, the distance-point method first published by Viator, that leads seamlessly into an exposition of the most elaborate design ideas of his time. Accolti's third book is entirely devoted to one of Barbaro's concerns, and a necessary corollary of the theory and practice of perspective, light and shade.[25]

Dubreuil's so-called 'Jesuit's perspective', addressed to jewellers, embroiderers and tapestry-makers as well as to painters, engravers, sculptors and architects, was published anonymously in Paris in the 1640s, and again in 1651.[26] Dubreuil's 'method of drawing Perspectives … without observing the Rules' takes Viator's application of perspective to numerous different scenarios to exaggeratedly pluralistic lengths, hundreds of objects of early modern life being illustrated in perspective, each from several angles. Dubreuil's *Perspective pratique* has been generously described by Martin Kemp as 'an effective and not overly technical introduction for artists'.[27] However, Lawrence Wright, himself writing for artists, has pointed out that the 'Jesuit's perspective' has 'no lack of' but on the contrary 'too many' illustrated examples, and has drawn attention to the impracticality of actually following Dubreuil's rule-free method.[28] We shall see that Pozzo shared Dubreuil's preference for copious imagery, while avoiding the latter's excesses.

Perspectiva pictorum et architectorum as illustrated book

Pozzo's *Perspectiva pictorum et architectorum* was directly dependent upon his artistic practice, revealing the methods of his spectacular works at S. Ignazio in Rome. The first volume was adjusted between the first and second editions to accommodate an engraving of Pozzo's ceiling in the nave of S. Ignazio, completed in the interim; the second volume also incorporates several engravings of Pozzo's other works at S. Ignazio and elsewhere.[29] One of his first biographers, Francesco Saverio Baldinucci, narrates that Pozzo's *Perspectiva* was economically a fruit of his own labours, being financed with the proceeds of his prolific painting activity.[30] The treatise is preceded by two engraved frontispieces, condensing Pozzo's achievement and intentions respectively. The first represents a triumphal arch, similar to Pozzo's designs for the Jesuits' *Quarantore* (Forty Hours) pageant in the Gesù, Rome,[31] but secularized to incorporate a dedication to Leopold II of Austria. In the manner of the tradition of *vedute* to which the engraving belongs, text is playfully represented as though inscribed onto the fragments of masonry that litter the foreground scene. In the centre foreground is the inscription 'Perspectiva Pictorum et Architectorum by Brother Andrea Pozzo … 1693'; to the left, being carved onto an empty plinth, is the signiature 'Vincenzo Mariotti, in practise of that faculty which he has learned from the author, engraved this' (see Figure 6.1a). The latter text is a key to the entire iconography of the *Perspectiva*, which was realized under the direct guidance of the author. Its inference of student loyalty to the teacher-author is corroborated by Baldinucci's account of Pozzo's 'school' above the Gesù in Rome as unprecedented for its combination of the study of architectural principles, drawing, painting and engraving, evidence that in turn concurs with the unobtrusive reliability of the main sequence of illustrations.[32] The second frontispiece displays some of the basic tools of self-education in perspective, and on a shelf above two books, one of which bears the title 'Arc[hittetura] di And[rea] Palladio';[33] on the table Vignola's *Regole* [a mistranscription!] *delli cinque ordini* is shown open at the title-page (see Figure 6.2a). Both Palladio's *Quattro libri* and Vignola's *Regola delli cinque ordini* are very relevant to the iconography of Pozzo's *Perspectiva*, wherein Pozzo's method is painstakingly applied to the five orders; accordingly in all editions of the *Perspectiva* Vignola's and Palladio's versions of the architectural orders are replicated together with Scamozzi's.[34] Throughout, so attentive are the engravings in the *Perspectiva* to the accurate representation of architectural vocabulary that Pozzo's book was (as the London edition would emphasize) as useful to architects as it was to painters.

The image-led method of Pozzo's *Perspectiva pictorum et architectorum* is, I suggest, principally informed by the illustrating strategies of Dubreuil and Accolti. While the sheer quantity of imagery, its primary role and its disposition on the right-hand side of each spread are derived (in the context of literature on perspective) from Dubreuil, the engravings in Pozzo's treatise are disposed in an order which, like that in the second part of Accolti's treatise, builds up from the simple to the complex. Pozzo makes explicit from the start the absolute necessity of following his didactic illustrations sequentially:

endeavour to understand the Second Figure thoroughly, before you proceed to the Third; and so of the rest: they being disposed in such Order, that the knowledge of the preceding figure is always necessary to a right Understanding of that which follows. If you meet with anything which at first seems difficult in the Description, a diligent Inspection of the Figure may relieve you: And on the other hand, if you find not in the Figure everything you desire, you may have Recourse to the Explanation.[35]

By means of this image-and-text didactic method, the reader is led from a demonstration of Viator's distance point method (Pozzo's figs 1–3), to its application to the square, rectangle and slightly more complicated geometrical shapes (figs 4–7), mastery of which is necessary for the perspectival depiction of a pedestal (fig. 8). The following five figures are devoted to the five orders of pedestal from Tuscan to Composite (figs 9–13). The same scheme governs Pozzo's demonstration of how to represent circles (fig. 14), columns (fig. 15), then the five orders of bases (figs 16–20) and of capitals (figs 20–25). His method thus systematically established, Pozzo retains its *modus operandi*, coupling the preparatory geometrical plans and elevations (figs 28, 30, 32, 34) for the perspectival projections of four orders of cornice (figs 29, 31, 33, 35). As his material becomes more complex, Pozzo becomes more flexible in the sequential organization of it. Thus in his exposition of how to combine pedestals, columns and cornices of each, after giving a geometrical plan and elevation (figs 40, 41), Pozzo establishes 'The Manner of avoiding Confusion in reducing Plans and Elevations into Perspective' (fig. 42); here like a good teacher he checks that the lessons of figs 10 and 11 have been retained, before revealing how to depict architectural ensembles in perspective (figs 43–6). His figs 45 and 46 broach a further practical consideration regarding the perspectival representation of architecture, by illustrating one half of the same Doric design, and then the other half, in all its 'Diversity of Light and Shadows'. As light and shadow were key issues in literature on perspective it is not surprising that Pozzo supplies this second view, a mirror image to its counterpart in all but light and shade (and incidental sculptural detail). On the contrary, it is remarkable that this view is appended as an afterthought, and that Pozzo, in the caption to it, observed that he 'might very well have omitted' his fig. 46.[36]

Pozzo's attitude that half a design was normally sufficient for the replication of the whole (comparable to Palladio's as described by Tavernor in his essay in this volume) emerges clearly from the passage in the *Perspectiva* on how to depict, and indeed how to invent, illusionistic *sotto in sù* architecture. Taking in this instance the Corinthian order, with his habitual thoroughness Pozzo devotes figs 79 to 85 to illustrating the *sotto in sù* view of the corbel (twice: first in plan and elevation, then with light and shadow), pedestal, shaft, capital and cornice. These are then combined in his engraving of a column seen from below (fig. 86). Pozzo is now nearing his characteristic product, the illusionistic ceiling, but as ever diligently leads his readership there via every 'necessary preparation' ('preparatio necessaria'). Fig. 87, the 'preparation necessary for the following figure, and for all other perspectives *di sotto in sù* in ceilings or in vaults', again reaffirms his method of in every case designing first the plan and elevation of a perspective view.

In the text to fig. 88, Pozzo is surprisingly candid about the perspectival system of his virtually balustraded room, admitting that 'if the vanishing point is close to the viewpoint, the design becomes quite stretched, and so has an ill effect; nevertheless try looking at it from its due distance [to] E [the vanishing point, from] O [the viewpoint], and any deformity will have disappeared'.[37]

Pozzo advises painters:

If you wish to deceive simple folk, having to paint works with too short a distance [between view- and vanishing points], you will do two drawings; one to show to all: and in this you put the vanishing point far from the viewpoint, as is necessary to escape any deformity; make hidden use of the other design in doing your own work.[38]

Pozzo's next design (fig. 89) divides a rectangular room into four, two quarters of which show quite different architectures viewed *di sotto in sù*, demonstrating that for rectilinear, high-ceilinged rooms one need execute only a quarter of the preparatory design which can then be replicated for each corner; the half-template discussed above has been halved again. Pozzo's suggestion of dividing the design of a rectangular room into four ignores issues of light and shade, and assumes a central viewpoint. The following image, of a fictive cupola seen in perspective *di sotto in sù* must, Pozzo explains, be executed from a complete geometrical design of the whole (fig. 90). This is because unlike his rectangular vault the circular cupola is planned from a viewpoint, in Pozzo's own words, 'outside the work, so that the viewer gets less exhausted, and one sees more architecture and artifice, which would not happen if the viewpoint was in the centre'.[39]

Pozzo omits the brackets from this engraving 'to avoid confusion' (see Figure 6.3a). These are then in part restored to the following engraving (fig. 91), at once a record of his previous illusionistic oil-on-canvas dome of 1685 and a means towards its replacement. The rest of the final decade of Pozzo's first volume concerns the illusionistic architecture in the nave of S. Ignazio.

The first half of the second volume of the *Perspectiva* is devoted to demonstrating the intersection rather than distance-point method.[40] Pozzo returns to the matter of representing cupolas *di sotto in sù* (figs 49–51). Fig. 49 addresses anew essentially the same problem as that of fig. 90 in the first part – keying the horizontal ribs of an illusionistic dome to the upper part of the actual architecture, while tilting the imaginary pilasters and thus the fictive dome itself to an off-centre vanishing point (see Figures 6.3a–6.3b). Pozzo's second take on the same problem clarifies the matter by opening it up graphically in two main ways. On the left, rather than the cramped solution of depicting the illusionistic dome above a sloping representation of the actual supporting architecture, the elevation of the supporting walls and the illusionistic cupola is drawn above a horizontal line dividing the drawing in half; lines are plotted from the upper design so that the distribution of the fictive ribbing is plotted in detail below the line. On the right, by way of control demonstration, the same scheme is plotted to a central viewpoint (see Figure 6.3b).[41] As well as being 'very easy' ('molto facile') in itself, the right-hand diagram also clarifies and facilitates the plotting of orthogonals and orientation of the pilasters to the point of convergence, 'O'.

In the following fig. 50, Pozzo again establishes the measurements of the dome by plotting lines down from the elevation of the actual-plus-imaginary space, once more according to a principal viewpoint outside the design of the cupola, towards a vanishing point well below the engraved image itself. Pozzo's text for fig. 50 explains the function of fig. 49 and thus also the importance of illustrations for his practice-orientated method:

> The previous figure was made so as better to clarify this one; because being composed of Architecture, it would have been difficult to explain, and understand. But try to do it, and thus maybe you will understand it better with practice, than with speculation.[42]

This is as clear a statement as any of the interplay between image and text in what has been termed the *Perspectiva*'s 'theory of praxis'.[43] The equivalence thus far in the *Perspectiva* of spreads of engraved imagery on one side and text on the other gives way, from spread 84 of the second volume to the culminating fig. 118, to a series of ideas for designs, each sequence of which is introduced by a single brief text. Imagery proves to be largely self-sufficient in the closing section of the *Perspectiva*, in a manner not without precedent in the works of seventeenth-century Roman 'empirical theorists of the new treatise through images'.[44] Pozzo's explanation of his series of appropriate models for doors and windows reveals that these sequences of engraved images are the fruit of careful selection.[45] In drawing attention to the passage in question, Marco Rosario Nobile has suggested that, while books containing engravings of portals, altars and windows were not a novelty, Pozzo's presentation of them established a much-emulated publishing typology.[46] While Pozzo's importance for subsequent developments in pattern books is in this respect unquantifiable, it is certain that its image-led graphic instruction and design ideas made the *Perspectiva* useful – more so than preceding treatises on perspective – to eighteenth-century artists in Europe, the Americas and Asia.

The European and worldwide diaspora of Pozzo's *Perspectivae Pictorum et Architectorum*

The third and final part of this essay considers the international fortunes of the *Perspectiva*, and the impact of its engravings on artists and architects in Europe and further afield. Rather than addressing the *Perspectiva*'s diaspora chronologically, or by considering first its publishing fortune and then its impact on other media, a geographical order best reveals the worldwide resonance of Pozzo's illustrated book. After brief consideration of Mediterranean usages of the *Perspectiva*, this diaspora will be followed northwards to Germany and England; westwards via Iberia to South America; and eastwards, through the agency of Jesuit missionaries, to India and China. This analysis of worldwide responses to Pozzo's *Perspectiva* aims to deliver an array of answers about the roles of book illustration in disseminating artistic ideas and models. Although extensive, it is by no means an exhaustive account of Pozzo's legacy to eighteenth-century artists. Pozzo's own art and architecture in mainland Italy,[47] in Ragusa-Dubrovnik,[48] in Austria where Pozzo and his workshop worked directly[49] and in Poland where two of his students were active[50] are disregarded since in these cases – bar Pozzo's design for the title-page of a pro-Habsburg panegyric[51] – book illustration is not the issue.

In Pozzo's own lifetime, variations on his artistic ideas as imaged in the *Perspectiva* were the prerogative of his students, such as Antonio Colli, whose illusionistic domes in the churches of the Gesù at Frascati and Montepulciano were both executed in the first years of the century.[52] While later fictive cupolas in remoter mainland Italian centres, such as Venanzio Mascitelli's of 1828 at L'Aquila,[53] testify to the enduring usefulness of the engravings in Pozzo's treatise, the best Italian case study for the reception of the *Perspectiva* is Sicily, where neither Pozzo nor any of his direct followers is known to have worked. An early-eighteenth-century altar at S. Caterina, Palermo, combining a pair of solomonic columns with four striated ones, recalls those engravings in the *Perspectiva* replicating Pozzo's painted altar at Frascati and of an altar that remained on paper.[54] Pozzo's images, especially his suggestions for the designs of window frames towards the end of volume II, were freely taken up by one of the architects of Noto, Paolo Labisi.[55] Elsewhere in the Mediterranean, the *Perspectiva* played a catalytic role in transforming religious painting in eighteenth-century Greece.[56] Panagiotis Doxaras (1662–1729) was best known in his lifetime for his (destroyed) illusionistic frescos of 1727 in the vault of S. Spyridon, Corfu. These have been described as having directly emulated Veronese's ceilings in the Doge's Palace in Venice.[57] It is likely that Doxaras – who by 1720 had translated the second part of the *Perspectiva* into Greek – also drew on Pozzo's visual method.[58]

NORTHERN EUROPEAN TRANSLATIONS OF THE *Perpectiva pictorum et architectorum*

The Bohemian publisher in Rome Johann Jakob Komarek,[59] first printer of Pozzo's treatise, was – presumably on the bases of the demand for the first edition of the first volume and of the expectation that Pozzo's well-illustrated book would appeal to readers in different languages – quick to recognize its commercial potential. In 1700 Komarek printed the second volume in Latin–German and Latin–French as well as Latin–Italian parallel texts, an early instance of a practice that became widespread only in the twentieth century, the simultaneous publication of the same text in several different languages but with identical illustrations.[60]

The history of the reception of Pozzo's *Perspectiva* in Germany dates from the year of the publication of the first volume, 1693, in November of which year a review in the Leipzig *Acta Eruditorum* praised Pozzo's book for the directness of its image-led explanation of 'how to accomplish by the fastest method and as succinctly as possible optical delineations of every kind, following the common rule, but one from which he has taken out all stumbling blocks of hidden lines'.[61]

There appears to have been a Vienna 1706 German translation of Pozzo's *Perspectiva*,[62] and in the same year the first volume of the Augsburg Latin-and-German parallel text was printed in Augsburg by Peter Detleffsen at the expense of Jeremias Wolff, with engravings closely resembling the Roman prototypes by Johann Boxbarth of Augsburg.[63] An early architectural response to Pozzo's graphic suggestions can be seen in the Kronentor (Crown Gate) of the Zwinger Palace at Dresden. Nicolas Powell plausibly suggested that Matthias Daniel Pöppelmann's design of an octagonal dome over an arched crossing was informed by fig. 60 in Pozzo's first volume;[64] furthermore, the Kronentor's reversed broken pediment interrupted by a cartouche was derived from a window frame at San Carlo Borromeo, Milan, illustrated in fig. 100 of Pozzo's second volume. Powell ignored the fact that the latter image is in Pozzo's second volume, which had been published in Latin-and-German, with engravings by Georg Conrad Bodenehr, in 1709, before Pöppelmann designed the Kronentor.[65] At least eight German editions, the great majority *quartos* aimed at students, but competently illustrated by Boxbarth, were printed by the end of the eighteenth century.[66] Moreover, Johann Jacob Schübler's *Perspectiva*, published in two volumes in Nuremberg between 1719 and 1720,[67] included full-page engravings that were intelligent adaptations of Pozzo's. 'Tabulae' 13 and 14 in the second volume of Schübler's *Perspectiva* replicate figures from Pozzo with an informed approximateness that concurs with Pozzo's own variety of models, and even self-proclaimed arbitariness.[68] In Schübler's 'Tabula 13', fig. 1 at the top synthesizes the ninetieth plate in the first volume of Pozzo's book (see Figure 6.3a) and the fifty-first from Pozzo's second volume, minus only the distracting indications of the positions of the columns surrounding the illusionistic dome viewed *di sotto in sù* (see Figure 6.4a). Fig. 4 of the same thirteenth engraving in the second volume of Schübler replicates, in mirror image, the left side of the forty-ninth engraving in Pozzo's second volume (see Figure 6.3b). Schübler's 'Tabula 14' also combines figures from Pozzo, and reinterprets these in a manner revealing of his cognitively engaged development of Pozzo's 'image-and-text' method. The main 'fig. 1' in Schübler's 'Tabula 14' is a variation, incorporating extra construction lines, of the ninety-first plate in Pozzo's first volume; its decorative variations of architectural details as well as a focal vase of flowers certainly reflect, and probably also informed, early-eighteenth-century taste in southern Germany (see Figure 6.4b). Condensing stages of Pozzo's didactic sequence, figs 2 and 5 at the top of the same engraving in Schübler closely derive from two figures in the twenty-fifth engraving in Pozzo's first volume, intended for the 'preparatio' of *sotto in sù* ceilings and vaults, while at the foot of Schübler's 'Tabula 14' fig. 3 is a slight variant of fig. 3 in the eighty-eighth engraving of Pozzo's first volume and Schübler's fig. 4 is a synthesis of figs 1 and 2 of the same engraving in the *Perspectiva*. These adjustments Schübler made to Pozzo's prototypes – and more than incidentally the author himself invented and designed the plates, as can be seen at the foot of Figure 6.4a here – are thoroughly in the spirit of Pozzo's own practice. Moreover, Schübler concurred with Pozzo in maintaining, 'you can master visual details much better through praxis than through theory'.[69]

Due primarily to the dissemination of his imagery in books printed at Augsburg, throughout the eighteenth century, Pozzo's illustrations – probably both directly and as mediated by the Nuremberg edition of Schübler – provided the models for much illusionistic fresco painting in southern Germany. Celebrated southern German examples, informed by Pozzo's ninetieth and ninety-first figures and/or Schübler's 'Tabulae' 13 and 14, of imaginary domes in perspective from an acentral viewpoint, include Cosmas Damian Asam's faithful replication at Freising of the 1720s,[70] and Josef Keller's interpretation of 1780 in the parish church of St Nikolaus Pfronten-Berg in the Bavarian province of Allgäu.[71]

Throughout the eighteenth century, translations of Pozzo's treatise were widely published. By 1798 there had been at least sixteen Latin–Italian editions.[72] In the first quarter of the century, Pozzo had been translated into six further modern European languages, for the most part in *quartos* deriving from the Augsburg 1708 Latin–German edition, illustrated with the above-mentioned replicas by Boxbarth of Pozzo's engravings.[73] A useful side-effect of Pozzo's method of visual exposition on the right supported by concise textual explanation on the left was the adaptability of the spacious layout of the text to parallel texts: usually the original Latin and a translation, although a French–Flemish parallel edition also went into three printings.[74]

The foreign edition which best emulates the handsome *folio* format of the Roman editions is the Latin-and-English edition, printed at London in 1707 and based on the *editio princeps* of 1693: a significant choice given its relative emphasis on architecture, compared to the second edition of 1702 which incorporated the fold-out engraving of Pozzo's frescoes in the nave of S. Ignazio.[75] Replicating the first edition to scale, among the very few adjustments to the content with respect to the original are a Preface recommending Pozzo's sequential method and, in the engravings, a couple of minor additions of architectural bent. The architectural emphasis of the iconography in the London edition is likely to have been determined by the fact that the translator, John James, was himself an architect,[76] and by the involvement of Christopher Wren, John Vanbrugh and Nicholas Hawksmoor, who approved the edition 'at the request of the engraver'.[77] The engraver was the art teacher John Sturt, who was also responsible for selling the book.[78] Both Sturt's general fidelity to, and his particular deviations from, the Roman prototype warrant analysis. With regard to the former, Sturt replicated not only the didactic sequence of engravings in the 1693 edition of the first volume, but also the two frontispieces. The frontispiece engraving immediately following the title-page reprises that of 1693, in reverse, with the inscription to Emperor Leopold omitted, and those on the slab and plinth adjusted rather than translated. In the place of Mariotti's eloquent 'in praxim facultatis authore' signature is the more impersonal 'LONDINI: juxta Exemplar ROMÆ Excusum' ('At London, after the version printed at Rome'); on the slab – a first hint of the bias of the London edition towards architecture – in place of the full title, 'Pozzo's Perspective for Painters and Architects', is written 'POZZO^s ARCHITECTURE IN [PER]SPECTIVE' (see Figure 6.1b).

The slight alterations to the otherwise mainly dutiful replications of the 1693 series reflect the translator's, editors', subscribers' and engraver's special interest in the architectural dimension of Pozzo's book. The second frontispiece engraving, which introduces Pozzo's method by illustrating his tools for the drawing of perpendiculars, reinforces the architectural emphasis of the original. The Roman editions illustrate Vignola's *Regole [sic] delli cinque ordini*, open on the desk, and two books on the shelf above it, the spine of one of which reveals it to be Palladio's *Dell'architettura*, the other being unidentified. In the London edition, Vignola and Palladio are again present, with the former's title corrected to *Regola …* , and the classical tradition of architecture informing both them and the London edition of Pozzo is accentuated by the identification of the third book as Vitruvius's *De architectura* (see Figure 6.2b). Vitruvius's currency in early-eighteenth-century England would be most creatively encapsulated in Colen Campbell's *Vitruvius Britannicus*, the first two title-pages of which are signed by the same John Sturt.[79]

The involvement of architectural authors and illustrators in the English edition of Pozzo reveals the extent to which they considered his *Perspectiva* to be part of their programme to disseminate European architectural models in Britain. This is further evidenced by the other addition of new text into a plate otherwise dutifully replicated in the London edition. In a variant of the London edition,[80] a replication of the same octagonal tabernacle illustrated in the Rome editions frames the legend 'A / TREATISE / *of the* / FIVE ORDERS / or/ Columns/ in/ ARCHITECTURE / *Viz t[he]/ Toscan,* / Doric, Ionic, / CORINTHIAN / *and* / Composite, / Written in French *by* / *Claude Perrault, Made English by* / JOHN JAMES / of Greenwich'. The inserted text alludes to James's translation of Perrault's Paris 1683 *Ordonnance des cinq espèces de colonnes*, which the same individuals responsible for the London Pozzo, John Sturt and Benjamin Motte, were to publish in London in 1708.[81] That is to say, this appearance of imagery-cum-text purporting to belong to one illustrated book in another differs from many such appearances in early modern books, normally due to the economizing re-use of an existing plate. In this case the reference to the extraneous work is a protention rather than a retention, heralding the forthcoming publication of an English-language edition of an illustrated European book on architecture. The advertisement for the not-yet-published edition of Perrault accounts for Sturt's exceptional omission in the plate of the information to which its accompanying text alludes, the tabernacle's elevation; duly illustrated in the Roman edition, and in most examples of the London one, this is omitted from plate 60 in the London variant.

IBERIA

Although no widely read Spanish-language edition of Pozzo's treatise was ever published,[82] Pozzo's *Perspectiva* was palpably influential in Spain and in Spanish America. In Spain, Antonio Palomino's *El museo pictorico y escala optica* carried versions of some of Pozzo's imagery. All of the engravings derived from Pozzo are in the second volume, first printed at Madrid in 1724, and were cut by the author's nephew Juan Bernabé Palomino. Antonio Bonet Correa deemed the engravings from Pozzo to be superior to those (by Boxbarth) in the Augsburg edition of 1708 and considered the fact that the same engravings were re-used for the second edition of 1795 – when the standards of book production were much higher – a testament to their quality.[83]

As Pozzo had done in some illustrations in the second volume, so as to compress as many examples as possible into few plates, the Palominos habitually divided engravings into separate figures. In doing so they took liberties with Pozzo's prototypes, some of their changes being more sensitive than others, as 'lamina X' in Palomino reveals (see Figure 6.5). At top left part of Pozzo's eighty-eighth figure, the quartered ceiling seen *di sotto in sù* is replicated, with the addition of marble finials but with the cognitive relation between the page and the room lost on account of the virtual edge of the quartered ceiling being aligned not with the edge of the page, but down the middle of it. However, in the main the Palominos deviate from the details of Pozzo's iconography in ways that demonstrate a thorough, if selective, understanding of Pozzo's image-led method. At bottom right of the same plate in the Spanish editions, the loss of the ground plan would only affect architects whom Palomino senior was hardly addressing; the halving of the image of a balustraded tabernacle seen from below is a departure from Pozzo's prototype in the manner of Pozzo himself.[84]

The 'Joanine' style, named after John V of Portugal (ruled 1707–50), was understood by George Kubler to be founded in 'the writings and plates of Andrea Pozzo and Ferdinando Galli Bibiena' (the latter a very important exemplar in Iberia, largely due to his presence in Barcelona in 1708–11, which in terms of an analysis of the impact there of book illustration confuses the issue).[85] José Fernandes Pereira's definition of the Joanine style describes the whole gamut of architectural innovations associated with the style – canopies and *baldacchini* combined with allegorical statues – as being derived from Pozzo's *Perspectiva*.[86] All of these, plus moreover Solomonic columns, are combined in the main altar in the chancel of Oporto Cathedral – by [Niccolò] 'Nicolau' Nasoni (?1691–?1773).[87] Although Nasoni, an Italian who moved to Portugal only in 1725, is very likely to have seen S. Ignazio, Rome, at first hand, there is no doubt that the *Perspectiva* itself was disseminated and studied in northern Portugal. Manuscript translations into Portuguese of both volumes of Pozzo's *Perspectiva* were made in Oporto during John V's reign, the first from the Latin text in one of the Augsburg *quartos* and like them intended for hard-up 'studiozos', the second from one of the Italian editions.[88] Moreover, revealing how thought-provoking Pozzo's images were for practising artists, the translator of the second volume, the painter José de Figueredo Seixas, also drafted a 'New Explanation of Figure 100 of the first tome' of Pozzo's *Perspectiva*.[89]

A negative measure of the *Perspectiva*'s central importance in the development of eighteenth-century ceiling painting in Portugal, and one that reveals the sort of limitation inherent to any artistic development sourced from a given illustrated tract, is the fact that much that is not adumbrated in Pozzo's book is also conspicuously absent from Portuguese perspective decorations. Reynaldo Dos Santos observed that 'notwithstanding the influence of [Vincenzo] Baccarelli (the Italian-born painter admired in early-eighteenth-century Portugal) in spreading the taste for architectonic perspectives, as published by Pozzo, Portuguese painters never assimilated the fundamental of aerial perspective'.[90] Dos Santos's observation can be rephrased: since Pozzo, the main source for the spread of perspective theory in Portugal, demonstrated architectural but not aerial perspective, the former was widely assimilated, the latter hardly at all. Examples of perspectival designs derived from Pozzo are the three painted ceilings in the library of the University of Coimbra. Both the one begun by Antonio Lobo in 1716 and those contracted in 1723 from Lobo's follower António Simões Ribeiro (whom we shall re-encounter as agent of Pozzo's dissemination in Bahia), adhered to a composition of balconies, balustrades and columns ultimately derived from Pozzo's *Perspectiva*.[91]

José-Augusto França characterized the continued interest in Pozzo in mid- to later-eighteenth-century Portugal (where as Nuno Saldanha has shown classical and early modern Italian art literature was extensively disseminated[92]) as a remedy to the traditional Portuguese ignorance of aesthetic ideas.[93] During the reign of D. José (1750–77) and beyond, Pozzo's models were persistently adapted in various media by the Benedictine brother José de Santo Antonio Ferreira Vilaça. R. C. Smith identified the concave disposition of the altars designed by Vilaça in the early 1760s for churches at Tibães and Lamego as informed by figs 36, 64 and 65 of Pozzo's second volume.[94] Vilaça, together with his fellow Benedictine Francisco de José 'de Pibidens', signed another translation of Pozzo (evidently from the rare Latin– Italian edition of 1717) into Portuguese, in 1768.[95] Portuguese Benedictine archives preserve evidence of Vilaça's successful petition to retain a copy of Pozzo's *Perspectiva* for the duration of his life; Vilaça adapted engravings in the *Perspectiva* for the illusionistic paintings he designed for the four lateral chapels at Santa Maria, Pombeiro.[96]

IBERIAN AMERICA

Evidence of the illustrations in Pozzo's book having been used as sources in eighteenth-century South America are found all over the continent.

Even by the standards of pre-Independence Spanish America, the visual arts of sixteenth- and seventeenth-century Quito were much informed by Flemish and Italian engraved imagery.[97] Some uses of book illustrations in Quito call into question the truism mentioned in the introduction to this volume, of the two-dimensional quality of Spanish American colonial architecture being due to the role of European engravings in their conception. The dynamic double-flighted staircase in front of S. Francisco, Quito, was appropriated via Serlio from Bramante's Belvedere project; the ground plan and thus the spatial quality of the church with which we will be mainly concerned, the Compañía, begun in 1606, were inherited from the Jesuit typology created by Vignola at the Gesù in Rome.[98]

In eighteenth-century Quitenian visual arts, especially architecture, the imagery in Pozzo's *Perspectiva pictorum et architectorum* recurs pervasively. The engravings in Pozzo's volumes were the single most important source for a characteristic component of the eighteenth-century *quiteño* architecture, the twisted 'solomonic' column.

Solomonic columns had featured in Vignola's *Regola delli cinque ordini* of 1562. Patritio Caxesi's translation of Vignola's *Regola* into Spanish had been published as early as 1593, and it was probably as a consequence of Caxesi's translation of Vignola that four years later small solomonic columns appeared in the tabernacle on the high altar of Seville Cathedral.[99] Already prominent in Mexican architecture by the mid-seventeenth century, and disseminated thence by means of engravings,[100] other Spanish-language illustrated manuals on architecture, such as Juan Caramuel Lobkowitz's *Arquitectura civil*, had contributed to the popularity of the motif; Caramuel included engravings demonstrating how to diminish spirals in such columns.[101]

In short there was no lack of potential sources for the earliest documented solomonic columns in Quito, the three on either side of the main portal to the Compañía, designed in 1722–25 by the Jesuit 'Leonardo' Deubler of Bamberg.[102] The columns, it is generally thought, replicate the architectural design (although not of course the heraldic decorations) of Bernini's supports for the *baldacchino* at St Peter's, Rome. Certainly the proportions of the shafts of the solomonic columns on the façade of the Compañía at Quito relate not to Vignola's (themselves based upon his and Bernini's common prototypes at St Peter's) but to Bernini's. To be precise, the Quitenian columns decidedly follow the fifty-second and fifty-third figures in all editions of Pozzo's *Perspectiva*, explicitly intended to make Bernini's artfulness widely and flexibly accessible.[103] The detail which to my mind reveals that Pozzo's *Perspectiva* was Deubler's source is the shape of the tall, elegant pedestals that the engraved solomonic columns in Pozzo's fifty-second and fifty-third figures and their sculpted counterparts have in common, in contrast not only to Vignola but also to the lower marble pedestals of Bernini's *baldacchino*. It is therefore highly probable (even without taking into account circumstantial evidence of Deubler's likely predisposition to a fellow Jesuit author) that Pozzo was the source for the solomonic columns on the façade of the Compañía.

The altars in the transepts of the Compañía are undoubtedly informed by the sequence in Pozzo's second volume of solomonic altars. Designed in the 1740s by the Tyrolese 'Jorge' [Georg] Vinterer, whose main altar of the previous decade is distinguished by solomonic columns recalling the Bernini–Pozzo formula, the transept *retablos* have long been identified as being derived via Pozzo's *Perspectiva* from his own transept altars in Rome.[104] However, it is worth scrutinizing the relationship between the engraved versions in Pozzo's book and those in the Compañía because doing so will more clearly reveal the limitations and thus the extent of the debt. The state of study is best summarized by referring readers to late-twentieth-century studies which compare the Roman and Quitenian designs. In *Summa artis*, the Quitenian Saint Ignatius altar is illustrated alongside a reproduction from fig. 62 of Pozzo's second volume, which replicates the altar dedicated to Luis Gonzaga at S. Ignazio.[105] From the overall architectural form right down to details such as the foliate decoration encircling the shafts, the juxtaposition is certainly convincing (see Figures 6.6a, 6.6b). However, the Luis Gonzaga altarpiece incorporated a marble relief sculpture by Pierre Legros, which, moreover, in the engraving in Pozzo's *Perspectiva* resembles a painting. Gabrielle G. Palmer pointed out that the statue of St Ignatius at Quito was derived, via fig. 60 in the second volume of the *Perspectiva*, from Pierre Legros's silver statue of the saint in the left transept of the Gesù in Rome, the Quitenian figure being a mirror image of the Roman one, either on account of being reversed in the process of copying from the Roman edition or due to having been sourced from the itself reversed image in the Augsburg edition (see Figure 6.6c).[106] In short, the St Ignatius altar at the Compañía in Quito synthesizes the most dynamic aspects of the two designs from Pozzo's *Perspectiva* (see Figures 6.6a, 6.6b, 6.6c).

The attention to ground plan as well as to frontal design in the engravings to Pozzo's *Perspectiva* was indispensable to the successful replication of his artistic ideas in the Ignatius and Francis Xavier altars of the Compañía, Quito. Figure 62 in the second volume is part of a series of illustrations of models for the solomonic-columned altar; fig. 60 represents the altar to St Ignatius in the transept of the eponymous Roman church; and fig. 61 its *vestigium* and *orthographia* or plan and elevation, fig. 63 supplying the same for fig. 62, while figs 64 and 65 show an alternative design for the altar of the Blessed Luis Gonzaga, and fig. 66 its plan and elevation.

The altars at the Compañía were much imitated within several churches in Quito, notably at the chapel of S. Ramon Nonato in the left crossing of the Merced and the altar of St John of God in the Iglesia del Hospital. The chapel at the Merced is of a squat format in which the solomonic columns comprise only three complete twists in comparison to Vignola's, Bernini's, Pozzo's and those at the Compañía, all of which are of five complete twists; almost certainly an approximation of the Compañía altars rather than their printed source, the S. Ramon Nonato altar lacks the elegant dynamism of its direct and indirect prototypes. The St John of God altar at the Hospital church reprises the shape, both in ground plan and in elevation, of the Compañía transept altars, but eschews solomonic columns.[107] Harold Wethey identified the St Ignatius altar at S. Pedro, Lima, as being informed by Pozzo, but via the Compañía, Quito. The hypothesis that the S. Pedro altar was copied from that in Quito rather than sourced from Pozzo's analytical illustrations tallies with the Liman altar's unexciting effect relative to either its Roman or its Quitenian prototypes.[108]

Second-generation 'European' designs that were derived from buildings themselves informed by illustrated books concern us insofar as a given model being widely followed reveals that its popularity was not circumscribed by the patronage circle with which it was initially associated, in the case of the Compañía the Jesuits. On the other hand, such repetitions of formulae originally informed by book illustration problematize the advantage which in the introduction to this volume was claimed for Spanish American architecture as a field of study of responses to book illustration. As soon as a given model is replicated for the second time in any centre, its currency changes from carefully selected import to accepted vehicle of local artistic competition. When examining the reception of print culture, once it becomes apparent that any image has become common currency in a given society, attention is best shifted elsewhere.

Several thousand miles to the south, Córdoba,[109] on the trade route from Potosí and Cusco to Buenos Aires, had in the seventeenth century been transformed by the Jesuits into a university city architecturally distinguished by the cosmopolitan missionary community's interpretations of European treatises including those by Dietterlin and Philibert de l'Orme.[110] An apologist for Pozzo in early-eighteenth-century Córdoba was the Italian-born Jesuit Andrea Bianchi (1677–1740), known in Argentina as 'Andres Blanqui'.[111] However, most architectural designs in and around Córdoba that were informed by Pozzo's book date from the second half of the century, and are almost certainly sourced directly from the *Perspectiva*. The doors to the presbytery at the church of the Jesuit ranch of Alta Gracía, near Córdoba, are modelled on the hundredth figure in the second volume of the *Perspectiva*, as was first recognized by Bonet Correa who also identified the similarity in sculptural detail between the exterior of the dome at Alta Gracía and engravings 109–10 in the same volume.[112] The portal to the Carmelite convent of Santa Teresa, of 1770, is, despite the adjustment to the volutes which curve downwards in the Roman book illustration and upwards in the Cordoban door frame, unmistakably derived from the seventy-ninth and eightieth figures in Pozzo's second volume.[113] The wide dissemination of Pozzo's ideas was initially due to the far-flung activities of his Jesuit Order, but due to their aesthetic appeal designs from the *Perspectiva* were also replicated in secular contexts. The same engravings in volume II of the *Perspectiva* informed the main door to the contemporary Casa de los Allende in Córdoba, the anonymous architect of which seems to have worked not from the Teresas portal but from the engravings in the work of Pozzo, whose suggested curvature of the volutes is observed in the Allende doorway.[114] The Cordoban realizations of Pozzo's designs are all derived from the second volume of his treatise. It therefore seems more than coincidental that inventories of the Jesuits in Argentina list only volume II of the *Perspectiva*.[115] Revealingly, while Pozzo's methodical first volume sufficed in Queen Anne's England, the southernmost Catholic colony in Argentina profited mainly, perhaps exclusively, from the second volume's eclectic miscellany. The common ground of the responses to the *Perspectiva* in London and Córdoba is that both treated Pozzo's book as a manual for constructing, and not just for representing architecture.

In the Portuguese colonies of present-day Brazil, as is fairly well known, the *Perspectiva* informed illusionistic ceiling paintings in the four main centres of artistic production: Rio, the Minas Gerais, Bahia and Recife. Referring the interested reader to literature on the three-tiered architectural perspective of João de Deus Sepulveda's decorations of the 1760s in the church of São Pedro dos Clérigos, Recife,[116] here it suffices to concentrate on Rio, the Minas and Bahia. In all three, as has not yet been fully acknowledged, characteristics of eighteenth-century architecture relate at least generically to Pozzo's book. Brazilian responses to the *Perspectiva* are connected with the missionary effort, but not especially with that of the Jesuit Order, the artistic activity of which in Brazil has been chronicled in some detail, but with no mention of Pozzo.[117]

In Rio, the Confraternity of the Ordem Terceira's contract for the decoration of their church of São Francisco da Penitência repeatedly emphasized the criterion of the best possible perspective painting,[118] realized – after a delay possibly due to the necessity of mastering the same, very likely with reference to Pozzo's book – by Caetano Costa Coelho.[119] Contemporary with Costa Coelho's ceiling, the side altars in the same church by the Portuguese Jesuit Francisco Xavier de Brito are framed by solomonic columns apparently informed by engravings in the *Perspectiva*.[120]

In the Minas Gerais, Italianate schemes for perspective painting were adapted in the mid-1750s (before Pozzo's book was available in Portuguese) by Antônio Rodrigues Belo, native of Porto, at the Matriz Nossa Senhora de Nazaré at Cachoeira do Campo.[121] Keyed to a central viewpoint, Manuel Rebelo e Souza's two illusionistic domes, painted in 1760 at the Cathedral in Mariana,[122] might plausibly derive either from printed imagery of earlier *sotto in sù* decorations such as Mantegna's in Mantua, or from Pozzo's *Perspectiva*, in which case the Brazilian artist was either disinclined or unable to address the complexity of Pozzo's suggestions for acentral illusionism. Pozzo's engravings of *sotto in sù* designs are manifestly the source for the early-nineteenth-century revival of perspective painting in the Ouro Prêto region, dominated by Manoel da Costa Athaide (Mariana 1762–1830).[123] It has been established that aspects of Athaide's work at São Francisco de Assis in Ouro Prêto are derived from European illustrated books,[124] and the illusionistic architectural compositions of Da Costa Athaide's frescos of the first quarter of the nineteenth century are recognizably (if freely) derived from Pozzo. Athaide's masterpiece, his tempera painting in brilliant local pinks and blues on the wooden ceiling of the nave of São Francisco de Assis in Ouro Prêto,[125] exemplifies both his debt to and his divergence from Pozzo. Although the articulation of the rectangular space by means of illusionistic architecture is clearly derived from Pozzo, Athaide's curvilinear imaginary scenography is quite distinct from Pozzo's. The perspective is constructed for a viewpoint at the centre of the nave, directly beneath the image of the Assumption, itself derived from a European engraving.[126] Insofar as it is framed and parallel with the picture plane, the *Assumption* is a *quadro riportato*, but behind the main figure the three sculptural tiers of clouds and the diminishing scale of the seemingly more distant figures sustain the perspectival illusion of the main framing decoration. Documents refer to Da Costa Athaide as 'professor of architecture and of painting', even though Athaide's attempt to found a school of art and architecture at Mariana in 1818 was unsuccessful.[127] The likelihood that Pozzo's *Perspectiva* was part of Athaide's projected didactic programme is suggested by his very conception of a school of architecture and painting. Certain evidence that the *Perspectiva* was circulating in the Minas in the first quarter of the 1800s is provided by the most detailed Brazilian emulation of Pozzo's demonstrations of how to depict architectural details, especially corbels, those of the early 1810s and 1820s by Joaquim José da Natividade in the area of São João del-Rei.[128]

In Bahia, Pozzo's models were circulated at Salvador from 1735 by the above-mentioned Antônio Simões Ribeiro,[129] and variations on Pozzo's scheme for the S. Ignazio ceiling are recognizable in the later eighteenth-century cycles associated with José Joaquim da Rocha.[130] The earliest of these is the much-admired nave painting at the Conceição da Praia in Salvador, of 1772–74. Illusionistic architecture of the Composite order frames the scene of the Immaculate Virgin ascending upwards from personifications of the four continents towards the Trinity. Notwithstanding the vertical dimension of the subject, like Athaide's ceiling painting at São Francisco de Assis, Ouro Prêto, the Ascension scene is parallel to the horizontal plane of the architectural opening. Also in common with Athaide's Ouro Prêto ceiling, at the Conceição da Praia the perspective of the fictional lateral columns and of the alcoves at each end is keyed to a central viewpoint; unusually in the Brazilian context the intended viewpoint is marked on the floor of the nave by a black marble star. The historiography of the Conceição ceiling, particularly Carlos Ott's account of Rocha's career, needs revisiting. On the basis of the ceiling's (as we have seen, only partial) resemblance to Pozzo's at S. Ignazio, Ott hypothesized that Rocha might have visited Italy; moreover, Ott described the four personifications of the continents as 'directly inspired by Pozzo's', when in fact they are much more likely to have shared the common source of Ripa's *Iconologia*.[131] The painted nave of the church of Ordem Terceira's de São Domingo (1780–82) at Salvador also displays elaborate architecture of the Composite order in convincing illusionistic perspective, within the central opening of which the saint's Vision of Christ is however depicted as a *quadro riportato*,[132] just as the slightly later decoration of the Augustinian church of Nossa Senhora da Palma in the same city is characterized by an architectonic framework around a scene of the Glorification of the Order of St Augustine, the imaginary space of which contradicts that of its setting.[133] While the repeated discrepancy between the perspective of architectural representation and that of the figures can be partially explained by the fact that Rocha and his circle worked from Pozzo's book, which demonstrates how to compose architecture but not figurative compositions in illusionistic perspective settings, constants in Bahian ceiling painting – above all the adoption of a central viewpoint, which is characteristic also of the Ordem Terceira de S. Domingo and Nossa Senhora da Palma ceilings – together amount to a local typology, which like that of the solomonic columns in Quito, while ultimately derived from Pozzo's *Perspectiva*, swiftly became self-propagating.

Brazilian architectural derivations from Pozzo were far from slavish, and have therefore in the main eluded comment; however, the marked incidence of free interpretations of Pozzo's models in the very churches with perspectival decorations informed by the *Perspectiva* amounts to accumulatively convincing evidence that the *Perspectiva* was widely used for the realization as well as the representation of architecture. The circumstantial likelihood that Brito's above-mentioned solomonic columns at São Francisco da Penitência, Rio, were sourced from Pozzo is corroborated by the fact that, as Marcos Hill has noticed, the pediment of Brito's second documented work, the main altar of Nossa Senhora do Pilar at Ouro Prêto, derives (via the *Perspectiva*) from Pozzo's St Ignatius altar at the Gesù in Rome.[134]

At São Francisco de Assis in Ouro Prêto, Athaide, whose perspectival decoration of the ceiling is discussed above, was also responsible for the architectural mouldings of the church. The doors at the choir end adapt the suggestion in Pozzo's second volume of paired ionic volutes as broken crowning devices.[135] In São João del-Rei, contemporary with Joaquim José da Natividade's Pozzo-sourced designs, the altar at Nossa Senhora do Pilar synthesizes engravings in Pozzo's second volume of the spacious arrangement of four solomonic columns framing his projected main altar at the Gesù, Rome, and the alternative design for the same, with angels above the broken-scroll pediments.[136]

Several of the churches at Salvador with ceiling paintings derived from Pozzo also have architectural details apparently sourced from the *Perspectiva*.

The four-columned solomonic transept altars at Nossa Senhora da Palma are generically related to Pozzo's ideas, and the octagonal towers at Nossa Senhora da Palma recall Pozzo's design for an octagonal tabernacle, perhaps in this case via the octagonal tower at the Conceição da Praia, which architecturally as well as in terms of painted decoration is the Bahian church most markedly informed by the *Perspectiva*. The four solomonic columns and overall proportions of the main altar at the Conceição are very comparable to Pozzo's Luis Gonzaga altar at S. Ignazio, while the altar of the Holy Sacrament in the same church recalls Pozzo's two-columned alternative design for the same, down to details such as the figures on the high cornice above the columns and the floral strips on the inner jambs.[137]

ASIA

Within a decade of the publication of the second volume of the *Perspectiva*, its fig. 60 of Pozzo's St Ignatius altar at the Gesú, Rome, had informed the main retable dedicated to the same saint at the sanctuary of Bom Jesus in Velha Goa where the pose of the statue of Ignatius exactly replicates that of the engraving.[138] José Pereira reasonably attributes the loss of three-dimensionality in the niche behind the statue to the Indian altar's derivation from print imagery.[139] Pereira also identified fig. 62 in the same volume, of Pozzo's Luis Gonzaga altar at S. Ignazio, as the source of the tripartate pediments of half a dozen mid-eighteenth-century Goan church façades; Pereira first tentatively then emphatically termed this type (notwithstanding its ultimate derivation from Michelangelo, Pietro da Cortona and Borromini) the 'Pozzoan pediment'.[140] That Pozzo, heir to a characteristically Roman form, has become so identified with it is a reminder of the crucial role of print imagery in the dissemination of early modern European design further afield.

In China, the *Perspectiva* informed both the eighteenth-century decorations of European churches in Beijing and the *Shixue*, a book of woodcuts that illustrated European ways of seeing (see Figures 6.7–6.10). These are best contextualized by first considering the influx of European illustrated books to China and the reasons – from both the European and the Chinese points of view – for the special currency of illustrated books on perspective.

The main propagators of print imagery in China, the Jesuits, were aware that the easiest way to 'impress ... the new faithful' around the world was 'by means of pictures'.[141] From their arrival in China, missionaries habitually requested illustrated literature as a key instrument for promoting Christian culture. In 1580 the leading Jesuit in China, Michele Ruggieri, wrote: 'I need illustrated books to help the mandarins of the King of China to understand the mysteries of our Lord.' The following year Ruggieri asked for a copy of

Arias Montanus's eight-volume polyglot Bible, printed by Plantin in Antwerp between 1568 and 1572 with twenty large engravings by Jan Wierix and others.[142] The publication that suited the Jesuits' purpose best of all, as witnessed by their 'enormous investment' in terms of both time and money from the mid-1500s to its publication in the 1590s, was the *Evangelicae Historiae Imagines* (*EHI*), a series of 153 large copper engravings printed both separately and with over 600 pages of annotations and meditations.[143] First applied for even before it was published,[144] immediately after one copy had arrived, another was requested by Ruggieri's successor, Matteo Ricci, head of the Jesuit mission from 1582 to 1610.[145] For the scholar of Sino-European publishing, Michael Sullivan, a salient feature of the *EHI* was their 'masterly perspective'.[146] In the seventeenth century, two editions deriving from the *EHI* were made in China itself; their replications of the European prototypes convey the perspective schemes very imperfectly, and adapt the scenes to an Asian environment.[147]

European illustrated books were also exported to China for diplomatic reasons, as Ricci's present of many Plantin and other editions to the Emperor reveals.[148] Mayching Kao has observed that the Jesuits habitually presented themselves to the Chinese 'not as humble men of God but as learned ambassadors of Western science and technical knowledge'.[149] According to the author of the *Hsi-Hsüeh Fan* or *Survey of Western Learning*, published in 1623, there were then some 7,000 European books in China.[150]

The most intriguing secular role of the books imported into China, and of Sino-European publishing, was the dissemination of scientific works. Matteo Ricci actively promoted Western secular learning, supporting an edition of Euclid by the Jesuit Christopher Clavius and works by the same author on mathematics and on the clock, astrolabe and sphere.[151]

The Jesuits' dissemination of books on the instruments for observational astronomy is a key instance of the reciprocity of Western and Eastern observational science. Jesuit proselytizers acknowledged that Chinese astronomy dated back to the very beginning of Imperial Chinese culture. Jean Baptiste Du Halde's early eighteenth-century *Description* of the Chinese empire dwelt at length on their astronomy by means also of a handsome double-page engraving of the Observatory at Beijing.[152] Notwithstanding the central importance of astronomy in Chinese culture, the armillary and equinoctial spheres, quadrants and sextants represented in the engraving of the observatory in Du Halde could not impress as they do were it not for the faultless perspective of their representation.

Bert S. Hall has shown how indispensable a working knowledge of perspectival conventions was for the comprehension of Western technologies such as those illustrated in the engravings to Agostino Ramelli's *Machine* (Paris 1588). This work supplied a high proportion of the illustrations in Fr

Johann Scheck's collection derived from Western machine books, published in 1627 as *Ji Qi Tu Shuo*; the practical usefulness of its illustrations was, however, limited by the Chinese illustrator's unfamiliarity with or indifference to perspective and other Western conventions, such as the cut-away view.[153] To Chinese men of letters, painters and their clients, perspective and its related conventions seemed merely mechanical; its applications were for the Chinese technical rather than artistic.[154]

Reflecting the usefulness of perspective both to the proselytizing agenda of the Jesuits and to the Chinese court, in the mid-seventeenth century one set of the Sicilian Jesuit Luigi Buglio's three 'tableaux' demonstrating the rules of perspective was exhibited in the Jesuits' garden and another was given to the Emperor.[155]

At least three churches built in Beijing in the years and decades following the publication of the *Perspectiva* drew on its designs. It emerges from Du Halde's account that the illusionistic dome of 1702 in the Cathedral at Beijing, by the maverick Italian painter Giovanni Gherardini who had been sent out to China by the Jesuits precisely because of his mastery of Pozzo's principles of perspective,[156] elaborated upon the models provided by Pozzo in a manner comparable to Sepulveda at Recife, by showing tiers of illusionistic architecture in perspective.[157] A contemporary engraving of the interior of Nossa Senhora da Assunção shows its solomonic altar and illusionistic dome, both presumably derived from the *Perspectiva*.[158] The Florentine Jesuit architect of the church of São José, Ferdinando Bonaventura Moggi, compared the high altar to that of Luis Gonzaga at S. Ignazio, Rome.[159] It is reasonable to assume that the cupola painted by Giuseppe Castiglione (Milan 1688 – Beijing 1766/8), self-professed follower of Pozzo,[160] drew on Pozzo's designs in the *Perspectiva*.

In the same year as his decorations of São José, 1729, Castiglione was acknowledged by the author in the preface to the first edition of the *Shixue ching-yün* (see Figures 6.7–10). The *Shixue*, which has been translated as 'instruction of how to see', *Visual Instruction* and *The Theory of Vision*,[161] was a court rather than a missionary initiative. In the early Qing, the Jesuits' principal missionary purpose was discouraged at court, but their scientific activities actively welcomed. According to Du Halde, the 'favourite passion' of Emperor Kanxi (1689–1722) 'was to acquire new knowledge every day'.[162] As Kanxi's reign progressed he increasingly prohibited the Jesuits from preaching, and allowed only a few scientifically expert Jesuits at court, such as one Father Grimaldi who demonstrated to him the principles of the *camera obscura*.[163] The Emperor during whose reign both editions of *Shixue* were published, Youngzhen (1723–36), tolerated Christianity only out of respect for his predecessor and expelled all missionaries except those working in Beijing who were put under house arrest.[164] There is no reason to suggest that Pozzo's *Perspectiva* was used out of deference to his Jesuit status, and all

Jesuit iconography is eliminated from the Chinese woodcuts. The essential difference between both the European editions and the Chinese variations on the *EHI* and the *Perspectiva* warrants emphasis. The *EHI* was a Jesuit collaboration, the *Perspectiva* as shown earlier in this essay Pozzo's own enterprise. The success of the former abroad was due to its usefulness for evangelization. Notwithstanding the devotional implications of perspective in Pozzo's own mind, its popularity was mainly due to the practicality of its visual method. Despite the fact that, as will emerge both here and in Cao Yiqiang's forthcoming study of Chinese artistic relations with the West from the Ming period to the early twentieth century, rather than an edition of the *Perspectiva* the *Shixue* is a compendium of Western book-illustrations of perspective leading to demonstrations of how to adapt it to Oriental motifs, the *Shixue* leads off from examples in the *Perspectiva* and thereafter recurrently adapts its consecutive visual method.

Both editions of the *Shixue* were curated by Nian Xiyao, the cultural superintendent at the court of Youngzhen, and director of the Ching-te Chen porcelain factory from 1726 to 1736, when the enamel decoration of ceramics was being revived and revised in a self-conscious attempt to match, even surpass early Ming porcelain.[165] In his preface Nian thanked Castiglione for enabling him to draw Chinese objects in Western style, and, it has been claimed, for helping with the illustrations to the *Shixue*.[166] The claim is misleading insofar as it is clear from their material characteristics and visual appearance that the woodcuts were sculpted by a Chinese engraver (or engravers). We shall return to the matter of the engraver's agency. As for the intended readership, Nian declared that he published *Shixue* mainly for the use of practising native artists.[167]

The second edition of 1735, enlarged with more woodcuts, had a preface in which Nian explained that while Chinese painters depicted landscape according to their inspiration and without being subjected to physical likeness, Western pictorial techniques and ideas were better suited to representing buildings and furnishings.[168] Cao Yiqiang's forthcoming study will reveal how this statement alienated subsequent Chinese readers.[169] The point made above, that to the Chinese the applications of perspective were more technical than artistic, is still reflected in Nian's admission of the usefulness of perspective for aspects of artistic practice. Among Yiqiang's many insights into the *Shixue* is the observation that Nian 'injected a touch of Chinese Taoism' into his analysis of the same set of pictures that Pozzo had presented as Christian.[170] This goes to show print imagery's amenability to different textual messages. Henceforth, the present enquiry is limited to scrutinising the engravings in the second edition. The oblong *folio* volume is far from luxurious; both copies consulted are bound, without a spine, between cardboard covers. The woodcuts are printed on one side of flimsy sheets of paper, the latter gathered so that double spreads of imagery tend to alternate with blank spreads. The cheap materials of the *Shixue* tally with Nian's claim that it was mainly for working artists, as does the frontispiece replicating with slight variations the design engraved for the European editions of Pozzo's *Perspectiva*, showing a table, set square and other materials for perspectival drawing (see Figure 6.7). However, the authors of the books, identified as Palladio and Vignola in the Roman frontispiece (see Figure 6.2a), and the same plus Vitruvius in the London one (see Figure 6.2b), remain unspecified in the *Shixue*. This is fitting. As we shall see, at least one of the figures in the *Shixue* is derived from Vignola-Danti but Nian drew on Viator, Serlio, and Dubreuil rather than on Palladio. Yiqiang has noticed that, as well as the frontispiece the first twenty-nine engravings in the *Shixue* are derived from volume I of the *Perspectiva*: to be precise from figs 2–27, 30–31 and 53. The dimensions of the woodcuts, measuring 32.5 by 21 cm, tally with the size of the engravings in *folio* editions of the *Perspectiva*, from which they have clearly been traced. The main difference is that figs 5–13, 15–27 and 30–1 in the *Perspectiva* all replicate the shadows thrown by the architectural elements represented by means of cross-hatching, while, for reasons addressed below, this *chiaroscuro* is omitted from the Chinese versions.

The size of engraved border inherited from the *Perspectiva* is retained throughout the *Shixue*; but no subsequent woodcut is directly traced from Pozzo's book. Nian does however more than once return to Pozzo's sequential visual method. The 140 engravings are arranged in a manner according even more primacy to imagery over text than in the European prototypes, brief descriptions being effected (thanks partly to the textual concision of Chinese characters) on the woodcuts themselves. As I have learnt from Yiqiang, Nian's text regarding the engravings in the *Shixue* does not set out to translate those of Pozzo's *Perspectiva* and his other sources; indeed Nian spoke no European language. The *Shixue* well exemplifies the didactic potential of images in books irrespective of their accompanying texts. In fact some of the 140 unnumbered woodcuts, for instance from pages '15' to '36' according to the manuscript pagination of the copy in the Bodleian Library, Oxford,[171] are entirely text-free, on the basis that they are self-explanatory. This section of the *Shixue*, the latter two thirds of that traced from the *Perspectiva*, retains Pozzo's sequential method of having one diagram inform those that follow it. The image combining three orthographic views of a circle-within-a-square with the scenographic perspective of each to a single vanishing point (*Shixue* 1735, p. '20'; Pozzo 1693, fig. 14) – which has Serlian and other precedents – leads directly into a series of demonstrations of how to represent the Western architectural orders, from the base and column up, in perspective.

The following sequence of woodcuts synthesises European expositions of the principles of perspectival representation (*Shixue* 1735, pp. '37'–'41'). The diagrams – the earliest published source for which is Viator's showing the distance-point method and the superimposition onto it of the staple of Renaissance picture space, the 'pavimento'[172] – recall rather than replicate graphic suggestions found in the treatises of Cousin, Serlio, Vignola-Danti, and Dubreuil (see Figure 6.8).[173]

Certain figures in the *Shixue* are directly copied from European sources. For instance the only cross represented in the *Shixue*, a double one of cubic proportions free of any Christian overtone, closely resembles one of Dubreuil's examples.[174] Slightly smaller than Dubreuil's precedent, the cross is probably copied rather than traced; as in the tracings from the *Perspectiva*, any indication of *chiaroscuro* or cast shadow is omitted. The same is true of another figure in the same woodcut, also close to one of Dubreuil's models, showing the elevation of a cube in perspective.[175] In the case of the Chinese woodcut of the cube, the keyed information on the diagram has been eliminated.

Such correspondences between particular images in the *Shixue* and in any of its European precursors are subject to a reservation akin to that aired before in the context of the reception of European print imagery in contact Spanish America: since the imagery in most European treatises on perspective is in turn indebted to that in another, any given image has more than one potential source.[176] More important in the present context is the strategic ordering of the images. For instance, a series demonstrating the diminution of circles and elipses (*Shixue*, pp. '92'–'97') ends with a graphic delineation akin to that in one of Danti's annotations to Vignola - albeit the Chinese version, in reverse and larger, thus evidently copied rather than traced, omits some of the dotted compositional guidelines as being superfluous since, as in its prototype, respective positions on the circle and its diminution are keyed.[177] This sequence informs the following two woodcuts showing how to depict in perspective two architectural ornaments the decorative details of which are thoroughly Chinese (*Shixue*, pp. '98'–'99'). That is, Nian has adapted Pozzo's sequential visual method, incorporated other Western sources into it, and applied it to his local cultural environment.

On the sole occasion other than the first thirty pages when the iconography of the *Shixue* imitates that in the *Perspectiva*, Pozzo's procedure is approximated. Three engravings (*Shixue*, pp. '102'–'104') illustrate Pozzo's method of designing illusionistic vaults in perspective to an off-centre vanishing point. They also exemplify how, not unlike Schübler's and Palomino's, the illustrations overseen by Nian Xayao adapted Pozzo's visual method flexibly. The first shows how to depict columns as seen from below within a square picture space; in the second the same architecturally non-specific columns are represented within a circular opening; in the third the architectural vocabulary is thoroughly orientalised (see Figure 6.9). Nian's aim of demonstrating how to represent Chinese subjects in the Western style becomes increasingly evident towards the end of *Shixue*. A high proportion of the later images in the Beijing 1735 book represent Oriental motifs, such as a Chinese theatre (*Shixue*, pp. '108'–'109'). An image which encapsulates *Shixue*'s position at the crossroads of Eastern and Western preoccupations with representation is that showing how to depict in perspective the habitual support of Chinese painting, the scroll (see Figure 6.10).

The final seven images of the *Shixue* show how to draw Oriental subjects in the Western shadow-casting mode. One such is a tiger in perspective;[178] while the tiger itself is represented convincingly enough, its shadow is less so, two alternatives seemingly being given by dint of a dotted and continuous outline respectively.[179] In the other six woodcuts showing Chinese subjects in the shadow-casting mode, the shadows themselves are indicated merely by dotted lines (very similar to the compositional ones in earlier plates) that mark their outer edges. That is, of the 'three points' about Western pictorial ideas and techniques detailed by Nian in his preface of 1735 – the single vanishing point, *chiaroscuro*, and the principle of cast shadows[180] – only the first is fully expressed in the woodcuts. Excepting some indication of light and shade on the shafts of the columns in the demonstrations of illusionistic domes (see Figure 6.9), *chiaroscuro* is not demonstrated at all, and the shadow casting principle is shown only schematically. Since this is clearly not due to authorial will and Nian Xiyao had an input into the engravings, Cao Yiqiang suggests that the fact that in the woodcuts *chiaroscuro* is mainly ignored and cast shadows are represented only by a dotted line (and in those traced from the *Perspectiva* not at all) may perhaps be 'both for clarity of demonstration and for the sake of the Chinese engraver, not yet accustomed to this European convention'.[181] That the engraver was able to represent *chiaroscuro* is indicated by the shading on the shafts in Fig. 6.9. Any unreadiness so to do is therefore likely to have been due less to technical inability than to aesthetic and cognitive choice. After all, woodcuts of a very linear character had been made in China for the best part of a millennium.[182]

A further remove from the illustrations to Pozzo but central to the issue of the illustrated book as conduit of artistic ideas is the role of the woodcuts in the *Shixue* in the emergence of *ukiyo-e* (floating world) imagery in Japan. In an important if flawed thesis Julian Jing Lee argued that the 'real origin' of the early *uki-e* phase of *ukiyo-e* was the *Shixue*.[183] This is historically plausible insofar as the importing of Chinese books on European science into Japan was permitted from 1720. Because free of Christian iconography, the *Shixue* would have qualified for the dispensation. At least one copy of the *Shixue* is preserved in Japan, and *ukiyo-e* itself can be dated from works of the later 1730s such as Torii Kiyotada's 1739 painting of the Ichimura theatre.[184] As we have seen the *Shixue* proposed oriental theatre designs. Lee's argument is that 'the multiple (or floating) vanishing points' of *ukiyo-e* 'derived from the fact that the illustrations in the Chinese prototype that are applicable to Chinese architecture ... are given in a piecemeal manner'.[185] A recurrent incongruity in the picture space of works by Kiyotada and subsequent *ukiyo-e* artists, that linear perspective is used for interiors and a bird's-eye view for surrounding exterior space may partly result from the fact that (for the reason explained by Nian in his preface of 1735) not a single illustration in the *Shixue* explains how to depict exterior scenery in perspective.[186] The disjunction between architectural and non-architectural space in *ukiyo-e* can thus be related to that here noted in Portuguese and Brazilian illusionistic perspective painting, as resulting ultimately from Pozzo's architectural agenda.

Lee supports his view that the *Shixue* was the main external source for *uki-e* with the observation that both are devoid of Western pictorial techniques such as hatching and *chiaroscuro*.[187] If Lee is at all right, the absence of hatching and *chiaroscuro* depends not so much on Nian's editorial advice as, most tellingly for our purposes, on the visual properties of the Chinese woodcuts.

Conclusion

At the start of this essay Pozzo's *Perspectiva* was described as culminating a tradition of illustrated books on perspective, and attention was drawn to its image-led method, which in turn was the main reason for its success in three continents. As remarkable as the geographical extent of the responses to Pozzo's *Perspectiva* is the variety of responses to a single set of book illustrations. In England the engravings in Pozzo's *Perspectiva* were nuanced towards architecture more than towards its representation; in Quito, engravings in the *Perspectiva* were at the root of the three-dimensional sculpturality of the transept *retablos* at the Compañía, while in Brazil it gave rise to a distinctive regional approach to perspective painting. In China, Pozzo's *Perspectiva* supplied the visual method for demonstrating some fundamentals of Western artistic practice.

The elasticity of Pozzo's illustrations as vehicles for theory as well as for practice is proven by the texts its imagery prompted, for instance De Figueredo Seixas's manuscript analysis of Pozzo's 'Figura 100', and by the textual nuances within the iconography of the London edition towards its agents' architectural agenda (see Figures 6.1b, 6.2b). On the other hand, perhaps the best proof of the efficacy of Pozzo's didactic imagery is the eloquence of the woodcuts in the Beijing edition, recognizably derived from Pozzo's, but not seen as requiring any text (see Figure 6.7).

Notes

1. A. Pozzo, *Perspectiva pictorum et architectorum*, 2 vols, Rome 1693 and 1700, I, text accompanying fig. 58: 'omnia ex diagrammatis inspectione clarissimè apparent', quoted in the title as translated in A. Pozzo, *Rules and Examples of Perspective proper for Painters and Architects, etc. In English and Latin ...* , transl. John James (printed by Benjamin Motte, sold by John Sturt), London 1707.

2. For perspective in classical antiquity see J. White, *The Birth and Rebirth of Pictorial Space* (1st edn 1957) London 1972, pp. 236–73; J. Onians, *Classical Art and the Cultures of Greece and Rome*, New Haven and London 1999, pp. 147–8; for China see W. H. Wells, *Perspective in Early Chinese Painting*, London 1935.

3. See, at least, E. Panofsky, 'Die Perspektive als "symbolische Form"', first publ. in *Vorträge der Bibliothek Warburg* 1924–25 (Leipzig and Berlin 1927), pp. 258–330 (Engl. edn *Perspective as Symbolic Form*, ed. and transl. C. Wood, New York 1991); M. H. Pirenne, *Optics, Painting and Photography*, Cambridge 1970; M. Kemp, *The Science of Art: Optical Themes in Western Art from Brunelleschi to Seurat*, New Haven and London 1990; and J. V. Field, *The Invention of Infinity: Mathematics and Art in the Renaissance*, Oxford 1997.

4. *Leonardo on Painting*, ed. M. Kemp, New Haven and London, 1989, p. 52.

5. R. Zwijnenberg, *The Writings and Drawings of Leonardo da Vinci: Order and Chaos in Early Modern Thought*, transl. (Dutch into English) C. van Eck, Cambridge 1999, p.122.

6. Vitruvius, *De architectura*, I, ii, 2.

7. A. Averlino 'il Filarete', *Trattato di architettura*, ed. A. M. Finoli and L. Grassi, Milan 1972, p. LXX.

8. V. Hart, 'Serlio and Representation', in *Paper Palaces: The Rise of the Renaissance Architectural Treatise*, ed. V. Hart and P. Hicks, New Haven and London 1998, pp. 170–85, esp. p. 179.

9. S. Serlio, *Tutte l'opere*, Venice 1619, 'Libro Secondo della Prospettiva', fols 23r, 24r, 26r, 28r–36r, 'Libro Settimo', every odd page from 3 to 243, bar only [p. 219; sic, for] p. 209, is entirely given over to imagery.

10. Pozzo (as in n. 1), II, 1700, pp. 84–7 (double-page spreads of ideas for S. Giovanni in Laterano), pp. 89–90 (for a 'Chiesa rotunda'), pp. 97–105 (doors and windows), pp. 114–18 (fortifications).

11. [J. Pélérin] Viator, *De artificiali p[er]spectiva*, Toul 1505, esp. sig. Avr. In the second edition, Toul 1509, the woodcuts are incorporated into the text and the corresponding diagrams found at sig. Avv.

12. D. Barbaro, *La pratica della perspettiva ... opera molto profittevole a pittori, scultori, et architetti*, Venice 1569, p. 5.

13. Barbaro (as above), 'Parte Terza', ch. XXXVIII, 'Descrittione del Torchio, ovvero Mazzocco', ch. XXXIX, pp. 125–8, 'La Perfetta Descrittione del Mazzocco', and especially the engraving on pp. 127–8, equip practising artists in Barbaro's readership to replicate the design of his headers.

14. Barbaro (as in n. 12), 'Parte Nona', pp. 187–93: 'Horario Universale'; on p. 188 woodcut after Dürer. See E. Panofsky, *The Life and Art of Albrecht Dürer*, Princeton NJ (1st edn 1943) 1955, pp. 252–3 on Dürer's discussion of perspective in the fourth book of his *Underweysung der Messung, mit dem Zirckel und Richtscheyt, in Linien Ebnen un[d] gantzen Corporen* (1st edn 1525) Nuremberg 1538, pl. 311 for Dürer's frame.

15. Barbaro (as in n. 12), 'Parte Quarta, ... Scenographia', pp. 129–53.

16. See, for instance, Barbaro (as in n. 12), 'Parte Quarta', ch. II: 'Descrittione et adombratione della base Toscana', pp. 131–3.

17. G. Barozzi da Vignola, *Regola delli cinque ordini d'architettura*, [Venice] 1562, fol. III: 'poi in ciò si procede per certe belle regole di Prospettiva la cui prattica è necessaria à questa, et alla Pittura insieme, in modo ch'io m'assicuro vi sarà grata, et spero anco di tosto donarvi'. See also M. Walcher Casotti, 'Nota introduttiva', in G. Barozzi da Vignola, commentary by E. Danti, *Le due regole della prospettiva*, Rome 1583, reprinted at Vignola 1974 (hereafter Vignola–Danti), n.p.

18. T. Frangenberg, 'Egnatio Danti on the History of Perspective', in *La perspectiva: fondamenti teorici ed esperienze figurative dall'antichità al mondo moderno* (Perspicere, 2), ed. R. Sinisgalli, Florence 1998, pp. 213–23, esp. p. 220 n. 7. Vignola–Danti (as above), fol. + 2r.

19. Vignola–Danti (as in n. 17), 'Prefatione', pp. [8–9], esp. p. [8]: 'Potranno ancora quelli artefici che piu si dilettano di operare, che di fare studio in diverse regole, lasciata in dietro la prima Regola del Vignola …, porre tutto lo studio nella seconda, & in quella fare grandissima pratica.'

20. Vignola–Danti (as in n. 17), pt II, ch. XVIII, p.132, 'Sagme per fare li corpi in Prospettiva', ch. XX, p.137, 'Sagme base', ch. XXI, p.139, 'Sagme capitelli'. Text is found on the left-hand page of each spread, engraved imagery on the right.

21. P. Accolti, *Lo inganno de gl'occhi, prospettiva pratica … trattato in acconcio della pittura*, Florence 1625 (repr. Portland OR 1972).

22. M. Daly Davis, *Piero della Francesca's Mathematical Treatises: The 'Trattato del abaco' and Libellus de quinque corporibus regularibus*, Ravenna 1977, p. 49. M. Daly Davis, 'Il disegno dei corpi regolari', in *Nel segno di Masaccio: l'invenzione della prospettiva*, exh. cat. Florence 2001, pp. 123–32.

23. Kemp (as in n. 3), p. 27.

24. Accolti (as in n. 21), 'Segunda Parte, De Corpi, e del levargli in disegno di Prospettiva', pp. 59–94: ch. I, Tetrahedron, pp. 59–60, chs II–III, Cube, pp. 60–2, ch. IV, Octahedron, pp. 62–4, ch. V, Dodecahedron, pp. 65–8, ch. VI, Icosahedron, pp. 69–70, ch. VII, 'qual si voglia Corpo', pp. 70–2.

25. Accolti (as in n. 21), 'Terza Parte, De lumi et ombre', pp. 95–152.

26. [J. Dubreuil], *La perspective pratique, necessaire a tous peintres, graveurs, sculpteurs, architects, orfevres, brodeurs, tapisseurs, et autres qui se messent de desseigner*, 3 vols, Paris 1651.

27. Kemp (as in n. 3), p.122.

28. L. Wright, *Perspective in Perspective*, Boston and London 1983, p. 159.

29. A. Pozzo, *Perspectiva pictorum et architectorum … pars prima*, (2nd edn) Rome: Antonio de Rossi 1702: fig. 100, 'DELINEATIO PICTURAE IN FORNICE TEMPLI S. IGNATII'; Pozzo (as in n. 1), II, 1700, figs 60–1, for Pozzo's altar dedicated to St Ignatius at the Gesù, Rome; figs 62–3 for the altar at S. Ignazio dedicated to B. Luis Gonzaga, fig. 82 for the main altar, figs 77–8 for his altar to St Sebastian at Verona, on which see B. Kerber, *Andrea Pozzo*, Berlin and New York 1971, p. 136.

30. F. S. Baldinucci, *Vite di artisti dei secoli XVII–XVIII* (MS. c.1725–30), ed. A. Matteoli, Rome 1975, p. 327: 'fece tant'altre pitture e quadri d'ogni sorte, potette, col guadagno – ascendente sopra duemila scudi – e con la debita licenza de' superiori, compire i bellissimi libri di prospettiva, che compose e diede alla luce, intitolati *Perspectiva Pictorum et Architectorum*'. See S. Samek Ludovici, 'Baldinucci, Francesco Saverio', in *Dizionario biografico degli Italiani*, V, 1963, pp. 498–9.

31. Pozzo reproduced his designs for the *Quarantore* in *Perspectiva* (as in n. 1), I, 1693, figs 69–70 and a further idea for the same in *Perspectiva* (as in n. 1), II, 1700, fig. 48. See P. Bjurström, 'Baroque Theater and the Jesuits', in R. Wittkower and I. B. Jaffe eds, *Baroque Art: The Jesuit Contribution*, New York 1972, pp. 99–110, esp. pp. 104–10, figs 54–6, 59–61, 63, 64 a–b.

32. Baldinucci (as in n. 30); see also L. Salviucci Insolera, 'Le prime edizioni del Trattato', in A. Battisti ed., *Andrea Pozzo*, (1st edn 1996) Milan and Trent 1998, pp. 207–14, esp. p. 208.

33. For an edition of Palladio's *Quattro libri* so entitled, see A. Palladio, *L'architettura … divisa in quattro libri … *, Venice: Marc'Antonio Brogiollo 1642.

34. Pozzo (as in n. 1), I, 1693, unnumbered engraving between figs 52 and 53; Pozzo (as in n. 29), I, 1702, 'Ultima Figura'; Pozzo (as in n. 1), 1707, 'Fifty-third Figure A'.

35. Pozzo (as in n. 1), 1707 edn, p. [11], 'Advice to beginners'. See also Pozzo (as in n. 1), I, 1693, p. [5], 'Avvisi a i principianti': 'che vi contentiate di ben intender la seconda figura prima di passare alla terza, e l'istesso dico di tutte le altre: Essendo disposte con tal ordine, che ciascuna di quelle che va avanti, è necessaria per capir quelle che vengon dietro. Se vi accaderà di non intender qualche cosa nelle spiegazioni, ajutatevi con rimirare attentamente le figure; e vicendevolmente, se nelle figure non trovate tutto quello che bramereste, ricorrete alle spiegazioni …'.

36. Pozzo (as in n. 1), I, 1693, text accompanying fig. 46: 'Lo potevo far di meno di disegnar l'altra metà della presente fabbrica'; Pozzo (as in n. 1), 1707 edn, text accompanying fig. 46, 'I might very well have omitted this Half of the Design.'

37. Pozzo (as in n. 1), I, 1693, text accompanying fig. 88: 'Essendo il punto della distanza poco lontano da quello dell'occhio, il disegno si stende assai, e non ha bella apparenza. Nondimeno provatevi a guardarlo dalla sua distanza EO, e sarà svanita ogni deformità'; Pozzo (as in n. 1), 1707 edn, text accompanying fig. 88.

38. Pozzo (as in n. 1), I, 1693, text accompanying fig. 88: 'Se volete gabbare la gente semplice, havendo a dipingere Opere con distanza troppa corta, farete due disegni; uno per mostrare a tutti; e in questo il punto della distanza mettetelo lontano da quello dell'occhio quanto è necessario per fuggire ogni deformità. Dell'altro disegno servitevene di nascosto nel fare il vostro lavoro'; Pozzo (as in n. 1), 1707 edn, text accompanying fig. 88.

39. Pozzo (as in n. 1), I, 1693, text accompanying fig. 90: 'Il punto dell'occhio l'ho messo fuori dell'opera, accioche quei che la mirano si stracchino meno, e si scopra più d'architettura e d'artifitio; il che non seguirebbe se la veduta fosse nel mezzo.'

40. Kemp (as in n. 3), p. 139.

41. On this, Pozzo's sole demonstration of a centrally viewed dome, see T. Frangenberg, 'Andrea Pozzo on the Ceiling Paintings in S. Ignazio', in P. Taylor and F. Quiviger eds, *Pictorial Composition from Medieval to Modern Art*, London 2000, pp. 91–116, esp. p. 94.

42. Pozzo (as in n. 1), II, 1700, text accompanying fig. 50: 'La passata figura fù fatta per dichiarar maggiormente questa; perche essendo composta di Architettura, sarebbe riuscita difficile à spiegarsi, & intendersi. Però provate à farla, e così forse l'intenderete meglio colla prattica, che colla speculativa.'

43. W. Oechslin, 'Pozzo e il suo trattato' in Battisti (as in n. 32), pp. 189–206, 'Scienza e arte: metodo sistematico e "teoria della prassi"', pp. 194–6, esp. p. 196 on Pozzo's systematic and accessible method.

44. G. Morolli, 'Un saggio di editoria barocca: i rapporti Ferri-De Rossi-Specchi e la trattatistica architettonica del Seicento romano', in *Gian Lorenzo Bernini e le arti visive*, M. Fagiolo ed., Rome 1987, pp. 209–40, esp. p. 217: 'teorici empirici del nuovo trattato per immagini', and Appendices X–XI, pp. 231–4.

45. Pozzo (as in n. 1), II, 1700, text accompanying fig. 97, 'Porte e finestre': 'hò cavato da molte fabriche varie inventioni, particolarmente di porte, e finestre, che mi sono parute più nobili, e che si scostino dalle volgari'. Between them figs 97–105 show 18 designs.

46. M. R. Nobili, 'Porte e finestre, un fenomeno editoriale del Settecento', in *Il disegno di architettura*, XVIII, 1998, pp. 38–41, esp. pp. 38–9. In relation to Pozzo's section on 'Porte e finestre' Nobili cites *Studio d'Architettura Civile sopra gli ornamenti di Porte e Finestre*, D. de Rossi ed., Rome 1702, and Filippo Juvarra's unpublished *Studio di architettura civile sopra gli ornamenti, porte e finestre* of 1725.

47. In Italy, Pozzo's designs were realized under his direct control at Arezzo, Belluno, Frascati, Mondovì, Montepulciano, Pistoia, Rome, San Sepolcro, Trent and so on.

48. See Kerber (as in n. 29), p. 194, pl. 98 for St Ignatius, Dubrovnik. On its authorship, see K. Prijatelj, 'Barocco romano in Dalmazia: il Duomo e la Chiesa dei Gesuiti in Ragusa', *Arte antica e moderna*, V, 1959, pp. 103–8, esp. p. 106.

49. On Pozzo in Vienna see R. Bösel, 'L'architettura sacra di Pozzo a Vienna', in Battisti (as in n. 32), pp. 161–76, and M. Koller, 'L'ultima opera di Andrea Pozzo a Vienna', ibid., pp. 177–81; on his student Christophorus Tausch, active in the Tyrol, see H. Dziurla, 'Christophorus Tausch, allievo di Andrea Pozzo', ibid., pp. 409–29.

50. See J. Kowalczyck, 'La fortuna di Andrea Pozzo in Polonia: altari e finte cupole', in Battisti (as in n. 32), pp. 441–51 on Pozzo's students Carlo Antonio Baii and Kaçper Bazanka in Poland.

51. G. Pettinati, *Quinquertium historicum sive Prolusiones historicæ de Bellis Augustissimæ Domus Austriacæ*, Vienna 1707; the lively title-page, 'A. Pozzo S.I. delin: – I.A. Pfeffel sculps. Vien.' is reproduced by Kerber (as in n. 29), p. 123.

52. M. Carta, 'Le finte cupole', in *Andrea Pozzo*, ed. V. De Feo and V. Martinelli, Milan 1996, pp. 54–65, esp. pp. 62–3 on Colli's illusionistic domes of 1701 and 1703. See also *Allgemeines Künstler-Lexikon* (hereafter *AKL*), Leipzig and Munich 1992–, XX, 1998, p. 296 on Colli.

53. Carta (as in n. 52), p. 63.

54. A. Blunt, *Sicilian Baroque*, London 1968, pl. 98; Kerber (as in n. 29), p. 210. For the altar's prototypes see Pozzo (as in n. 1), II, 1700, figs 69, 79–80.

55. S. Tobriner, *The Genesis of Noto: An Eighteenth-Century Sicilian City*, London 1982, pp. 193–4, pl. 173, pp. 222–3 n. 37, on Labisi's 15 drawings of doorways and windows, appended to Francesco Sortini's translation into Latin (MS dated 1746, Biblioteca Comunale, Noto) of C. Wolff, *Elementa Matheseos Universae* (German *princeps*, first Latin edition 1713–15). The lintel and keystone in the design reproduced by Tobriner, and the method of their depiction, resemble the middle figure of three in Pozzo (as in n. 1), II, 1700, fig. 105.

56. A. Procopiu, *La peinture religieuse dans les Isles Ioniennes pendant le siècle XVIII: essai sur la transformation de la peinture byzantine en baroque*, [Paris] 1930.

57. A. Charalampidis, 'Doxaras, Panagiotis', in *The Dictionary of Art*, London 1996, IX, pp. 205–6, esp. p. 205.

58. Biblioteca Marciana, Venice, MS Codex Marciano Gr. IV (= 1117), 1720, entitled *Techni Zografias* (The Art of Painting), comprises translations of Alberti's *Della pittura*, Leonardo's *Trattato della pittura* and at least some of the second volume of Pozzo's *Perspectiva*. Chryssa Damianaki Romano presented initial research on the manuscript at the conference 'The Fortuna of Leonardo da Vinci's *Trattato della pittura*', at the Warburg Institute, London, 13–14 September 2001.

59. A. Tinto, 'Giovanni Giacomo Komarek tipografo a Roma nei secoli XVII–XVIII', *La Bibliofilía*, LXXV, 1973, pp. 189–225.

60. M. Carta and A. Menichella, 'Il successo editoriale del Trattato', in *De Feo and Martinelli* (as in n. 52), pp. 230–3, esp. pp. 230, 233 n. 6 and 7.

61. *Acta Eruditorum*, November issue, 1693, pp. 498–9, esp. p. 498: 'opticas quorumvis ordinum delineationes, adhibita communi regula, sed ex qua omnia linearum occultarum offinidula sustulit, expeditissima methodo quam succintissime perficere docet'.

62. Kerber (as in n. 29), p. 268.

63. *AKL* (as in n. 52), XIII, 1996, p. 445 on Boxbarth (Augsburg 1671–1727), best known for his engravings in editions of the first volume of A. Pozzo, *Perspectiva Pictorum atque architectorum / Der Mahler und Baumeister Perspectiv*, Augsburg 1706, 1708; cf. Kerber (as in n. 29), p. 268, nos IV, 2, 3.

64. N. Powell, *From Baroque to Rococo: An Introduction to Austrian and German Architecture from 1580 to 1790*, London 1959, p. 80, pl. 31a, on Pöppelmann's Kronentor (Crown Gate), commissioned in 1710 and built 1713–15.

65. *AKL* (as in n. 52), XII, 1996, p. 74 on Bodenehr (Augsburg 1663–1710). Kerber (as in n. 29), p. 268 no. IV, 4 on the first Augsburg edition of the second volume of A. Pozzo, *Perspectivae pictorum atque architectorum / Der Mahler und Baumeister Perspectiv*, Augsburg 1709.

66. See Kerber (as in n. 29), pp. 268–9 for translations of Pozzo into German.

67. J. J. Schübler, *Perspectiva. Pes Picturae. Das ist: Kurtze und leichte Verfassung der practicabelsten Regul, zur perspectivischen Zeichnungskunst*, 2 vols, Nuremberg 1719–20.

68. Pozzo (as in n. 1), II, 1700, fig. 54: 'Tholus alter, arbitrariæ structuræ / Cupola di diversa figura'.

69. Schübler (as in n. 57), II, p. 39: 'man die Optischen Kleinigkeiten viel leichter aus der Praxi als aus der Theorie überkommen könne'.

70. P. Vignau Wilberg, 'Le finte cupole e la loro recezione nella Germania meridionale', in Battisti (as in n. 32), pp. 215–23. See also H. Tintelnot, *Die barocke Freskomalerei in Deutschland*, Munich 1951, pp. 60, 62, and H. Trottmann, *Cosmas Damian Asam 1686–1739, Tradition und Invention im malerischen Werk*, Nuremberg 1986, s.v. Pozzo, on Pozzo and Asam.

71. H. Bauer, *Der Himmel im Rokoko: Das Fresko im deutschen Kirchenraum des 18. Jahrhunderts*, Regensburg 1960, p. 19, pl. 5 and 6 for the Pfronten-Berg frescoes; see U. Thieme and F. Becker, *Allgemeines Lexikon der bildenden Künstler*, 37 vols, Leipzig 1907–50 (hereafter Thieme–Becker), XX, p. 111 on Keller.

72. Kerber (as in n. 29), pp. 267–8.

73. Kerber (as in n. 29), pp. 268–70 on the editions in German, French, English, Flemish, Spanish and modern Greek, and p. 268 no. IV, 3 on *Perspectiva Pictorum atque Architectorum... / Der Mahler und Baumeister Perspectiv...* , Augsburg 1708, and using the same engravings by Johann Boxbarth, the Flemish/French edition of the first volume, *Eerste Deel. van de Perspective / Première partie de la perspective*, Brussels [1711], the latter cited by Kerber, p. 269, and in *Architecture and its Image: Four Centuries of Architectural Representation*, ed. E. Blau and E. Kaufman, Montreal 1989, p.190.

74. Kerber (as in n. 29), p. 269.

75. Pozzo (as in n. 29), I, 1702, fig. 100.

76. See S. Jeffery in *The Dictionary of Art*, XVI, London 1996, p. 893 on John James (1673 –

Greenwich 1746), whose work as architect and surveyor included being clerk of the works for Hawksmoor's Royal Hospital for Seamen at Greenwich.

77. See Pozzo (as in n. 1), 1707, p. [11]: 'The Approbation of this Edition'.

78. In Pozzo (as in n. 1), 1707, the latter part of the title-page information reads: 'Engraven in 105 ample folio Plates, and adorn'd with 200 Initial Letters to the Explanatory Discourses: Printed from Copper-Plates on ye best Paper by John Sturt … Sold by John Sturt in Golden-Lion-Court in Aldergate-Street.' John Sturt (1658–1730) ran a drawing school in St Paul's Churchyard from 1697 to after 1710.

79. C. Campbell, *Vitruvius Britannicus, or the British Architect*, 3 vols, I, London 1717, title-page 'J. Sturt sculp.', II, 1717, title-page 'J. Sturt sculp.'.

80. Pozzo (as in n. 1), 1707, fig. 60: the copy in the National Art Library at the Victoria and Albert Museum (NAL), call-mark 99.D.22, fig. 60 has the inscription quoted in the text; other consulted copies of the London edition (e.g. NAL 99.D.22A, BL 744.d.19 and the New York 1971 reprint) do not.

81. C. Perrault, *Ordonnance des cinq espèces de colonnes*, Paris 1683, and *A Treatise of the Five Orders of Columns in Architecture*, transl. John James (printed by B. Motte, sold by John Sturt), London 1708.

82. Kerber (as in n. 29), p. 270, cites 'Potey, De Perspectiva y Arquitectura, Roma 1700'; however, I have found no reference to this edition in the Spanish-language literature.

83. A. Bonet Correa, 'Láminas del Museo Pictórico y Escala Óptica, de Palomino', *Archivo Español de Arte*, XLVI, 182, 1973, pp.131–44, esp. p. 134. On Palomino's book see also A. Gallego Gallego, *Historia del grabado en España*, Madrid 1979, pp. 234–5.

84. Pozzo (as in n. 1), II, 1700, fig. 55: 'un pezzo di Architettura di sotto in sù per linee rette'.

85. G. Kubler and M. S. Soria, *Art and Architecture in Spain and Portugal and their American Dominions 1500 to 1800*, Harmondsworth 1959, p. 192. See ibid., pp. 59, 358 n. 59 on Bibiena's sojourn in Barcelona in 1708–11, and the debt to him of the Morató family of architect-decorators, as manifested by the *camarín* of Santa Teresa at Vich of 1750 by Carlos Morató Brugaroles (1721–85), based on illustrations in Bibiena's *L'architettura civile*, Parma 1711; see ibid., p. 115, on Bibiena and the Bom Jesus shrine of Barga, Portugal.

86. J. F. Pereira, 'Joanine Style', in *Dictionary of Art*, XVII, London 1996, p. 595: 'Concentric arches were abandoned in favour of canopies and baldacchini of architectural form; combined with allegorical statues … taken from *Perspectiva Pictorum et Architectorum*'.

87. On Nasoni, see R. C. Smith, *Nicolau Nasoni, arquitecto do Porto*, Lisbon 1967. On Nasoni's altar at Oporto Cathedral, see A. Delaforce, *Art and Patronage in Eighteenth-Century Portugal*, Cambridge 2002, p. 257.

88. 'Parte I da perspectiva de pintores & architetos … em Roma pello Sr. Andre Pozo S.J. … agora a favor does studiozos desta arte pouco rricos incolhida por mos mais deminuto e Composta nesta forma por João Boxbarte, chalcographo Augusta vindelicorum. A custa de Jeremias Wolffio…Traduzido tudo de Latim em Portugues pelo P. João Sarayva, da Cidade de Porto' (University of Coimbra Library, MS. 222, fols 1r–37v); 'Perspectiva de Pintores Architectos de André Poço … Parte II … Traduzido da Lingua Toscana no nosso idioma portugues por Jose de Figueyredo pintor na Cidade do Porto,…1732' (ibid., fols 38r–82r). On both these manuscripts, see R. C. Smith, *Frei José de Santo Antonio Ferreira Vilaça*, Lisbon 1972, p. 305, n. 20.

89. J. De Figueredo Seixas 'Pintor de Architectura', 'Nova Explicação da Figura 100 do Primeyro Tomo desta Obra' (University of Coimbra Library, ms. 222, fols 91r–98v); Smith (as in n. 88), p. 305 n. 20. On Seixas, see Smith (as in n. 87), pp. 177–9.

90. R. Dos Santos, 'A Pintura dos Tectos no Século XVIII em Portugal', *Belas artes*, XVIII, 1962, pp. 13–22, esp. p. 14.

91. Dos Santos (as in n. 90), p. 17. On Simões Ribeiro at Coimbra, see also F. de Pamplona, *Dicionário de pintores e escultores portugueses*, V, (2nd edn) Lisbon 1987–88, p. 49.

92. N. Saldanha, *Artistas, imagens e ideias na pintura do século XVIII*, Lisbon 1995, pp. 203–13 on eighteenth-century artistic literature in Portugal.

93. J. A. França, *Lisboa Pombalina e o Illuminismo*, Lisbon 1965, p. 169.

94. Smith (as in n. 88), p. 228 relates Pozzo's figures to the altar of c. 1760 at São Martinho, Tibães, on which see also Delaforce (as in n. 87), pp. 276–7; see Smith p. 419 on the relation of the same to the concave *retablo* at Nossa Señhora de Remedios, Lamego.

95. 'Este Livro de Perspectiva, e he tambem de Architectura de Andre Pozo … dous belumes de folio grande feito em Latim, e Italiano; e agora vertido, ou traduzido em Portuges pelo D. P. Fr. Fran.co de Sam Joze, de Pibidens … 1768. Do uzo de Fr. José de S.to Antonio Vilaça. Tibães' (Biblioteca Nacional, Lisbon, MS F. 6, fols 69r–108r). See Smith (as in n. 88), p. 86, for the indication that the translation was made from an edition of 1717; p. 296 n. 143 for the Benedictine librarian's note on the lack of *figuras* in the manuscript. See Kerber (as in n. 29), p. 267, for the only edition of Pozzo dated 1717, the seventh Latin–Italian edition, 'Ex Typographia Antonii de Rubeis, in Platea Cerensis', Rome. On the 1768 translation see also Saldanha (as in n. 92), p. 211.

96. See Smith (as in n. 88), p. 703, fig. 316, for the Pombeiro paintings of 1773–77.

97. See G. Gasparini, *América, Barroco y arquitectura*, Caracas 1972, pp. 269–72, on the 'contamination' of Quitenian architecture by means of engraved reproductions in books of Michelangelo's and Vignola's models; H. Crespo, F. Samaniego Salazar, and J. M. Vargas, *Arte ecuatoriano*, 2 vols, Barcelona and Quito 1976, II, p. 48, on the use of Michelangelo's design of a portal for the Villa Grimani, via P. Caxesi's Madrid 1593 Vignola, at the Compañía, Quito, and on the use there of Cornelis Floris's designs, and pp. 135–6 on Serlio's reception in Quito; and S. Sebastián, 'La influencia de los modelos ornamentales de Serlio en Hispanoamerica', *Boletino del Centro de Investigaciones Históricas y Estéticas* (hereafter: *BCIHE*) VII, 1967, pp. 30–67, esp. pp. 55–8, on supports derived from Serlio at Quito. See also M. S. Soria, *La pintura del siglo XVI en Sudamérica*, Buenos Aires 1956, p. 104, and J. M. Vargas, *El arte ecuatoriano*, Puebla (Mexico) 1960, p.101, on Vredeman de Vries's influence on the sixteenth-century caryatids at S. Domingo, Quito.

98. See J. de Mesa and T. Gisbert, 'Un diseño de Bramante realizado en Quito', *BCIHE* (as in n. 97), VII, 1967, pp. 68–73, and S. Sebastián, 'Notas sobre la arquitectura manierista en Quito', *BCIHE* (as above), I, 1964, pp. 113–20, esp. p.117 and fig. 60, on the appropriation, via Serlio, of Bramante's staircase for the front of the church of S. Francisco. See Gasparini (as in n. 97), pp. 171–233 on spatial and planar design ideas transmitted by means of engraving and p. 274 fig. 380 and p. 276 for the Compañía ground plan.

99. G. B. Barozzi da Vignola, *Regla de las cinco ordenes de Architectura*, transl. P. Caxesi, Madrid 1593, pl. 31; see Kubler and Soria (as in n. 85), p. 369 n. 23, on the Sevillan solomonic columns of 1597 and some subsequent uses of the order in Spain.

100. See *Los Siglos de Oro en los Virreinatos de América 1550–1700*, exh. cat. Madrid 1999–2000, pp. 265–6, for Juan de Noort's engraving of 1651 for the Altar de los Reyes, Puebla.

101. J. Caramuel Lobkowitz, *Arquitectura civil recta y obliqua*, Vigevano 1678, 1st series, pl. LIX, 2nd series, pl. II, fig. II, for solomonic columns.

102. See Vargas (as in n. 97), p. 75, and Crespo et al. (as in n. 97), II, p. 156, for the inscription on the façade of the Compañía, and J. M. Vargas, *Convento de la Compañía de Jesus*, Quito 1960, pp. 21–22, on Deubler.

103. Pozzo (as in n. 1), 1707, text accompanying fig. 53: 'The wreath'd columns describ'd in the fifty-second Figure, being divided into twenty-four equal parts, want very much of that elegancy of contour, which is visible in those brass [sic] pillars, made by the famous Cavalier Bernino, for St Peter's Sepulcher in the Vatican. Wherefore I lay before you three several ways of diminishing the spaces through the whole height of the column.'

104. Gasparini (as in n. 97), p. 277. See J. G. Navarro, *La Iglesia de la Compañía en Quito*, Madrid 1930, p. 47 fig. 24, for Vinterer's design of 1735 for the main altar at the Compañía, Quito.

105. *Summa artis: Historia general del arte: arte iberoamericano desde la colonización a la Independencia (Segunda parte)*, XXIX, (4th edn) Madrid 1992, p. 384, figs 424–5. For the Luis Gonzaga altar at S. Ignazio, see V. De Feo, 'Le cappelle e gli altari', in De Feo and Martinelli (as in n. 52), pp. 114–43, esp. pp. 133–9.

106. G. G. Palmer, *Sculpture in the Kingdom of Quito*, Albuquerque 1987, p. 72. See De Feo (as in n. 105), pp. 129, 132, and R. M. Dal Mas, 'L'altare di sant'Ignazio nel Gesù di Roma: cronache del progetto', in De Feo and Martinelli (as in n. 52), pp. 144–55, for the altar of St Ignatius.

107. See Navarro (as in n. 104), p. 71, fig. 41, for the altar of St John of God at the Merced, p. 73, fig. 43, for the altar to Ramon Nonato at the Hospital church. Kubler and Soria (as in n. 85), p. 175: they 'set a model imitated … at the Hospital Church, at the Merced, and most gracefully at the Cantuña'.

108. H. E. Wethey, *Colonial Architecture and Sculpture in Peru*, Cambridge MA 1949, pp. 223–4, fig. 326.

109. A. Bonet Correa, 'El Padre Pozzo y la Arquitectura Argentina', *Anales del Instituto de Arte Americano e Investigaciones Estéticas*, XXIII, 1970, pp. 28–35, esp. pp. 29–30 on the background to the visual arts in Córdoba; J. E. Burucúa, *Nueva historia Argentina*, vol. I: *arte, sociedad y política*, Buenos Aires 1999, pp. 79–84; M. J. Buschiazzo, *Historia de la arquitectura colonial en Iberoamérica*, Buenos Aires 1961, pp. 139–42.

110. See Bonet Correa (as in n. 109), p. 33, for the response in Córdoba to W. Dietterlin, *Architectura*, Nuremberg 1598; on p. 30 he identifies the 'libro impreso entre los galos' used by Philippe Lemaire for the construction of the *Compañía*, Córdoba, as Philibert de l'Orme, *Nouvelles inventions*, (Paris 1561) 2nd edn Paris 1576.

111. See V. Gesualdo, *Enciclopedia del arte en América: biografías* I, Buenos Aires 1968, n.p., under 'Bianchi' for the Jesuit Andrea Bianchi, born Milan 1677, heard of in Rome in 1716, then in Paraguay, in Buenos Aires from 1717 to 1729, and in Córdoba 1729 until his death in 1740.

112. Bonet Correa (as in n. 109), pp. 32, 34.

113. Bonet Correa (as in n. 109), fig. 5, and Buschiazzo (as in n. 109), opp. p. 147, reproduce the portal to the convent of Santa Teresa, Córdoba; comparison with the pediment of the altar illustrated in Pozzo (as in n. 1), II, 1700, figs 79, 80, unmistakably reveals the derivation.

114. See Bonet Correa (as in n. 109), fig. 6, for the Casa Allende portal; and see p. 30 for the 'absoluta seguridad' that the two doorways are by the same architect, the certitude rather being that they are both sourced from the same engravings in Pozzo.

115. Bonet Correa (as in n. 109), p. 34.

116. See J. Carduso, 'Notas sobra a Antigua Pintura Religiosa em Pernambuco', *Revista do Serviço do Património histórico e artistico nacional* (hereafter *RSPHAN*), III, 1939, pp. 45–62, esp. p. 46 and the fourth unnumbered fig. after p. 54, for Sepulveda's S. Pedro dos Clérigos ceiling.

117. See S. Leite, *Artes e oficios dos jesuitas no Brasil 1549–1760*, Lima and Rio de Janeiro 1953.

118. N. Batista, 'Caetano da Costa Coelho e a pintura da igreja da Ordem 3a de S. Francisco da Penitência', *RSPHAN* (as in n. 116), V, 1941, pp. 129–54, esp. pp. 131, 139–40, 145; see p. 131 on the 'pintura de todo o teto que há de ser da melhor perspectiva'.

119. G. Bazin, *L'architecture religieuse baroque au Brésil*, 2 vols, Paris and São Paulo 1956–58, II, p. 52; C. del Negro, *Contribuição ao estudo da pintura mineira*, Rio de Janeiro 1958, p. 135, on Pozzo as source for Caetano de Costa Coelho's ceiling fresco at São Francisco da Penitência, Rio de Janeiro. See *AKL* (as in n. 52), XX, 1998, pp. 119–20, on Costa Coelho (Rio 1709–49) for the 1737–43 date of the ceiling fresco.

120. Bazin (as in n. 119), p. 52, pl. 155. See R. Pontual, *Dicionário das Artes Plásticas no Brasil*, Rio de Janeiro 1969, p. 90, and M. Hill, 'Francisco Xavier de Brito: um artista desconhecido no Brasil e em Portugal', *Revista do Instituto de Filosofia, Artes e Cultura* (Ouro Prêto), III, 1996, pp. 46–51 on Brito (d. Ouro Prêto 1751).

121. M. Ribeiro, 'A pintura de perspectiva em minas colonial', *Barroco*, X, 1978/79, pp. 27–37, esp. p. 31; see Del Negro (as in n. 119), pp. 21–3, pl. opp. p. 24, for Belo's decoration of the ceiling of the choir at the Matriz de Cachoeira do Campo, dated 1755–56. For Antônio Rodrigues Belo's place of birth, see the documents in J. Martins, in *Dicionário de artistas e artífices dos séculos XVIII e XIX em Minas Gerais*, 2 vols, Rio de Janeiro 1974, I, the two documents at pp. 111–12, both describing him as a native of Porto, the latter as aged 40 in 1742.

122. See Ribeiro (as in n. 121), figs 4–5.

123. M. Andrade Ribeiro de Oliveira, 'Pintura de perspectiva em Minas colonial – ciclo Rococó', *Barroco*, XII, 1983, pp. 171–80, esp. p. 173. On Athaide, see I. P. de Menezes, *Manoel da Costa Athaide*, Belo Horizonte 1965, F. Teixeira de Salles, *Vila Rica do Pilar (um roteiro de Ouro Prêto)*, Belo Horizonte 1965, p. 128, and Martins (as in n. 121), I, pp. 79–97.

124. See De Menezes (as in n. 123), p. 10 and figs 1–4, for Athaide's accurate copies from L. A. Demarne, *Histoire sacrée de la Providence*, 3 vols, Paris 1728, I, pls 42, 46, the Annunciation of the Birth of Isaac (after Raphael) and the Sacrifice of Isaac (after Rubens) in the choir at São Francisco de Assis.

125. See De Menezes (as in n. 123), p. 15, and Andrade Ribeiro de Oliveira (as in n. 123), pl. 9–12, esp. pl. 9, for the painting in the nave of São Francisco de Assis dating from 1801–12.

126. Teixeira de Salles (as in n. 123), p. 126.

127. See De Menezes (as in n. 123), p. 43, p. 99 doc. 49 and p. 108 doc. 58; Andrade Ribeiro de Oliveira (as in n. 123), p. 173 and p. 179 n. 12, implied that the school was founded; José

Arnaldo, Professor of Art History at the Universidad Federal in Mariana, is convinced that Athaide never realized this aspiration (verbal communication, at Mariana, February 2001).

128. Andrade Ribeiro de Oliveira (as in n. 123), pp. 176, 179 n. 24; and pls 26–9.

129. Pontual (as in n. 120), p. 451, on Simões Ribeiro's activity at Salvador for twenty years up to his death there in 1755.

130. Ribeiro (as in n. 121), p. 30, and see Pontual (as in n. 120), p. 455, on Rocha (? 1737 – Salvador 1807).

131. See C. Ott, 'José Joaquim da Rocha', RSPHAN (as in n. 116), XV, 1961, pp. 71–108, esp. pp. 78–80 and fig. 1, on the Conceiçao ceiling; see p. 80 for Ott's hypothesis of Rocha's Italian journey. See C. Ripa, Iconologia, Padua 1603, pp. 332–9 (Padua 1611, pp. 355–61; Padua 1624, pp. 437–43) for Ripa's personifications of the continents.

132. Pontual (as in n. 120), p. 451.

133. See Ott (as in n. 131), pp. 84–5 and fig. 3, for these decorations of c. 1785.

134. See Hill (as in n. 120), p. 50 and figs 6–10, on the Pilar altar of 1746–51.

135. See De Menezes (as in n. 123), p. 26, on Athaide's gildings and mouldings, and fig. 22 for his doorways at São Francisco de Assis, which relate to Pozzo (as in n. 1), II, 1700, fig. 104 (the designs on the left and right), fig. 105 (the design on the right).

136. Compare D. Garcia Figueira, Cidades históricas e o Barroco Mineiro, Belo Horizonte 2000, p. 155, fig. 89, with Pozzo (as in n. 1), II, 1700, figs 61, 63.

137. See Pozzo (as in n. 1), II, 1700, fig. 62, for the Luis Gonzaga altar; fig. 64 for the two-columned design.

138. Compare Pozzo (as in n. 1), II, 1700, fig. 60, with the Ignatius altar at the Bom Jesus sanctuary, Goa, reproduced in J. Pereira, Baroque India: The Neo-Roman Religious Architecture of South Asia: A Global Stylistic Survey, New Delhi 2000, pl. 7.

139. J. Pereira, Baroque Goa: The Architecture of Portuguese India, New Delhi 1995, pp. 84–5.

140. See Pereira (as in n. 139) p. 34, for the first coining of 'Pozzoan pediment', of the façades of the Espirito Santo at Morhgoum, St Aleixus at Kurhtori and S. Joaquim at Morhgoum-Bod-ddem; and Pereira (as in n. 138), pl. 28a–d and fig. 43c, for further 'Pozzoan pediments'; also ibid. p. 86 on Pozzo's sources.

141. P. Rheinbay, 'Nadal's Religious Iconography Reinterpreted by Aleni for China', in 'Scholar from the West': Giulio Aleni S.J. (1582–1619) and the Dialogue between Christianity and China, T. Lippiello and R. Malek eds, Brescia and Sankt Augustin 1995, pp. 323–31, esp. p. 326.

142. M. Sullivan, 'Some Possible Sources of European Influence on Late Ming and Early Ch'ing Painting', in Proceedings of the International Symposium on Chinese Painting, Taipei 1972, pp. 595–625, esp. p. 604. On Ruggieri (b. Naples 1543, China 1579–88, d. Salerno 1607), see H. Cordier, Bibliographie des ouvrages publiés en Chine par les Européens au XVIIe au XVIIIe siècle, Paris 1901, pp. 42–3, and H. Bernard, 'Les adaptations chinoises d'ouvrages européens: bibliographie chronologique depuis la venue des Portugais à Canton jusqu'à la Mission Française de Pékin', Monumenta Serica, X, 1945, pp. 1–57, 309–88, and XIX, 1960, pp. 349–83, esp. p. 26.

143. M. Nicolau, Jerónimo Nadal, S.I. (1507–1580); sus obras y doctrinas espirituales, Madrid 1949; see Rheinbay (as in n. 141), p. 325, on the EHI as 'enormous investment'.

144. Rheinbay (as in n. 141), p. 326.

145. On Ricci see M. Sullivan, The Meeting of Eastern and Western Art: From the Sixteenth Century to the Present Day, London 1973, pp. 47–58. See also Sullivan (as in n. 142), p. 605, and Rheinbay (as in n. 141), p. 326.

146. Sullivan (as in n. 142), p. 605.

147. See Nicolau (as in n. 143), pp. 180–85 on Chinese editions of Nadal, and pls V–XV for comparisons of their iconography with that of their prototype; G. A. Bailey, Art on the Jesuit Missions in Asia and Latin America, 1542–1773, Toronto 1999, pls 53–5, 57 for juxtapositions of engravings from the EHI and woodblocks in the edition by Ricci's colleague Juan de Rocha for the Metodo de Rosario / Song nian zhu gui cheng of 1608. See Rheinbay (as in n. 141), p. 329, for Dong Qichang's 'probable' authorship of the woodcuts.

148. Sullivan (as in n. 142), p. 605.

149. M. Kao, 'European Influences in Chinese Art, Sixteenth to Eighteenth Centuries', in China and

Europe: Images and Influences in Sixteenth to Eighteenth Centuries, T. H. C. Lee ed., Hong Kong 1991, pp. 251–303, esp. p. 253.

150. Yang T'ing-yün, *Hsi-Hsüeh Fan*, cited after Kao (as in n. 149), p. 253.

151. Bernard (as in n. 142), p. 45.

152. G. B. Du Halde, *Description geographique, historique, chronologique, politique et physique de l'Empire de la Chine*, 4 vols, Paris 1735, see III, pp. 271–89 on astronomy, engraving between pp. 288 and 289, and his *A Description of the Empire of China*, 2 vols, London 1738–41, esp. II, pp. 128–39.

153. B. S. Hall, 'The Didactic and the Elegant: Some Thoughts on Scientific and Technical Illustrations in the Middle Ages and Renaissance', in *Picturing Knowledge: Historical and Philosophical Problems Concerning the Use of Art in Science*, ed. B. S. Baigrie, Toronto 1996, pp. 3–39, esp. pp. 24–5 for a comparison of the illustration of a windlass crankshaft in A. Ramelli, *Le diverse et artificiose machine*, Paris 1588, and in *Ji Qi Tu Shuo*, Beijing 1627.

154. Bailey (as in n. 147), p. 82.

155. Du Halde, *Description* (as in n. 152), III, p. 269; see Cordier (as in n. 142), pp. 8–10, on Buglio (b. Mineo 1606, arr. China 1637, d. Beijing 1682).

156. Thieme–Becker, XIII, pp. 523–4, *AKL Bio-bibliographischer Index*, 10 vols, Leipzig and Munich 1999–2000, IV, p. 145, for Gherardini (b. Modena 1654, China c. 1698–1702, d. 1723). See Sullivan (as in n. 145), pp. 60–1, on Gherardini's brief sojourn in China.

157. Du Halde, *Description* (as in n. 152), III, p. 116: 'Le platfond est tout-à-fait peint: il est divisé en trois parties: le milieu représente un dôme tout ouvert d'une riche architecture: ce sont des colonnes de marbre, qui portent un rang d'arcades surmonté d'une belle balustrade. Les colonnes sont elles-mêmes enchassées dans une autre balaustrade d'un beau dessin, avec des vases de fleurs fort bien placez.'

158. See Bailey (as in n. 147), p. 110, fig. 61, for the interior of 1703.

159. Bailey (as in n. 147), pp. 109–10.

160. On Castiglione (b. Milan 1688, arr. Beijing 1715, d. Beijing 1766/8), see C. and M. Beurdeley, *Giuseppe Castiglione: A Jesuit Painter at the Court of the Chinese Emperors*, (1971) transl. from French by M. Bullock, London 1972. For Castiglione's professed apprenticeship to Pozzo see G. R. Loehr, 'Un artista fiorentino a Pechino nel Settecento', *Antichità viva*, II, 3, 1963, pp. 43–56, esp. p. 44, citing Archivo Romano Societatis Jesu, Jap. Sin. 184, p. 41; and see R. Kanz in *AKL* (as in n. 52), XVII, p. 226, on the uncertainty whether Castiglione studied from Pozzo directly or via the *Perspectiva*.

161. Loehr (as in n. 160), p. 44; Beurdeley (as in n. 160), p. 136. Cao Yiqiang, *Anxiety and Expedience: A Study of Chinese Artistic Relations with the West from the Ming to the Early Twentieth Century*, forthcoming, prefers *The Theory of Vision*. I am grateful to Yiqiang for having shown me a draft towards his Chapter II , 'An Effort without a Response: Nian Xiyao (? – 1739) and his study of scientific perspective'.

162. Du Halde, *Description* (as in n. 152), III, p. 268; Du Halde, *A Description* (as in n. 152), II, p. 126.

163. Du Halde, *Description* (as in n. 152), III, pp. 268–9; Du Halde, *A Description* (as in n. 152), II, p. 126; C. Clunas, *Art in China*, Oxford 1997, p. 78.

164. Bernard (as in n. 142), XIX, 1960, pp. 364–75 on Emperors Kanxi and Youngzhen's attitudes to Western culture and Sino-European publishing. Beurdeley (as in n. 160), pp. 32–7 on Youngzhen.

165. Beurdeley (as in n. 160), pp. 27, 47, 136; Yiqiang (as in n. 161) on Nian Xiyao; Clunas (as in n. 163), p. 78 on Qing cultural politics.

166. Beurdeley (as in n. 160), p. 142.

167. Loehr (as in n. 160), p. 44.

168. Loehr (as in n. 160), p. 44. *Shixue*, ed. Nian Xayao, (1st ed. Beijing 1729) Beijing 1735. The preface to the edition of 1735 is translated into bad English in J. J. Lee, 'The Origin of Japanese Landscape Prints: A Study in the Synthesis of Eastern and Western Art', PhD thesis, University of Washington 1977, pp. 602–5, esp. p. 602. I am grateful to Asao Sarukawa for drawing my attention to Lee's thesis.

169. Yiqiang (as in n. 161).

170. Ibid.

171. Bodleian Library, Chin. Douce B. 2.

172. Viator (as in n. 11), 1505, sig. Avr–v; Viator (as in n. 11), 1509, sigs Avv, Bir.

173. The sequence in *Shixue* from pp. '38'–'40' relates to Vignola-Danti (as in n. 17), 'Teorema Primo', p. 17. Compare, for instance, *Shixue*, p. '38' diagram at top left with J. Cousin, *Livre de Perspective*, Paris 1560, sig. B iv 'Pavé' (pavement) design. Similarly, compare *Shixue*, p. '39' bottom right with Serlio (as in n. 9), fol. 36v; also *Shixue*, p. '41' top left with Serlio (as in n. 9), fols 23r and 24r and Dubreuil (as in n. 26), I, 'Traité II Pratiques des Plans en Perspective', esp. p. 34.

174. Compare *Shixue* (as in n. 168), p. '43' diagram at bottom left with Dubreuil (as in n. 26), I, 'Traité III Pratiques des Elevations Perspectives', esp. p. 48, top.

175. Compare *Shixue* (as in n. 168), p. '43' diagram at top left with Dubreuil (as in n. 26), I, 'Traité III Pratiques des Elevations Perspectives', esp. p. 45, top.

176. R. Palmer, 'Adaptations of European Print Imagery in two Andean *Sillerías* of circa 1600', in *Raising the Eyebrow: John Onians and World Art Studies*, ed. L. Golden, Oxford 2001, pp. 229–52, esp. p. 229.

177. Compare *Shixue* (as in n. 168), p. '97' with Vignola-Danti (as in n. 17), 'Annotatione Terza Della digradatione del cerchio nel secondo esempio', pp. 77–8, esp. p. 77.

178. *Shixue* (as in n. 168), p. '146'.

179. See Lee (as in n. 168), fig. 130.

180. Lee (as in n. 168), p. 604.

181. Yiqiang (as in n. 161).

182. On early Chinese woodcuts, see M. Cohen and N. Monnat, *Impressions de Chine*, Paris 1992, esp. pp. 42–4 and 46–7 for woodcut scrolls which the authors date to the eighth century; on the woodcut dated the equivalent of 868 AD of *The Buddha Discoursing to Subhuti*, see L. Binyon, *A Catalogue of Japanese and Chinese Woodcuts Preserved in the Sub-Department of Oriental Prints and Drawings in the British Museum*, London 1916, p. 576; for woodcuts of the tenth century, R. Whitfield & A. Farrer, *Caves of the Thousand Buddhas, Chinese Art from the Silk Route*, London 1990, pp. 101–4, 106–7.

183. Lee (as in n. 168), 'The Real Origin of Uki-e', pp. 219–45.

184. Lee (as in n. 168), p. 240 n. 72 on the copy of the *Shixue* formerly in the collection of Naitó Konan (1866–1934), Professor of Chinese Studies at the University of Kyoto; fig. 51 for Kiyotada's painting of the Ichimura theatre.

185. Lee (as in n. 168), p. 235.

186. Lee (as in n. 168), p. 236.

187. Lee (as in n. 168), p. 238.

6.1a   Engraving by Vincenzo Mariotti after Andrea Pozzo, first frontispiece to
Perspectiva, vol. I, 1693

6.1b   Replica of 1693 frontispiece, in reverse with alterations to text, engraving after Pozzo, in *Rules and Examples of Perspective*, London 1707, first frontispiece

6.2a   Engraving after Andrea Pozzo, second frontispiece to *Perspectiva pictorum et architectorum*, vol. I, 1693

ARCH. VITRUVE
ARCH. ANDR. PAL LA DIO
Vides tabellam rectangulam A, cui
agglutinata est pagina et regulam
B quæ cum assere transverso normam
componit: Si applices asserem late-
ribus tabellæ, regulà designabis
quotcunque volueris lineas pa-
rallelas aut normales.
A
On the Table A exactly squar'd, as
you see here, fix the Paper, and
the Rule B, having a Cross-stock
serves as a Square, by the applica-
tion of which Stock to the Sides
of the Table, you draw by the
Rule what Parallel or Perpen
-dicular Lines you have amind
to.
B
REGOLA
DELLI CINQVE
ORDINI
D'ARCHITETTURA
DI M. IAC. BAROZZIO
DA VIGNOLA.

6.2b Second frontispiece to Andrea Pozzo, *Rules and Examples of Perspective*, London 1707 edition, second frontispiece

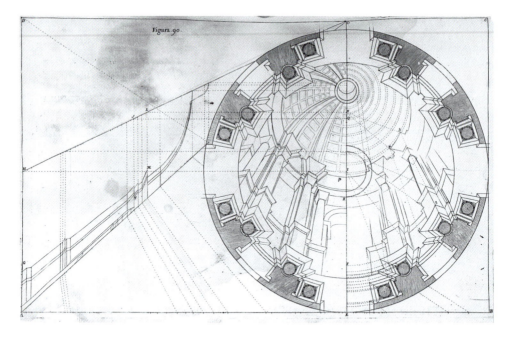

6.3a Demonstration of how to design a fictive cupola to an acentral viewpoint, engraving in Pozzo, *Perspectiva*, I, 1693, fig. 90

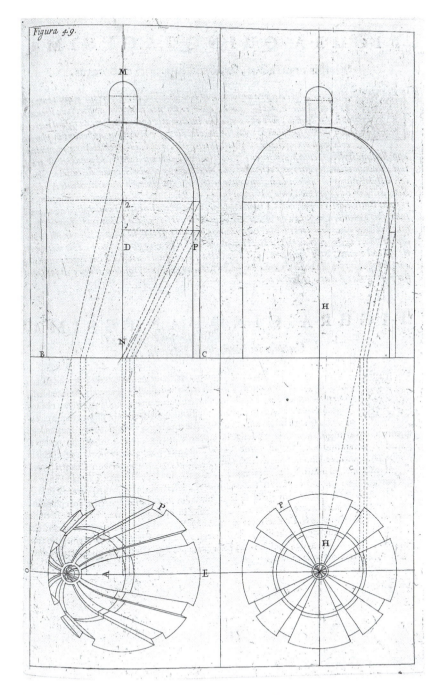

6.3b   Demonstrations of how to design fictive cupolas to acentral and central viewpoints, engraving in Pozzo, *Perspectiva*, II, 1700, fig. 49

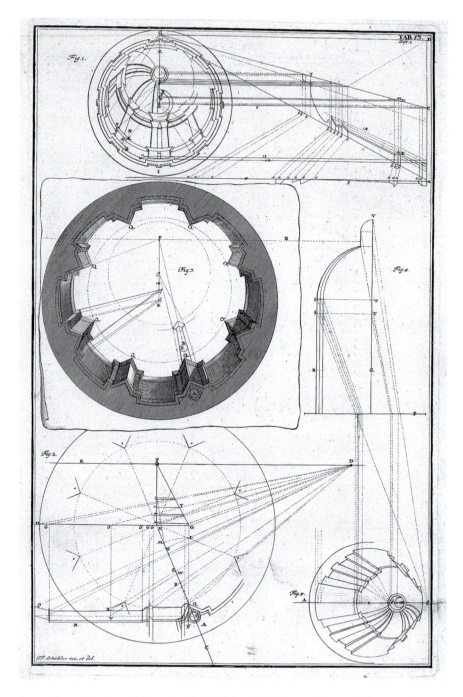

6.4a   Engraving from Johann Jacob Schübler in his *Perspectiva*, vol. II, 1720, pl. 13: adaptations of figures from Pozzo, *Perspectiva*, I–II, 1693–1700

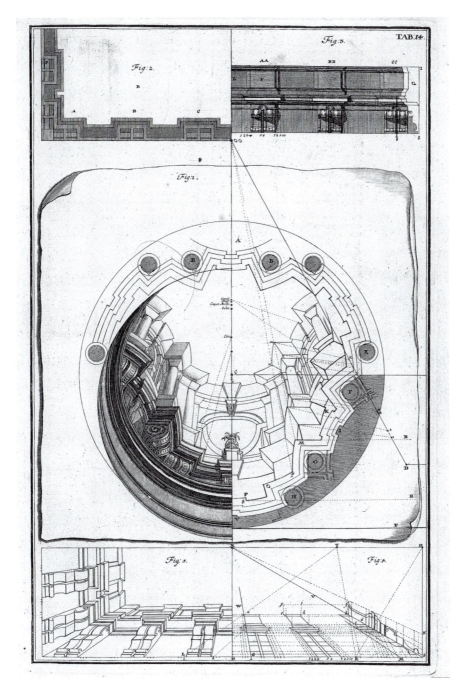

6.4b   Engraving from Johann Jacob Schübler in his *Perspectiva*, vol. II, 1720, pl. 14: adaptations of figures from Pozzo, *Perspectiva*, I, 1693

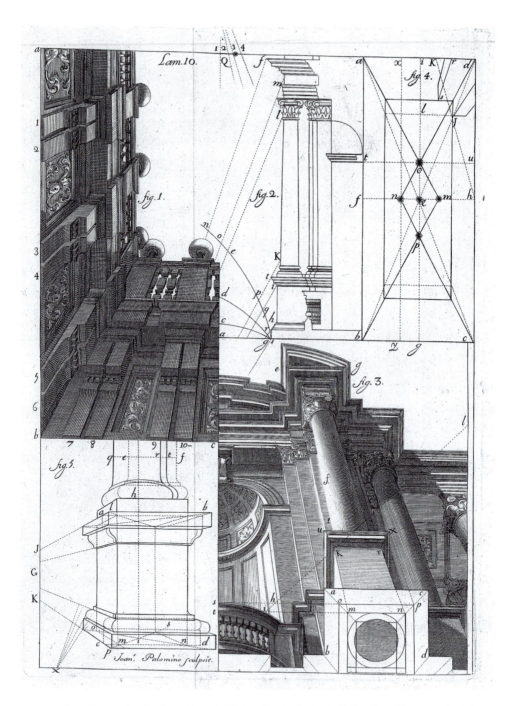

6.5   Engraving by Juan Bernabé Palomino in Antonio Palomino, *El museo pictórico, y escala optica*, vol. II, 1724: adaptations of figures from Pozzo, *Perspectiva*, I–II, 1693–1700

6.6a   Georg Vinterer, altar of St Ignatius, Quito, Compañía, transept, 1740s

6.6b   Georg Conrad Bodenehr, engraving of Pozzo's altar to the Blessed Luis
Gonzaga, S. Ignazio, Rome, via Pozzo, *Perspectiva*, II, 1700, fig. 62 in the Augsburg
1709 edition, vol. II

6.6c   Georg Conrad Bodenehr, engraving of Pozzo's altar of St Ignatius, S. Ignazio, Rome, via Pozzo, *Perspectiva*, II, 1700, fig 60 in the Augsburgh 1709 edition, vol. II.

6.7   Nian Xiyao, *Shixue*, 1735 edition: frontispiece, derived from that to Andrea Pozzo, *Perspectiva*, I, 1693 (but omitting text), woodcut

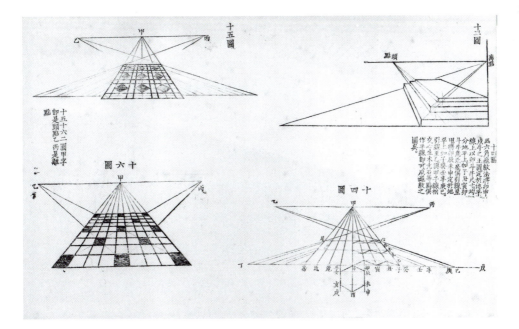

6.8   Nian Xiyao, *Shixue*, 1735 edition: p. '40', demonstrations of distance-point perspective, woodcut

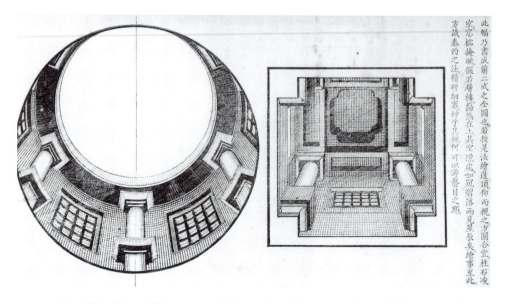

此幅乃畫成前二式之全圖也若按是法繪蓬頂仰而視之弓圓合宜柱石凌
空窓櫺掩映微若層樓歸然在上其空隙處如冠碧落而見星辰矣繪事至此
方識泰西之法精研御密神乎其神何可以游藝目之耶。

6.9   Nian Xiyao, *Shixue*, 1735 edition: p. '104', demonstrations of illusionistic domes in perspective, woodcut

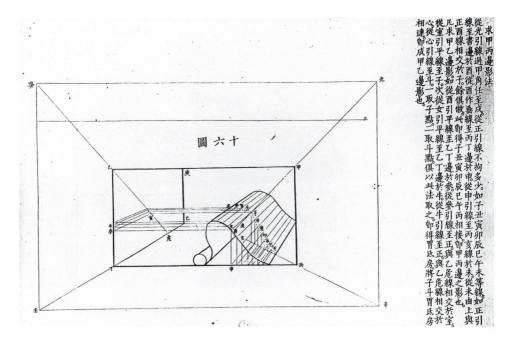

求甲丙邊影法
從光引線過甲角任
線至書邊於甲從
正酉線相交於甲從
凡求甲乙邊影如
從室引平線至子次
心從心引線至斗一取
相連即成甲乙邊影也

從光引線過甲角任至戌從正引
線至書邊於甲從酉作垂線至丙即得申
正酉線相交於甲餘倣此如子丑寅卯辰
凡求甲乙邊影如從酉引平線得子丑於室
從室引平線至子次從女引平線至乙丁邊於室
心從心引線至斗一取子點二取斗點俱以此法取
相連即成甲乙邊影也

線引正從如線等未午巳辰卯寅丑子如少多拘不線
即得胃氏房將子丑胃氏房於室交相線危乙與線引甲於接相丙午巳引午丙至線引申於未上由未從亥至線引巳於申從電正得即丙至線引丁從酉

6.10   Nian Xiyao, *Shixue*, 1735 edition: p. '134', demonstration of how to represent a
scroll in perspective, woodcut

7

Photography in nineteenth-century art publications

Anthony Hamber

The significance of the photographic reproduction of works of art during the middle of the nineteenth century is still an emergent field of enquiry.[1] This use of probably the most influential image process yet to be invented was seen by both its inventors and early practitioners to be one of its most prominent applications. Roger Fenton (1819–70), one of the leading English photographers of the 1850s, placed much emphasis on the kudos bestowed by his becoming the first official photographer at the British Museum. The mid-Victorian photographic art publication was a primary channel through which a knowledge of art covering a wide gamut of periods, schools and geographic regions was disseminated to an eager public.

This essay aims to demonstrate the scope, diversity and impact of photographic reproduction of Renaissance art from 1840 to 1880. Publications with photographic reproductions of Renaissance art began to appear in small but significant numbers during the early 1850s. The 1860s saw an explosion in photographic publications and by 1870 the impact this development had on scholars of Renaissance art was being acknowledged in print. Many thousands of photographs were commercially available and these were disseminated through an international network of dealers. Evaluation of the contemporary impact of photographic reproductions is still in its infancy. The career of John Charles Robinson (1824–1913) at the South Kensington Museum during the middle years of the nineteenth century allows a revealing case study. This essay will set the scene by describing the diversity of photographic publications circulating in mid-nineteenth-century England, and analyze Robinson's contribution.

While the announcements in 1839 of the discovery of photographic processes by Louis-Jacques-Mandé Daguerre (1787–1851) and William Henry Fox Talbot (1800–77) caused a considerable stir within scientific circles, for a variety of technical and economic reasons the 1840s saw little use of photographic illustration in book, serial or periodical publications. However, by 1840 the possibility of photomechanical illustrations accompanying text had been demonstrated by the publication in Vienna of Joseph Berres's *Phototyp nach der Erfindung des Prof. Berres in Wien*.[2] Berres (1796–1844) was Professor of Anatomy at the University of Vienna. He developed a photomechanical heliogravure process based on the chemical etching of Daguerreotype plates. Probably because only a limited number of prints could be pulled from the etched Daguerreotype plates, *Phototyp*, which contains a short text and five photo-mechanical illustrations, had an estimated print run of around 200 copies. The five illustrations show a sculpture entitled *Amor*, an anonymous copperplate engraving depicting *Judith and Holofernes* and three views of Vienna, including the Cathedral of St Stephen and Ferdinand's Bridge on the Danube Canal. These images were separately printed and were not inserted into text pages.

In *Phototyp*, Berres stated that

The path which was opened through my new art of etching pictures (gravure) – when used properly – can hardly be measured in advance, nor can the extent [of its significance] be grasped:

1) All 'visible' objects can, in a clear light, be photographed and etched, and all views of towns, landscapes, military positions etc. can therefore be communicated quickly through print.

2) With the 'Hydro-Orygengas-Microscope' the unaided eye can have 'invisible' objects enlarged, photographed, etched and duplicated.

3) Copper-plates can be produced either in an object's original size or in any other desired form and in every other size and can be multiplied in the new format.

4) The same also applies to maps, situation drawings, hand-written and printed materials etc. It will thus be possible to produce identical copies of old, rare and out of print copper-plates and typographical works, without damaging the original in the slightest degree.

5) Also oil paintings, portraits of living people and illustrations of diverse natural-historic objects can be reproduced faithfully, etched and used in print and distributed.[3]

Although very few examples of Berres's publication and of his other photomechanical experiments survive it seems that he did make images of a significant proportion – if not all – of the subjects he described. While Berres extensively marketed his process, sending samples to institutions and journals in major European capitals, he did not spawn an immediate uptake of photomechanical reproduction. Nonetheless, Berres's *Phototyp* had clear implications for art reproduction, a point underlined by the fact that when he presented his process to the Imperial Society of Physicians in Vienna on

30 April 1840 he included a print after an engraving of a girl with a butterfly by 'Stöber'.[4]

The first photographic publication to make a major impact was Talbot's *The Pencil of Nature*, published in several parts by Longman, Brown, Green and Longmans of London between June 1844 and April 1846. It set a tangible benchmark in that the forthcoming publication was advertised, and it received reviews in periodicals such as the *Athenaeum*. Most of the 24 images in *The Pencil of Nature*, hand-mounted original photographic paper prints from paper negatives on separate pages, were of exterior views of buildings. However, Talbot's text to plate XI, 'Copy of a lithographic print', stated that 'this application of the art is a very important one … because it enables us at pleasure to alter the scale, and to make the copies as much larger or smaller than the originals as we may desire'.[5] Plate XXIII is a reproduction of a lithograph by Johann Nepomuk Strixner (1782–1855) after a sketch of *Hagar in the Desert* by Pier Francesco Mola (1612–66) from Strixner's *Les Œuvres lithographiques. Contenant un choix de dessins d'après les grands maîtres de toutes les écoles des Musées de sa Majestè le Roi de Bavière*, published in Munich between 1810 and 1816 under the direction of Johann Christian von Mannichlich, the Director of the Bavarian Royal Museums and Galleries. Talbot wrote of such use of photography: 'Fac-similes can be made from original sketches of the old masters, and thus they may be preserved from loss, and multiplied to any extent.'[6]

The Pencil of Nature received mixed reviews and its publication was effectively discontinued after Part VI though the initial advertisement for Part I, published in June 1844, stated: 'It is proposed to publish the Work in Ten or Twelve Monthly Parts, in Royal quarto, price Twelve Shillings each, each Part containing Five Plates, with descriptive letter-press.'[7]

During the 1840s Talbot was involved in three other ventures that promoted the photographic illustration of art publications. While these were valiant failures they did highlight the possibilities of photographic illustration both for the specialist and for more mainstream art publications. In 1846 Talbot agreed to produce sample photographs for insertion in the June issue of the serial publication *Art-Union*, later renamed *Art-Journal*. Around 6,000 photographs, of different subject matter and size, were produced for this venture. Since all the photographs had to be hand printed using daylight, Talbot was driven, for reasons of productivity, to use almost any suitable negative available, though he avoided paintings, engravings and graphic art. Many images depict architecture and a few sculptures. One such image was a copy of *The Rape of the Sabine Woman* by Giambologna. However, once again Talbot failed to inspire either the public or publishers to adopt his reprographic process. The *Art-Journal* did not adopt photographic or photomechanical illustration and continued to use engraving until the last decade of the century.

In spite of the setbacks that befell him, Talbot continued with his attempts to promote the use of his photographic process for book illustration. In 1848 the fourth volume of William Stirling's *Annals of the Artists of Spain*, containing 66 Talbotype photographs, was issued.[8] Stirling's book was a scholarly work that had a significant effect on the understanding of Spanish art in England. Most of the photographs were from reproductions (mainly lithographs and engravings) of originals, but some of the Talbotypes were from original works, many of which were in the collection of Richard Ford whose highly influential *A Hand-Book for Travellers in Spain* had been published in 1845. The illustrations also included two small bas-reliefs (purchased by Stirling in Seville in 1832 and now in the Brinsley Ford collection), which Stirling stated were 'perhaps the sole specimens of the national Spanish sculpture in England, [and] are probably the first which have as yet been reproduced by a mechanical process',[9] three original drawings by Murillo (plates 56, 57, 58) and one by Alonso Cano (plate 41). Stirling also stated that 'I believe I may safely assert that the drawings by Cano (41) and Murillo (56, 57), are the only original works of these masters ever copied by the Sun.'[10] Another significant feature is that four of the Talbotypes are from reduced oil copies by Pedro Roldán of works by Murillo in the Museum at Seville. Whether these were made specifically for this publication is unclear. However, two photographs were taken directly from two paintings by Goya, *Boys playing at Soldiers* and *Boys playing at See-Saw*, in Stirling's own collection. This edition of Stirling's publication was clearly targeted at a very specialist and scholarly sector of the art publishing market. Unfortunately, it was not widely reviewed at the time of its publication.

Talbot's concentration on specialist art books with a very limited print run was underlined in 1849 by a publication entitled *Specimens of Portraits Engraved in Spain during the Seventeenth Century and now Reproduced by the Sun*. Published by Henneman and Malone in London, with a text by William Stirling and illustrated with ten photographs of seventeenth-century Spanish engravings, it failed to receive extensive reviews.[11]

During the 1850s art publications with photographic illustrations began to appear in greater numbers, but photography was still mainly used for scholarly rather than popular purposes. In 1853, with the aid of the *catalogue raisonné* in Johann David Passavant's biography of Raphael, which had been published in 1839, Prince Albert began a campaign to create an album of prints of all of Raphael's works.[12] Later, the scope of the project was extended to include related drawings and engravings, intended to show the evolution of a painting from the first sketch to the final work. Albert contacted owners of Raphael drawings so that the 'Raphael Collection' in Windsor might be as complete as possible. Since many of Raphael's works had never been reproduced in any form, the Prince perceived that photography might be brought into use. As Carl Ruland, a librarian who was responsible for the material in the Print Room in Windsor Castle and who completed the project after the Prince Consort's death, wrote in the introduction to the finished publication, 'most fortunately the newly invented art of photography stepped in to supply the means for the introduction into the collection of facsimiles of unimpeachable fidelity'.[13]

Owners often did not send photographs of their own accord, thus necessitating the commissioning of photography both at home and abroad. In England the contracted photographers included William Bambridge, Leonida Caldesi, Joseph Cundall, Philip Delamotte, Robert Howlett, Frederick Molini, Gustave Rejlander and Charles Thurston Thompson. Elsewhere, photographers included William Lake Price and Pietro Dovizielli, who carried out work in Rome, the Alinari brothers in Florence and Robert Bingham, who photographed in the Louvre. The set of volumes resulting from this project entitled *The Works of Raphael Santi da Urbino as Represented in the Raphael Collection in the Royal Library at Windsor Castle, Formed by H.R.H. the Prince Consort, 1853–1861 and Completed by Her Majesty Queen Victoria* is one of the first applications of photography to the creation of an illustrated *catalogue raisonné* of a major Italian Renaissance painter.

A quarter of a century after the publication of *The Pencil of Nature* photography was acknowledged to have brought about a revolution in the study of art. John Charles Robinson succinctly described this phenomenon in the introduction to his catalogue of the drawings by Michelangelo and Raphael in Oxford, published in 1870.[14] This book, which is completely unillustrated, was described by Francis Haskell as 'perhaps the single most important contribution to scholarly connoisseurship made by an Englishman in the nineteenth century'.[15] Robinson wrote in his introduction:

But the invention of photography has in our own time effected an entire revolution: the drawings of the ancient masters may now be multiplied virtually without limit: and thus, what was before a practical impossibility, namely, the actual comparison of the numerous dispersed drawings of any particular master, has become quite practicable. For the purpose of his present undertaking, the writer has been enabled to make use of photography in the most complete manner. ... The comprehensive work of Passavant, though abounding in errors, a great proportion of which the art of photography, had it been available in that writer's time, would have enabled him to avoid, was of great service.[16]

There are two key points to underline in this quotation: first, that by 1870 the scale and scope of photographic dissemination of Italian Renaissance drawing had had a profound effect on the academic study of this subject; secondly that Robinson's reference to the 'complete manner' of his use of photography documents the diversity of the forms of photographic publishing at the end of the second third of the nineteenth century. However, Robinson seems to have been unusual in his emphatic appreciation of photography as a primary professional tool and only considerably more research will indicate to what degree it was shared amongst his peers.

The purchases of photographs by the South Kensington Museum during the second half of the 1860s, as recorded in the museum's Photograph Register, indicate some of the photographic resources Robinson had available to him. For instance, in April 1868 the museum purchased from Williams & Norgate, the specialist London dealer of German language books, for £1. 7s., J. Sighart's photographically illustrated *The Lord's Supper. Christ and His Twelve Disciples. From the Original Crayon-Drawings of Leonardo da Vinci in the Possession of Her Royal Highness the Grand Dutchess of Saxe-Weimar by John Neissen*. This title had been published by Frederick Bruckmann in London the same year. In May and June the following year the museum purchased 384 mounted photographs by Adolphe Braun of 'drawings and sculpture by the Old Masters' and that October it purchased from the dealer Colnaghi *Drawings of the Old Masters in the Collection of the Duke of Rutland, Belvoir Castle. Photographed from the Originals. By Lt. Col. Stuart Wortley.*[17]

Robinson's use of photographic illustration can be dated from as early as 1856 when he wrote the *Catalogue of the Soulages Collection; Being a Descriptive Inventory of a Collection of Works of Decorative Art, Formerly in the Possession of M. Jules Soulages of Toulouse, Now ... Exhibited to the Public at the Museum of Ornamental Art, Marlborough House*, published by Chapman and Hall, London. This book contained ten mounted albumen print photographs.[18] In 1862 Robinson's catalogue to the South Kensington Museum's Italian sculpture collection was published by Chapman and Hall and was illustrated with line engravings based on photographs.[19] An important catalogue, it was still being issued as prizes to the Schools of Art over thirty years later. An edition with photographic illustrations, produced at the same time or later, included up to twelve albumen prints, and later editions included carbon prints taken from the same negatives. Curiously, the photographs used for these extra-illustrated editions frequently duplicated the existing line-engraved illustrations, that is, they were the very images from which the line engravings had been copied. (see Figures 7.1, 7.2). One of the photographs used in Robinson's catalogue of 1862 also appeared as a mounted carbon print in Charles Christopher Black's *Michael Angelo Buonarroti, Sculptor, Painter, Architect. The Story of His Life and Labours*, published in London in 1875 by Macmillan and Co.

In the title of this essay, the term 'art publications' was preferred to 'art books' since there were many different forms and contexts in which photographic reproductions of works of art were published during the second half of the nineteenth century, and which it is pertinent to elaborate upon here. Art publications illustrated with photographs included loose photographic prints and special formats such as the carte de visite and the Cabinet card.

Loose photographic prints

These varied considerably both in size and price. They might be purchased mounted on card or into albums, or left unmounted within portfolios built up by the owner. Small, thumbnail-size photographic images – frequently created by photographing engravings after original paintings – were marketed for use as border decoration within albums during the 1860s and 1870s. At the other extreme, very large photographic images, measuring more than half a metre square, were also sold as loose prints. Photographic publishers such as the Alinari brothers and Giacomo Brogi (in Florence), Adolphe Braun (of Dornach in Alsace), Frederick Bruckmann and Franz Hanfstaengl (both of Munich) and Carlo Naya (in Venice), amongst others, vigorously exploited these possibilities.

Some publishers aimed to cover as many market sectors as possible. One of the most successful photographic publications of the Department of Science and Art, based at the South Kensington Museum, during the late 1850s and early 1860s was the series of photographs taken by the department's photographer Charles Thurston Thompson (1816–68) directly from the Raphael Cartoons while they were still hung at Hampton Court. It was first advertised in the 1859 *Price List of Reproductions of Works of Art*; sizes ranged from 19.6 × 12.25 cm prints priced between 5d. and 7d., depending on the cartoon, through 36.75 × 27 cm, 56.35 × 36.75 cm and 76 × 51.5 cm to 117.6 × 73.5 cm photographs, the most expensive of which was 15s. 7½d. The photographs could be bought either in sets or singly. In comparison with engravings and other prints, the largest photograph was extremely cheap and sold so successfully that the photographs were republished in 1864 by Cundall & Downes, another photographic company specializing in photography of art and architecture.

Large-sized photographs, some coloured, were also produced for framing and hanging on the walls of houses throughout the country. The Arundel Society, founded in 1848, promoted such usage for its expensive chromolithographs, and experimented intermittently with photographic processes.[20]

Special photographic formats

THE CARTE DE VISITE

The carte de visite was patented in France by A. A. E. Disdéri (1819–89) in November 1854 and became particularly popular from the late 1850s onwards. Although primarily intended for the commercial portrait photography market, the format was extensively employed for the reproduction of the fine and decorative arts and of architecture. While it is difficult to determine to what extent carte de visite photographs were collected and used by mid-nineteenth-century art historians, they were clearly seen as a significant resource. The Photograph Register of the South Kensington Museum indicates that on several occasions John Charles Robinson acquired cartes de visite for the museum's photographic collection. These included eleven views of Burgos Cathedral, a single image of the Cathedral at Bordeaux and 57 images of 'celebrated paintings by the Old Masters' (probably from the Prado).[21] Most cartes de visite included printed information on both sides of the card on which the photographic image was mounted. There might be a caption beneath the image while on the verso of the card details of the photographer and publisher were frequent. It is significant that institutions such as the Department of Science and Art purchased the carte de visite to promote its aims and objectives, though it did not publish in this format. Cartes de visite of paintings were frequently created from prints rather than the original, though there are significant examples of cartes using negatives taken directly from the original itself, such as the reproduction of Leonardo's *Last Supper* (Figure 7.3). Widespread photographic 'piracy' in the illegal copying of cartes de visite significantly increased the influence of this format.

THE STEREOSCOPIC VIEW

Popular from the early 1850s, this format was used primarily to reproduce three-dimensional subject matter, such as sculpture and architecture (see Figure 7.4). Images could be purchased individually though they frequently formed part of named series, a fact prominently emphasized in the printed text on the front of the mount. Some publishers used the verso of the card for printed texts, sometimes printed directly onto the card, in other cases printed on paper that was trimmed and then manually pasted on. Serial publications of stereoscopic views accompanied by texts appeared from the late 1850s onwards; one of the most famous was *The Stereoscopic Magazine: A Gallery of Landscape Scenery, Architecture, Antiquities, and Natural History, Accompanied with Descriptive Articles by Writers of Eminence*, published in London between 1858 and 1865 by Lovell Reeve.

Large series were produced, such as the one published by the London Stereoscopic Company, devoted to the 1862 International Exhibition. By April 1863 it was reported that some 300,000 stereoscopic views of the interior and the exhibits had been sold, and the *Art-Journal*, with reference to the views of sculpture, stated that it was 'impossible to estimate too highly the importance of such works as these photographs as agents for refining and elevating the public taste'.[22]

In the mid-1860s, William England, one of the photographers who had carried out a large amount of the photography for the London Stereoscopic Company at the 1862 International Exhibition, published a series entitled *Gems of Statuary by Eminent Sculptors* that documented the work of contemporary British sculptors. However, sets of cartes de visite of Italian Renaissance sculptures do not appear to have been mass-produced. This was perhaps largely due to the geographic distribution of the original sculptures themselves.

Another series, published in 1864 by Cundall, Downes & Co. of London, underlines in its title the range of subject matter available. *One Hundred Stereoscopic Illustrations of Architecture and Natural History in Western India, Photographed by Major Gill and Described by James Fergusson* was just one of a number of books with photographic illustrations on Indian architecture for which James Fergusson (1808–86) wrote scholarly texts. Curiously, Fergusson did not use photographic illustration for his publications dealing with Western European architecture.

THE CABINET CARD

The Cabinet format, measuring 13.5 × 9.8cm, was proposed in England in 1866 in an attempt to stimulate the market for commercial photography that had boomed during the early 1860s and then fallen into a recession from 1863. Significantly larger than the carte de visite or the stereoscopic view, the verso of Cabinet cards was deployed by some publishers to print extended text describing the scene or object depicted. Albums designed to house this photographic format proliferated; one frequently finds albums that mix subject matter, for instance family portraits with those of royalty. Fine art and architectural reproduction was particularly popular and all the prominent photographic firms specializing in this market exploited this format. For instance, Goupil et Cie. made systematic use of the Cabinet card to market photographs of the paintings that had appeared in the annual Salon.

Portfolios of photographs

The convention of the portfolio of photographs followed in the tradition of publications of engravings. Photographers and photographic publishers would create large lists of photographs for sale. Individual photographs, which could be purchased separately as required, might then be selected and assembled by the publisher into sets or portfolios (some with accompanying short texts). The firm of Adolphe Braun of Dornach led the field in the creation of luxurious portfolios of photographs of the drawings and paintings of Italian Renaissance masters. The set of 25 carbon-print photographs of the Sistine Chapel by Adolphe Braun issued in 1869 proved to be one of the landmarks in the influence of photography on art historical scholarship. Not only did members of the art establishment become aware of this publication,[23] but institutions such as the Royal Academy and the South Kensington Museum acquired copies. However, the set was not cheap, the South Kensington Museum paying £50 for its copy. The museum was to acquire many of the portfolios in double-Elephant (up to 102 × 68 cm) format published by Braun during the 1870s and 1880s.

Art books with photographic illustrations

During the period covered by this essay the vast majority of art books with photographic illustrations included one of the three following types of photographic print: individually pasted-in, hand-printed original photo-graphs (primarily in the form of albumen prints); permanent photographs (using the carbon process); or photomechanical prints (such as the collotype or Woodburytype).

Many books were illustrated only with a photographic frontispiece; for instance, Herman Grimm's *Life of Michael Angelo*, published in 1865 by Smith, Elder and Co. of London, included a photographic frontispiece replicating a portrait of Michelangelo in the Vatican collection. The following year the same publisher issued Alfred von Wolzogen's *Raphael Santi. His Life and His Works*, which included a reproduction of an engraved head-and-shoulders portrait of Raphael (Figure 7.5). Revealingly, neither Wolzogen nor Grimm, both acknowledged scholars in the field of Italian Renaissance art, explicitly referred to the influence of photography.

Many books of the mid-nineteenth century had their photographic illustrations mounted on separate sheets of paper that were inserted into the printed text signatures. It was common to use a heavier stock to mount the photographs, usually on the recto of the sheet, leaving the verso unused. Sometimes the photographs were given a title and numbered. This form of construction was primarily practical; it enabled publishers to illustrate existing texts photographically, or to produce editions of the same text both with and without photographic illustrations. As we have seen, J. C. Robinson's *South Kensington Museum: Italian Sculpture of the Middle Ages and Period of the Revival of Art* of 1862 is one such example.

However, there were some notable exceptions to the design and production techniques outlined above. In 1860 the London-based French photographer Camille Silvy (1834–1910) published a photographic facsimile, the *Manuscrit Sforza: Fac-simile d'après le manuscrit original appartenant à M. le Marquis d'Azeglio, Ambassadeur de Sardaigne à Londres. Photographié et publié par C. Silvy.*[24] This publication was a facsimile of the entire manuscript to scale and the photographs were printed both on the recto and the verso of the pages. Unusually, the photographs were also full-page, that is, no paper support is visible. In the introduction, a reprint of a paper given by J. Vincent to the French Académie Impériale des Inscriptions et Belles-Lettres on 21 September 1860, Vincent indicated some of the advantages of photographic reproduction of manuscripts. These include the ability to reproduce the original in the exact dimensions, to enhance and restore faded text, and thus to facilitate scholarly research and the exchange of facsimiles between libraries, to the benefit of the general public.[25]

The inclusion of photographic illustrations on text pages had been considered as early as 1850. In that year *Promenades poétiques et daguerriennes. Bellevue (Seine-et-Oise). Avec sept vues prises au daguerréotype et reportées sur papier photographique, par Louis-Auguste Martin, Sténographe de l'Assemblée Nationale* was published by the photographer in Paris. In this sixteen-page publication photographs are mounted within the text. While this style of layout was not extensively used, there were some notable examples such as William and Mary Howitt's *Ruined Abbeys and Castles of Great Britain*, published by A. W. Bennett of London in 1862. The photographic illustrations – in the form of individual albumen prints – were pasted in blank spaces left for them on text pages.

In some instances different photographic and photomechanical processes were combined for use in book illustration. In others, a particular process was chosen to achieve the desired effect. In the salt paper print, going back to Talbot's calotype (or Talbotype) and popular into the mid-1850s, the photographic image is formed within the paper structure of its support. This process was specifically selected to mimic the originals it reproduced. In 1853, Goupil published Benjamin François Delessert's *Notice sur la vie de Marc Antoine Raimondi, graveur bolonais, accompagnée de reproductions photographiques de quelques-unes de ses estampes.* It is not clear how many photographs made up this publication though it would appear that up to 99 salt paper prints of photographs taken from engravings by Marcantonio Raimondi in Delessert's own collection were sold in around seven *livraisons*. These photographs were printed by Louis-Désiré Blanquard-Evrard (1802–72) who revolutionized the industrialization of photographic print manufacture at his works in Lille. In 1854 a second edition of this work was jointly published by Goupil of Paris and P. & D. Colnaghi of London. In an explanatory note Delessert wrote:

I wished to make all the negatives of these plates myself; all have been made on paper. Some individuals have advised me on the types of albumen on glass, or collodion; I could have obtained more fineness and clearness; but I would not have been able to avoid, I believe, a harshness and a coldness that does not exist in the prints of Marcantonio; these processes, in my opinion, are principally suited to the engravings of the school of Pontius, of Bolswert, of Wille.[26]

The albumen print began to replace the salt paper print from the mid-1850s. Like the salt paper print the albumen print is an original photograph and required manual printing, usually using daylight. The benefits of the salt paper print that were appreciated by Delessert were sacrificed to the consumers' preference for sharp, clear images devoid of the effects introduced by the structure of the paper support.

A variety of issues occupied the minds of publishers of books with photographic illustrations. First was the logistics of producing photographic images of sufficient number and durability to serve a rapidly increasing demand. The albumen print remained a highly labour-intensive manual printing process throughout the nineteenth century. The development of more expedient photomechanical processes came to be perceived as a priority during the 1850s, but it was not until the end of the 1860s that the albumen print was supplemented by the carbon process of Joseph Swan and by the Woodburytype.[27]

One advantage of the carbon print was that different-coloured carbon tissue could be used, thereby creating a 'coloured' photographic image restricted to a single hue. The firm of Adolphe Braun, amongst others, exploited this technique when reproducing monochrome drawings by Old Masters. In England the process was developed by Bernard Bolingbroke Woodward (1816–69), who had been appointed librarian at Windsor Castle in 1860, and had set about reorganizing the collections under the supervision of Prince Albert. The year after Woodward's death, particularly fine use of photographic illustration is found in his *Specimens of the Drawings of Ten Masters, from the Royal Collection at Windsor Castle. Michel Angelo. Perugino. Raphael. Julio Romano. Leonardo da Vinci. Giorgione. Paul Veronese. Poussin. Albert Dürer. Holbein* (London: Macmillan and Co. 1870) (see Figure 7.6). This work was illustrated with coloured carbon prints published by Edwards & Kidd under licence from the Autotype Company. In 1871 Edwards & Kidd printed and published a work issued in parts, the *Drawings from the University Galleries at Oxford. Printed in Permanent Colours*, which included carbon prints from works by Raphael and Michelangelo.

In the early 1870s *The Portfolio. An Artistic Periodical*, edited by Philip Gilbert Hamerton and published in London by Seeley, Jackson, and Halliday, was illustrated with a variety of permanent photographic and photomechanical illustrations. According to its advertisements, the etched illustrations to this serial publication were its leading feature, though the publication would avail itself 'of every New Process which has genuine artistic qualities' (see Figure 7.7).[28] *The Portfolio* used carbon, Woodburytype and also collotype processes for its illustrations. The last of these processes, in which the photographic image was printed in ink directly onto paper, had been perfected by the photographer and printer Joseph Albert (1825–86) of Munich in 1868. By 1874 Albert was printing collotypes in colour, though few publications using this process appeared until the end of the century.

The texts of mid-nineteenth-century art books with photographic illustrations varied considerably in length, scholarly slant and factual accuracy. The mediation of the original by its photographic reproduction produced some curious cases of textual exegesis, for example in two photographically illustrated books on the works of Raphael by the Reverend Richard Henry Smith: his *Expositions of the Cartoons of Raphael*, published in London in 1860 by James Nisbet and Co. and illustrated with seven small albumen prints, and his *Expositions of Raphael's Bible*, published in 1868 by A. Miall of London, which included twelve albumen prints by (possibly Edward) Dunmore.[29]

The *Cartoons* book, an early monograph with photographic illustrations on a highly acclaimed artist, was aimed at a popular gift-book market. In the preface to the book Smith discussed the fidelity of photography, which he considered 'may be safely trusted in a literal translation of the originals'.[30] The seven albumen prints were of photographs taken directly from the original cartoons and not after reproductions, although the photographer is not named. Smith's descriptions are individual homilies, but their peculiar fascination lies in the fact that they are descriptions of the photographs rather than the originals. Of *The Charge to St Peter*, he wrote, 'The peculiar weird-like effect of photography is in strange keeping with the scene here depicted' (see Figure 7.8).[31] Of the cartoon of *Paul and Barnabas at Lystra*, he noted that

A necessity was laid upon the photograph to reproduce the convoluted forms of the various objects; it has, however, done its best, by deepening the shadows, to deaden the distracting effect of the original, and by concentrating and heightening the light that falls upon those who are hastening and those who are interrupting the sacrifice, it gives a premature revelation of the secret.[32]

Furthermore, in discussing the cartoon of *Peter and John healing the Lame Man*, Smith concluded that 'Photography has kindly and cleverly hidden the injuries of carelessness and the ravages of time.'[33]

Given the extraordinary lengths to which Smith went to discuss the photographs of the Raphael Cartoons, his comment on the photographs used in his *Expositions of Raphael's Bible* of 1868 is paradoxical. The photographs are all of 'Early impressions of plates, printed at Rome in 1674'[34] save for a 'Raphael drawing' of *The Dream of Jacob* that forms the frontispiece (see Figure 7.9). Smith made a single enigmatic comment on the photographs in the last line of the unpaginated preface. It reads, 'The Photographs may be fairly left to speak for themselves.'

There are a number of important characteristics of mid-nineteenth-century photographic publications of works of art. Many photographs showed reproductions (engravings, lithographs and so on) after the original. This could be because direct access to the original work was not feasible or it was technically impossible to photograph the work in question. For example, in the preface to his *The Madonnas of Raphael* (New York: Leavitt & Allen 1860) (see Figures 7.10, 7.11) James Perkins Walker reveals that he considered engravings as an essential resource, albeit of limited scope; he wrote: 'a limited number of the original pictures have ever been reproduced by the engraver; and of those at any time engraved, – amounting in all to about thirty – several are so rare as not to be obtainable in this country [the USA], or only inferior copies of them'.[35]

In some instances an engraving, rather than the original from which it was derived, was acknowledged as source of the reproduction. In 1866 Bell & Daldy of London published *The Great Works of Raphael Sanzio of Urbino; a Series of Thirty Photographs from the Best Engravings of His Most Celebrated Paintings; with Descriptions, Translated from Passavant's "Rafael von Urbino und sein Vater": Vasari's Life of Raphael, Translated by Mrs. Jonathan Foster: and an Appendix, Containing a Classified List of the Principal Paintings of the Artist,* edited by Joseph Cundall. In the preface it was stated that the photographs were from the 'famous engravings from his [Raphael's] most celebrated works, by Raphael Morghen, Longhi, Desnoyers, Garavaglia, Müller, Toschi, and other eminent men' and that the 'marvellous power of Photography had rarely been more beautifully shown than in the reproduction of these magnificent engravings'.[36] This observation underlines the esteem that engravings retained throughout the century.

By the mid-1860s photographic piracy was badly affecting the engraving trade and was taken seriously enough by the British government for a review to be carried out by the 1866 Art Union Law Select Committee. To copy a print or any existing photograph was cheap and posed few technical or logistical problems. So far no detailed research has been carried out on the degree to which publishers of books with photographic illustrations availed themselves of 'illegal' prints to aid production of their publications.

Until the early years of the twentieth century black and white photographic materials had limited spectral sensitivity and produced distorted results. Photographing from achromatic engravings or prints overcame these limitations, though photographic companies specializing in art reproduction endeavoured to increase the spectral sensitivity of the photographic emulsions they used, creating more accurate reproductions and thus building a competitive edge. In England, one of the most significant art publications with photographic illustrations of the late 1860s was *The Pictures by the Old Masters in The National Gallery, Photographed by Signor L. Caldesi; with Letterpress Descriptions, Historical, Biographical, and Critical,* by Ralph Nicholson Wornum. It contained 360 photographs taken directly from the paintings and was issued as a part work. Although less than half the gallery's paintings were reproduced, it is significant that they were exclusively of the Italian school. Surprisingly, given the status of the collection documented, the publication received few contemporary reviews. Several prints displayed the problems of the limited spectral sensitivity of the photographic emulsion used. For instance, Pollaiuolo's *Martyrdom of St Sebastian* is almost illegible and its inclusion can only be justified by the fact that the picture was considered to be a very important work.

Many publications with photographic illustrations were issued as serials or part works that could be collected to form a complete book. The firm of Sampson Low & Co. was one of the prominent publishers of such part works. One of their most popular series of volumes was entitled *The Picture Gallery*. These were illustrated by Woodburytype photomechanical prints of reproductions after the original works. The first appeared in 1872 and was followed by variants entitled *Picture Gallery of Sacred Art*, *Picture Gallery of Modern Art* and *Picture Gallery of British Art*. *The Academy* stated that the number of the *Picture Gallery* for January 1875 was

devoted to Sir Joshua Reynolds, and contains permanent photographs from four of his most celebrated works. We are told that this cheap and well-got-up publication is so much appreciated by the artisan classes in the North of England, that there is quite a rush for it on the day that it arrives in one or two of the principal manufacturing towns. The publishers, Messrs. Sampson Low and Co., propose this year to give short biographies of all our best English artists, illustrated by photographs from their most important works. Such an undertaking merits recognition for it popularises art without degrading it.[37]

However, the *Athenaeum* was less complimentary, stating that the work had 'tolerable photographs' and that 'as a publication for lovers of albums, of a very "popular" sort of art-books, this work will doubtless be welcome'.[38] This comment highlights the different target markets of art publications with photographic illustrations. At a populist level, the Christmas market was specifically targeted by publishers of illustrated art books and in some instances publishers, such as Sampson Low, reissued a part work as a complete title, frequently with two options for the binding.[39]

To return to the career of Robinson: it highlights a number of the facets of mid-nineteenth-century photographic art publications. Robinson was to become the principal architect of the South Kensington Museum's medieval and Renaissance collections. During the 1850s photography became a standard tool for Robinson, as witnessed by his *Catalogue of the Soulages Collection* of 1856, and for some of his contemporaries. In 1858 Ottavio Gigli, in an attempt to entice prospective purchasers, had a catalogue with 117 photographs of his late-medieval and early-Renaissance Italian sculpture collection published. This he took on a trip to London, Paris and St Petersburg. When the South

Kensington Museum purchased part of the collection in late 1860, Gigli gave a copy of this book to the museum.[40] This was not the first such publication to play a part in the history of the South Kensington museums; Henri D'Escamps' catalogue of the Greek and Roman sculpture in the Museo Campana, Rome, of 1856,[41] including 88 albumen prints of up to 30 x 39 cm each, was given to the South Kensington Museum after it had purchased some pieces from this collection.[42]

There is evidence to suggest that in 1859 Robinson was actively involved in what was intended as an art serial with photographic illustrations. The National Art Library of the Victoria & Albert Museum has a copy of the fascicle *Museum of Art, South Kensington: Photographic Illustrations of Works in Various Sections of the Collection*, which includes 49 albumen print photographs 'selected by J. C. Robinson' and photographed 'by C. Thurston Thompson'.[43] The fascicle cover is marked 'Parts 1–12' and the price (of each fascicle) was 10s. 6d., which made it an expensive publication. It is stated on the title-page that the publication was 'To be completed in Twelve parts'. The *Museum of Art* was to be published under the auspices of the Department of Science and Art, which controlled the South Kensington Museum. No further copy has been located, suggesting that this venture did not progress.

Robinson's other art books with photographic illustrations are also significant. *The Art Wealth of England. A Series of Photographs, Representing Fifty of the Most Remarkable Works of Art Contributed on Loan to the Special Exhibition at the South Kensington Museum, 1862* (London: P. & D. Colnaghi, Scott & Co. 1862), contained 50 albumen prints; the project indicates his involvement with temporary exhibitions.[44] His *Notice of the Principal Works of Art in the Collection of Hollingworth Magniac, Esq.*, Cundall, Downes & Co., London 1861 (24 albumen prints) underlines his close relationship to collectors.[45]

Under the directorship of Henry Cole, the Department of Science and Art made enthusiastic use of photography. It acquired a large photographic collection (numbering some 50,000 images by 1880) and had many photographically illustrated publications in its library; it photographically documented collections and temporary exhibitions and published a wide variety of photographic images. The Department subsequently formed a close working relationship with the Arundel Society that led to a substantial number of photographic publications, such as *Examples of Art Workmanship of Various Ages and Countries*, a series of volumes in *folio* published in London between 1868 and 1871, and a high level of sales of loose photographs.[46] Robinson was actively involved in all of these activities.

The scale and scope of the nineteenth-century market for photographic art publications has yet to be fully evaluated. Similarly, the contemporary impact of these publications with photographic illustrations requires considerable further research. Contemporary reviews frequently offer a perspective significantly different from the accepted historiography of art.

What is clear is that the Italian Renaissance was one of the most popular subject areas for photographic publishers. The works of Raphael were extensively published in photographic form though many of these photographs were after reproductions rather than the originals themselves. The comparative absence of the Baroque in nineteenth-century art publications with photographic illustrations primarily reflects the greater interest shown by contemporaries in other periods of art history, notably the Gothic and the Italian Renaissance. However, further research is likely to show that the level of photographic publications of Baroque art was higher than is currently perceived.

After a quarter of a century, by the 1870s art publications with photographic illustrations were plentiful. Their richness and diversity is remarkable even to those who specialize in the study of this field. Perhaps the most important consideration is the impact these publications had on the study of art, an aspect of the historiography of art that remains almost completely unwritten. Robinson may be seen as an exemplary user of photographic publications. The challenge to future art historians is to clarify the extent to which Robinson's approach to photography was shared by his contemporaries and peers.

Notes

1. See A. Hamber, *'A Higher Branch of the Art': Photographing the Fine Arts in England, 1839–1880*, Amsterdam 1996.

2. J. Berres, *Phototyp nach der Erfindung des Prof. Berres in Wien* [Vienna 1840], published by the author. A *folio* edition of this work may also have been planned since some sample prints were recently discovered in Austria; they were offered at auction as Lot 6 of the sale held at the Dorotheum, Vienna, in December 1998.

3. English translation by M. Rees from the copy in the British Library, as cited in C. Bloore, 'Photography and Printmaking 1840–1860', PhD thesis, Department of Typography and Graphic Communication, University of Reading 1991, p. 369; Berres (as in n. 2), n.p.

4. Berres (as in n. 2, n.p.) mentions the 30 April 1840 meeting with the Imperial Society of Physicians, Vienna. Translations of his paper were printed in the *Literary Gazette* and in the *Journal des Belles Lettres*, 24 May 1840, p. 331. I presume that 'Stöber' is Franz Stöber (1760–1834).

5. H. Fox Talbot, *The Pencil of Nature by H. Fox Talbot, F.R.S.*, London: Longman, Brown, Green and Longmans [1844–46], published on 29 January 1845, pt 2, text to pl. XI, n.p.

6. Ibid., text to pl. XXIII, n.p.

7. Unpaginated piece of ephemera, private collection.

8. W. Stirling, *Annals of the Artists of Spain*, 4 vols, London: Parker, vols I–III 1847, vol. IV 1848.

9. Stirling (as in n. 8), IV, n.p.

10. Ibid.

11. The copy in the collection of the Royal Photographic Society includes a letter, dated May 1901,

that states that this copy was formerly in the Library of John Leighton of the Royal Institution and that the work had been executed for Sir William Stirling Maxwell. Henneman had been Talbot's manservant and photographic assistant; he had worked as the manager of Talbot's photographic establishment originally set up in Reading but then transferred to London.

12. For an account of this unique undertaking see J. Montagu, 'The "Ruland/Raphael" Collection', *Visual Resources*, III, 3, 1986, pp. 167–83.

13. *The Works of Raphael Santi da Urbino as Represented in the Raphael Collection in the Royal Library at Windsor Castle, Formed by H.R.H. The Prince Consort 1853–1861 and Completed by Her Majesty Queen Victoria*, text volume and 50 portfolios, London 1876, text volume, p. xii.

14. J. C. Robinson, *A Critical Account of the Drawings by Michel Angelo and Raffaello in the University Galleries, Oxford*, Oxford: Clarendon Press 1870.

15. F. Haskell, *Rediscoveries in Art: Some Aspects of Taste, Fashion and Collecting in England and France*, London 1980, pp. 203–4 n. 75.

16. Robinson (as in n. 14), pp. x–xi.

17. Photograph Register nos 58,138–58, 150, 67,956–67, 979 and 66,666–67,049. The set of 24 images from Belvoir Castle cost £2. 12s. 6d. and the Braun prints cost 2 shillings each.

18. The albumen print was the dominant photographic printing process during the mid-nineteenth century. In this process the image was formed in chemicals suspended in a layer of albumen applied to the paper. It therefore differed from earlier processes, such as the Talbotype (also known as the calotype) and the salt paper print, all of which had the photographic chemicals within the paper structure.

19. J. C. Robinson, *South Kensington Museum: Italian Sculpture of the Middle Ages and Period of the Revival of Art*, London: Chapman and Hall 1862.

20. The three publications with photographic illustrations of the Arundel Society are *Notices of Sculpture in Ivory, Consisting of a Lecture on the History, Methods and Chief Productions of the Art Delivered at the First Annual General Meeting of the Arundel Society, on 29th June, 1855*, London 1856; *Descriptive Notice of the Drawings and Publications of the Arundel Society from 1849 to 1868 Inclusive, Illustrated by Photographs of All the Publications, 1/5 Their Original Size*, London 1869; and *Descriptive Notice of the Drawings and Publications of The Arundel Society from 1869 to 1873 Inclusive; (Being a Continuation of "Twenty Years of the Arundel Society"). Illustrated by Photographs of All the Publications, Arranged in Order of Their Issue*, London 1873.

21. Photograph Register nos. 46182–46192 and 42019–42073.

22. 'Photographs of the Sculpture of the Great Exhibition', *Art-Journal*, April 1863, p. 68. The number of images used by the London Stereoscopic Company for the stereoscopic views series will never be known. The company printed the numbered and captioned cards and then pasted variant images of the same object on cards with the same number. In some cases over twenty separate views of one piece of sculpture have been identified.

23. In December 1869 William Boxall (1800–79), director of the National Gallery from 1865 to 1874, was visiting Munich and met with Dr Carl Ruland, formerly librarian to Prince Albert, who showed him photographs by Adolphe Braun of the Sistine Chapel.

24. This manuscript is not the Sforza Hours, British Library Add. MS 34294. I thank Dr Michelle Brown of the British Library for corroborating this information for me. I am grateful to Dr Rowan Watson of the National Art Library who has informed me that this manuscript is believed to be MS 75 in the Biblioteca Reale, Turin.

25. *Manuscrit Sforza: Fac-simile d'après le manuscrit original appartenant à M. le Marquis d'Azeglio, Ambassadeur de Sardaigne à Londres. Photographié et publié par C. Silvy*, London 1860, pp. 4–5. Another relevant example of a photographic reproduction of a Renaissance manuscript was *Facsimile des Miniatures contenues dans le Bréviaire Grimani conservé à la Bibliothèque de St. Marc (Venise) exécuté en Photographie par Antoine Perini avec explication de François Zanotto et un texte français de M. Louis de Mas Latrie*, Paris: A. Perini 1866.

26. 'J'ai voulu faire moi-même les négatifs de ces planches; tous ont été faits sur papier. Quelques personnes m'ont conseillé des types sur glace par l'albumine ou le collodion; j'aurais obtenu plus de finesse et de netteté; mais je n'aurais pu éviter, je crois, une dureté et une sécheresse qui n'existent pas dans les estampes de Marc Antoine; ces procédés, selon moi, conviennent principalement aux graveurs de l'école de Pontius, de Bolswert, de Wille'; Benjamin Delessert, *Notice sur la vie de Marc Antoine Raimondi, graveur bolonais, accompagnée de reproductions photographiques de quelques-unes de ses estampes par M. Benjamin Delessert*, 2nd edn, Paris and London: Goupil; P. & D. Colnaghi 1854, p. 27.

27. The carbon print was a 'permanent' print but each one needed to be manually created. The Woodburytype, first marketed in 1869, was the photo-relief process of Walter Bentley Woodbury (1834–85). Extensively used for photographic illustration during the 1870s and 1880s this process, which produced a permanent ink-on-paper print, was labour-intensive. Both the carbon print and the Wooburytype had to be mounted onto a support, the Woodburytype also requiring trimming before mounting.

28. *Athenaeum*, MMCCII, 8 January 1870, p. 46.

29. *A Directory of London Photographers 1841–1908*, Watford 1994, p. 56, lists Edward Dunmore as a photographer of Camden Road in 1871.

30. R. H. Smith, *Expositions of the Cartoons of Raphael*, London: James Nisbet and Co. 1860, p. vi.

31. Ibid., p. 16.

32. Ibid., p. 67.

33. Ibid., p. 37.

34. R. H. Smith, *Expositions of Raphael's Bible*, London: A. Miall 1868, 'Preface', n.p.: 'Early impressions of plates, printed at Rome in 1674, have therefore been secured.'

35. J. P. Walker, *The Madonnas of Raphael*, New York: Leavitt & Allen 1860, p. [vii].

36. *The Great Works of Raphael Sanzio of Urbino; a Series of Thirty Photographs from the Best Engravings of His Most Celebrated Paintings; with Descriptions, Translated from Passavant's "Rafael von Urbino und sein Vater": Vasari's Life of Raphael, Translated by Mrs. Jonathan Foster: and an Appendix, Containing a Classified List of the Principal Paintings of the Artist*, ed. J. Cundall, London: Bell & Daldy 1866, p. [v].

37. *The Academy*, VII, 23 January 1875, p.101 (short note).

38. *Athenaeum*, MMCCCCLXVI, 30 January 1875, p. 168 (short note in 'Fine-Art Gossip').

39. The cheaper binding was in cloth while the de luxe binding was in morocco that could be twice as expensive. The *Athenaeum* was one of the primary channels through which book publishers advertised.

40. A. Migliarini, *Museo di sculture del Risorgimento raccolto e posseduto da Ottavio Gigli, coi tipi di Felice Le Monnier*, Florence 1858. Victoria & Albert Museum, Department of Sculpture (PR 36749) (X.353) (incomplete).

41. H. D'Escamps, *Description des marbres antiques du Musée Campana à Rome par M. Henry D'Escamps. Sculpture Grecque et Romaine*, Paris: Henri Plon 1856.

42. Victoria & Albert Museum, Photo. Reg. 36,584.(X.186) (now in Print Dept.).

43. Victoria & Albert Museum, NAL, VA. 1859.0003 (X.200 old cat. no.).

44. 'The Art Wealth of England' was a highly successful exhibition organized by J. C. Robinson. *The Times*, in a substantial, almost full-column review published on 28 May 1863, stated that almost one million people had visited the exhibition; it also observed that 'Perfect photography – such as Mr. Thurston Thompson's – was never better applied than on this selection of 50 choice examples.'

45. Hollingworth Magniac (1786–1867) was a merchant and connoisseur of medieval art. His collection formed a loan exhibition at the South Kensington Museum on which this book was based. While exhibited at South Kensington the collection was extensively photographed. The Victoria and Albert Museum has a number of these photographs (35252–35320).

46. For a detailed outline see Hamber (as in n. 1), Appendices B and C.

7560.   MICHAEL ANGELO.   *Cupid, life sized Statue in Marble.*

7.1   'Michelangelo', *Cupid, life sized Statue in Marble'*, line engraving in J. C. Robinson, *South Kensington Museum. Italian Sculpture of the Middle Ages and Period of the Revival of Art*, 1862, pl. opposite p. 133 or 134

7.2   Albumen print by [Charles] Thurston Thompson, of *Cupid (Narcissus)* (then attributed to Michelangelo), in J. C. Robinson, *South Kensington Museum. Italian Sculpture of the Middle Ages and Period of the Revival of Art*, 1862 or later, pl. opposite p. 134

7.3   T. Pozzi, carte de visite (albumen print), photograph of Leonardo da Vinci, *The Last Supper*

7.4   Photograph of Michelangelo, *Moses*, 'No.665. Moses of Michel Angelo. Church of S. Pietro in Vincoli', stereoscopic view, albumen print, published by the Libreria Spithöver, Rome

7.5   Anonymous engraving after Raphael Self-portrait in the Uffizi, Florence
(albumen print, L. Caldesi & Co.), frontispiece to A. von Wolzogen, *Raphael Santi –
His Life and His Works*, 1866

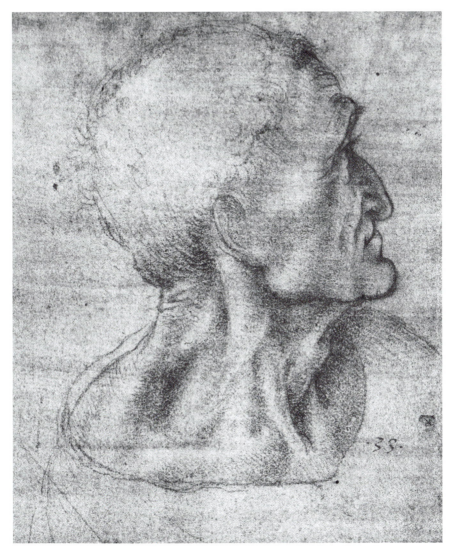

7.6   Carbon print, printed by Edwards and Kidd, under licence of the Autotype
Company Limited, of Leonardo da Vinci, *Head of Judas*, in B. B. Woodward,
Specimens of the Drawings of Ten Masters ..., 1870, pl. opposite p. 50

THE RAISING OF LAZARUS.

REDUCTION IN AUTOTYPE OF A RED CHALK DRAWING BY

MICHELANGELO.

7.7   Carbon print, printed by the Autotype Company, of Michelangelo, *The Raising of Lazarus*, in P. G. Hamerton, ed., *The Portfolio. An Artistic Periodical*, 1871, pl. opposite p. 53

7.8   Albumen print, printed by Negretti and Zambra, of Raphael's cartoon, *The Charge to St Peter*, in R. H. Smith, *Expositions of the Cartoons of Raphael*, 1860, pl. II

7.9   Albumen print of Raphael's *The Dream of Jacob* (now ascribed to Gianfrancesco Penni), in R. H. Smith, *Expositions of Raphael's Bible*, 1868, frontispiece

7.10   Albumen print by E. Hufnagel, (after Raphael) title-page of J. P. Walker, *The Madonnas of Raphael*, 1860

7.11   Albumen print by E. Hufnagel of an engraving after [A. G. L.] Desnoyers, after Raphael's *Vierge au berceau*, in J. P. Walker, *The Madonnas of Raphael*, 1860, pl. accompanying p. 23

8

'Still a makeshift'? Changing representations of the Renaisssance in twentieth-century art books

Valerie Holman

Neither a history of illustration, which suggests the prior existence of text and the subordinate role of imagery, nor a history of technological advance, with its implicit assumption of an ever-narrowing gap between original and representation, can adequately account for the changing function and status of reproductions in twentieth-century art books. Colour plates have become a defining feature of contemporary publications on painting and sculpture, and in a culture that is increasingly characterized as visual, they may be required to function in a number of different ways. Reproductions not only stand in for the missing object, but direct the eye to specific features of the original, while through the designer's judicious layout and sequence of images they can reinforce the argument of a text, suggest a dialogue between verbal and visual, or create a discrete, even discordant, narrative.[1] Furthermore, the history of illustration in art books runs parallel to, but is not necessarily to be identified with, particular approaches to the history of art, or individual attitudes to the function of the photograph.

I shall consider first some of the major changes that have taken place over the past hundred years in how the Italian Renaissance has been presented visually in art books. Secondly, and more specifically, I shall focus on the significance of the publishing context in which these images have appeared, and argue for a heightened awareness of the reproduction as an element of material culture, subject to economic forces and political constraints that have little to do with either the art world or the history of the Italian Renaissance.

The need for books on art to be illustrated has not always been seen as self-evident. For the greater part of the nineteenth century, standard reference works on Italian art and artists were largely unillustrated. Luigi Lanzi's six-volume *History of Painting in Italy*, translated into English in 1828, Franz Kugler's *Handbook of the History of Painting in Italy*, published in English in

1842 and in its sixth edition by 1890, and Jacob Burckhardt's *Die Kultur der Renaissance in Italien* of 1860 are cases in point.[2] Histories of art that were illustrated might contain no more than a few simple line engravings to indicate the subject of a particular painting or sculpture. For instance, Anna Jameson's *Sacred and Legendary Art*, first published in 1848 with figures drawn by the author and her niece, gives no sense of the tonal contrast, texture, or individual style that marked the original painting.[3] High-quality engravings cost the publisher money; thus texts accompanied by full-page plates tended to remain the preserve of wealthy patrons and collectors. Handbooks and introductory histories were specifically designed to be carried by tourists and museum visitors when travelling to see original works of art: verbal description sufficed. Even the more substantial histories sought to engage the reader not by illustration but by the power of the prose and the force of the argument, while compilations of artists' biographies simply prefaced each chapter with a portrait of the artist, a practice dating back to the Renaissance and exemplified by the second edition of Vasari's *Lives*, discussed in the second essay in this volume by Sharon Gregory.

By the second half of the nineteenth century, Italian art, especially in Germany and England, became subject to new strategies of identification and new ways of presenting the latest scholarship to a much wider readership. What was believed to constitute worthwhile material for study also expanded, a point forcibly made by David Brown in his catalogue to an exhibition illustrating Bernard Berenson's connoisseurship: 'Like antiquities in the Renaissance, early Italian paintings offered evidence to the nineteenth century of a vast uncharted tract of human creativity.'[4] To the desire for a systematic account of history was added the lure of virgin territory.

Among the first to take up this challenge were Joseph Archer Crowe, a journalist who covered the Crimean War and the Indian Mutiny, and his associate Giovanni Battista Cavalcaselle who had originally worked as a picture restorer. Their study of art was based on eye and experience, a direct approach to which Giovanni Morelli, doctor, soldier and statesman, sought to add a new and more scientific dimension. Beginning his career as an amateur writing about Italian art in German galleries, he adapted what he had learned from comparative anatomy, and looked for evidence of artistic identity not in documents and written records but in the painting itself, developing a technique of visual analysis that, with the work of Crowe and Cavalcaselle, laid the foundations of twentieth-century connoisseurship and came to fruition in published form as the *catalogue raisonné*. To make a correct attribution and to distinguish the genuine from the fake or copy, he looked not at the picture as a whole but at its component parts. In *Italian Painters: Critical Studies of Their Works*, translated into English in 1892, Morelli expressed his belief that each artist was unique in his treatment of such relatively overlooked anatomical details as fingernails or ear lobes, and to identify characteristic portrayal of hands and ears he made his own drawings after Renaissance artists.[5] Morelli's readiness to single out specific features and study them separately may be seen as paving the way for the introduction of photographically enlarged details into twentieth-century art books, and more generally as signalling the need for extremely clear and accurate reproduction. Comparison was the basis of his method. Like that of Crowe and Cavalcaselle, Morelli's approach depended on having the means to travel and see original works of art, and the ability to remember and record in minute detail what he had observed in different parts of the world over a long period of time.

In 1864, John Murray published *A New History of Painting in Italy from the Second to the Sixteenth Century* by Crowe and Cavalcaselle, who stated in their preface:

We believe that the history of Italian art has received such valuable additions from a direct comparison of extant works among each other … that no new edition of Vasari, even with the completest commentary, would satisfy the demands which may justly be made upon the writers of the present day.[6]

Their comparative method was not, however, visually supported by the engravings, most of which had already appeared in Franz Kugler's *Handbook of the History of Painting in Italy* and which revealed nothing of the scale, form, texture, tone, colour, or context of the works reproduced. Crowe and Cavalcaselle pointed out in their preface to the second, photographically illustrated, edition of 1903 that the success of the first edition could not have been due to the outward form of the volumes, for '*The History of Painting in Italy* had few of the adornments of the modern art book'.[7]

Meanwhile in 1897 George Bell *had* published a new edition of Vasari which paid explicit tribute to photography as a catalyst for the study of art history. Art-lovers, observed the editors, were less indebted to recent literature than 'to the discovery of those photographic processes which have utterly changed the character of the data for study'.[8] In the past, reproduction had been subject to a series of separate processes, each undertaken by a specialist with a particular skill. Before the image could be printed, it had to be copied by a draughtsman and then engraved in the style of the period or that of an individual workshop. The invention of photography appeared to offer a more accurate copy, an immediate likeness, and much fuller information than had previously been possible using images or words, for 'In the study of the plastic arts even a poor photograph is worth more than pages of description.'[9] In the mid-sixteenth century when Vasari wrote his *Lives*, as Patricia Rubin has pointed out, 'The assumed link between perception and cognition made it possible for [him] confidently to produce a book about images without illustration.'[10] Through his use of language, Vasari could appeal to the imagination and expect his descriptions to recreate a work of art in the mind of his reader.

By the late nineteenth century, such assumptions were no longer widely held, and there were moreover a number of firms producing photographs that were far from poor. As the editors of the 1897 edition of Vasari were at pains to point out, 'The most complete and admirable collection of photographic reproductions of art works existing in the museums, churches, streets, palaces and squares of the Peninsula is that of the Alinari Brothers, of Florence ... . The photographs of Brogi are also excellent.'[11] The rival of the Alinari, Giacomo Brogi, was an engraver turned photographer who specialized in portraits and sites of architectural interest, especially in the Near East. His son Carlo continued the family business; to these two photographic dynasties was added a third: James Anderson, a contemporary based in Rome, initially catered for tourists seeking views of the Holy City, but later his firm too became celebrated for its reproductions of art.

To the Victorians, photography offered the potential of truth to nature and scientific exactitude. As Rosanna Pavoni has observed:

Between 1840 and 1870 critics were practically unanimous in their opinion that photography was an absolutely faithful reproduction of the objects framed by the lens, and they committed the typically positivist error of viewing it as a technical procedure devoid of creativity.[12]

Furthermore,

Photography had a significant and specific role to play in the revival of the Renaissance [which], with its proportions, with its rules, with the unutterable perfection and complexity of its ornamentation, required descriptive accuracy and analytical precision ... [13]

Through photography, architecture could be seen in all its decorative detail; sculpture could be lit to bring out three-dimensionality; the tonal qualities of painting could be rendered to an extent impossible with line engraving; most important of all, photographs could be bought off the peg from catalogues and circulated internationally. The speed with which nineteenth-century Italians took up and mastered photography proved highly advantageous at the time of the unification of Italy, when images of art and architecture from the fifteenth and sixteenth centuries were employed to consolidate a successful self-image. A number of Italian firms founded at mid-century, notably Alinari, Anderson and Brogi, also capitalized on the beginnings of mass tourism. Those who took advantage of the huge market for such photographs were able to undercut rivals in other countries well into the twentieth century when art book publishing became heavily dependent on access to cheap illustrations.

One of the first scholars to reflect on photographic reproductions as coded, problematic images, and not simply as the result of technical processes, was Heinrich Wölfflin who succeeded Burckhardt as Professor of Art History at the University of Basle in 1893. In an early article, he expressed strong resistance to the current vogue for 'aesthetic' or 'picturesque' photographs of Renaissance sculpture taken from the side which, he believed, militated against the artist's intention and working practice by destroying the silhouette according to which the sculpture had been created. The cultivated Renaissance eye would have found the one position from which the sculpture's whole meaning was revealed, and which also dictated the viewing distance. Wölfflin believed that the way sculpture, and particularly relief, was lit should approximate to paintings of the period. Light striking the work from the wrong direction could accentuate an unintended part of the image; *chiaroscuro* that was too pronounced, especially in side-lit work, could falsify a formal unity characteristic of the fourteenth century; strong contrast could change the mood from calm to dramatic.[14] Much of this criticism is valid, not least in highlighting the nature of the photograph as a distinct artefact subject to the changing taste of photographers, viewers, and historians.[15]

To illustrate Wölfflin's contention, an engraving of Donatello's relief *The Ascension with Christ giving the Keys to St Peter* from J. C. Robinson's *Italian Sculpture of the Middle Ages and the Revival of Art* of 1862 can usefully be compared with photographic reproductions in two twentieth-century books: Paul Schubring's *Donatello* (1922) from the long-running German series 'Klassiker der Kunst' (see Figure 8.1a) and Paul Williamson's *European Sculpture at the Victoria and Albert Museum* published in 1996 (Figure 8.1b). In *The Birth and Rebirth of Pictorial Space*, first published in 1957, John White situated this relief in the context of a particular problem: how to 'incorporate a new degree of realism without disrupting the decorative surface'.[16] Donatello's solution lay in his treatment of aerial perspective, and in his creation of an undulating surface, unified by soft modelling throughout. In the engraving, none of this can be seen, but a comparison of the two photographs, one lit from the left and one from the right, shows a strongly modelled image that focuses in one case on facial expression and in the other on the drama of the narrative. Both exaggerate the depth of the relief, and neither recreates the pale luminosity and harmony of the original.

It is important to bear these criticisms in mind, because Alinari photographs in particular, with their characteristically dramatic *chiaroscuro*, have been common to several major twentieth-century books on the Renaissance, including one of the most substantial multi-volume projects on Italian art, Adolfo Venturi's *Storia dell'arte italiana* published by Ulrico Hoepli in Milan between 1901 and 1940.

In the second volume of his trilogy *An Introduction to Italian Sculpture*, published by Phaidon in 1958, John Pope-Hennessy particularly recommended Schubring's book for forming 'an invaluable corpus of photographs of Donatello's sculpture', and commented on the then recent publication by Princeton University Press of *The Sculpture of Donatello* by H. W. Janson: 'This book provides the best available series of reproductions of the work of any Italian sculptor.'[17] Janson's express aim had been 'a pictorial corpus elaborate enough to provide a satisfactory record of every facet of Donatello's achievement': no fewer than 12 photographs of the *Gattamelata* were specially commissioned by Janson and taken by Brogi on site.[18] It was no longer the 'correct view' that determined the choice of image but comprehensiveness and approximation to the viewer's experience.

Phaidon too had sent their photographer to re-photograph the same work for Ludwig Goldscheider's book on Donatello, published in 1941. It had become a special feature of Phaidon books on both painting and sculpture to focus on a detail, usually the head or hands, and to photograph at eye-level from so close that the frame was filled by a painted or sculpted surface revealing above all its texture and facture. The process of making and the skill of the artist were thereby given precedence over reproduction of the viewing experience: Gattamelata's head would normally be seen from below and at a distance, but on this occasion the photographer paid for the services of the local fire brigade who had the only ladder long enough to permit a close-up shot of the face (see Figure 8.2).[19]

Despite the availability of so many different views of the *Gattamelata*, books such as Michael Levey's *Early Renaissance* in the 'Pelican History of Art' series, published in 1967, still showed the original image from Alinari, dramatically silhouetted against a blank sky. The choice of an early Alinari image did not necessarily represent reversion to a previous way of seeing, but was more probably dictated by cost.

That the reliance of authors and publishers on a limited stock of relatively cheap photographs has a long history is suggested by the example of correspondence associated with Bernard Berenson's *Florentine Drawings*, a book first published in 1903 by John Murray in a limited edition that contains 180 collotypes from photographs by Brogi and by Braun, the Alsatian firm celebrated for reproductions of old master drawings. A proposed second edition became the subject of long discussions with the Clarendon Press between 1924 and 1936 when the University of Chicago Press finally took over the project and offered to publish it according to the author's wishes, with as many plates as he wanted.[20] A note of an internal meeting at the Clarendon Press in 1924 states that

The question of photographs and their copyrights is an extremely important one … Braun charges £1 fee for the use of each photograph, Alinari 10 shillings. So you see that if the 300 reproductions for the book were all to be taken from Braun's photographs it would add £300 to the cost of the book, if from Alinari's, £150.[21]

Astonished, the Berensons commented, 'This is the first time we have ever heard of Alinaris charging a fee for reproducing their photos.'[22] Already reproduction rights were being added to the purchase price of individual photographs which were now firmly located in a highly commercial world shortly to enter the Great Depression. The printer wrote to Berenson later the same year, 'I am fresh myself from a tussle with Messrs Braun, who have the audacity to ask for 25 shillings for a single use of their photographs.'[23] Berenson envisaged R. Van Marle's *Development of the Italian Schools of Painting*[24] as a model for his *Florentine Drawings*, but Charles Bell wrote to dissuade the Clarendon Press from acceding to Berenson's wishes:

As his [Van Marle's] text and illustrations are all mixed up together the whole book had to be printed on 'Art' paper, which is heavily loaded with china clay, making the volumes insufferably heavy. The loading of this paper furthermore makes it certain to disintegrate entirely within relatively few years.[25]

Bell's comment reminds us that reproductions are neither to be identified with originals nor to be seen as disembodied images: they exist on paper, have a texture, date, economic value, and even weight of their own, all of which can have a determining effect on the type of book in which they appear, and hence on the audience the author or publisher is trying to reach.

Ten years after preliminary discussions, the political and economic situation had altered immeasurably, and Anglo-Italian trade in 1934 was particularly hard-hit. Clarendon Press had the difficult job of persuading Berenson that their publishing decisions were affected by the state of the international book trade, and that the thousands of poor students ready to spend their last shilling on the latest Berenson were a figment of his imagination.[26]

The rise of European dictatorships in the 1930s and the Second World War had the unexpectedly positive effect of forcibly relocating a number of art historians and publishers who forged new alliances or acquired new supporters and sponsors that ultimately made possible more innovative publication of Renaissance scholarship in different forms. Adolfo Venturi's son Lionello was one of only eleven Italian academics who refused to swear an oath of allegiance to Mussolini, and so lost his chair in Art History at the University of Turin. He moved to Paris where in 1936 he met Albert Skira who became his publisher and son-in-law. Panofsky was in the USA when stripped of his German professorship in 1933, so *Studies in Iconology* was published not in Germany but by Oxford University Press in New York in 1939. In the Spring of 1938, just before the annexation of Austria, the Viennese publishers Bela Horovitz and Ludwig Goldscheider nominally sold the

Phaidon Press to Sir Stanley Unwin to ensure its survival, and a fellow publisher from Vienna, Walter Neurath, also moved to Britain where in 1949 he launched the firm of Thames and Hudson. During the War, a number of influential works on the Italian Renaissance were published or in progress, many the result of close collaboration between authors and publishers who shared a special interest in how art books should be illustrated. Skira's partnership with André Malraux, for example, had a lasting impact on the author's subsequent editorial work and the development of his ideas on art in reproduction.

Photographs are, as Malraux well knew, objects that can be manipulated, and when used to reproduce art can either reveal or conceal what is visible in the original. In 1935, Cambridge University Press had published Kenneth Clark's two-volume catalogue of Leonardo da Vinci's drawings at Windsor Castle, in which four images were frequently fitted onto a single page. When the catalogue was revised and published by Phaidon in 1969, the images were given more space, and in some cases printed darker to reveal what previously had been hard to distinguish, for example the lion in the corner of 12502 (see Figures 8.3a and 8.3b). Images can be made to emerge more fully, or extraneous details to disappear completely if they detract from the form and impact of a work of art.

Anthony Blunt's *Artistic Theory in Italy*, first published in 1940 by the Clarendon Press, was illustrated entirely with Alinari and Anderson photographs, but the blocks were destroyed during the War and, for the second edition, published in 1956, the question of illustration had to be considered afresh. Blunt's queries to his publisher can be deduced from the reply:

Plate 9. [In the 2nd edition, plate 6.] Like you, we prefer the Brogi print, and we think it should be possible to use it by trimming the block vertically so as to exclude a good part of the background. What remains we propose to leave as it is. We do not think it will be distracting since so little of it will be left.[27]

In the version eventually published, Michelangelo's *Rondanini Pietà* no longer casts a shadow on the wall behind it, but stands out against a uniformly black background divorcing the sculpture from its architectural context but emphasizing the photographer's choice of silhouette. Publishers could adapt photographs bought off the peg to their own ends: crop judiciously, select details, or let the layout tell the story.

It was this last option that characterized André Malraux's *The Psychology of Art* published by Albert Skira in three volumes between 1947 and 1950, and appearing in English as *The Voices of Silence* in 1949/50. The first draft had been written shortly after a close reading of Walter Benjamin's essay 'The Work of Art in the Age of Mechanical Reproduction', but the final version was also indebted to Malraux's own essay on the psychology of film published in 1946. In the *Psychologie de l'art*, Malraux acknowledged the separateness of the image, maintaining that he did not conceive of illustration as an accompaniment to description but as a replacement whose framing and sequence throughout the book created a parallel cinematic text. He even had one plate printed upside-down, so that the image would not distract from a point he wished to make about the sculptural effect of Giotto's painting *The Raising of Lazarus* (see Figure 8.4). More importantly, he argued that knowledge had become dependent on what could be known from photographs: for example, while books were illustrated only with black and white photographs, periods of art characterized by changes in the use of colour remained neglected or simply unknown.[28]

Malraux and Skira both sought to heighten the reader's awareness of the art book as the culmination of a long and highly skilled process, a collective enterprise subject to external constraints of an often surprising kind. In 1950 Skira launched the trilogy of *Italian Painting* with critical studies by his father-in-law, Lionello Venturi, and historical survey by his wife Rosabianca. An address to the reader at the beginning of the first volume is typical of Skira's concerns:

The making of this book synchronized with the celebration of the Holy Year in Italy, and the fact that churches and art museums were thronged with pilgrims and visitors throughout the year might well have hampered the work of our photographic experts and engravers: a work necessitating both meticulous attention and the most delicate precision.[29]

Since the early 1930s Skira had been dedicated to the pursuit of excellence in colour reproduction, and this concern now coincided with public demand. Tipped-in colour plates had become a feature of successful art publishing, for not only did they appeal to the reader but (as with black and white photography) the same image could be used with texts in different languages, thereby enlarging the edition and bringing down the unit cost. Interviewed in 1967, Skira explained what was involved: to achieve true colours and accurate tonal relationships, corrections were made in front of the original picture, but even then the reproduction of paintings was not an exact science; variations in light and weather also played a part for, depending on whether it was snowing, raining, or sunny, the colours would appear to be different. The battle for a 'true' reproduction was won only when it faithfully rendered the relationship between colours and captured the 'soul' of the original. Furthermore, to achieve a satisfactory result was not just a question of how a photograph was taken, but also of the surface on which it was printed, and the inks and printing process selected.[30]

Bernard Berenson made similar observations on the importance of texture in original and reproduction, but reached quite different conclusions about the role and value of the photograph. Whereas early in the twentieth century

Wölfflin had chastised Alinari for a use of lighting that was historically incorrect (giving the example of early Florentine sculpture), Berenson praised Alinari's photographs for their quality of revelation, observing that they had made available to connoisseurs Venetian paintings hung in the semi-darkness of chapels where they were 'absolutely invisible except by candlelight'.[31] Already in 1890 Berenson had seen photographs as 'the most important single aid in this new science'[32] (connoisseurship), because they permitted comparison of two objects located in different places. For him, the important point was that they were tools for study, but in no way substitutes for original works of art.

The essays that were to become the four volumes of Berenson's *Italian Painters of the Renaissance* were first published between 1904 and 1907; in 1932 an illustrated edition was brought out by the Clarendon Press in Oxford with thirty black and white illustrations, all but one by Alinari, Braun or Anderson. The book was reprinted in 1939 and again in 1949, reaching sales of 6,000 copies. Berenson had been seeking a publisher to produce a much more richly illustrated cheap edition for the USA, but in 1951 told Oxford University Press in Britain that he had twice been turned down by their branch in New York. He had, however, embarked on a new venture: 'I approached the Kress Foundation and told them I would like to get out a new edition of the book with 400 illustrations on condition that it would be sold for no more than five dollars.' The Foundation 'agreed to spend at least 15,000 dollars on getting out an edition of about 20,000 copies'.[33] Phaidon was approached to produce a book for both England and America but, to avoid undercutting the Clarendon edition that was still in print, had to agree that theirs would be sold for not less than twice as much.

Having amassed an extensive personal collection of photographs, Berenson felt compelled to explain his views on reproductions when they featured so prominently in the edition of his essays published by Phaidon in 1952:

Unhappily pictures cannot as yet be printed ... exactly as they are painted, in the way a writer's manuscript can be, without losing the quality of the original. The reproduction of a picture is still a makeshift, and may remain so for a long time, even if accurate and satisfactory colour reproductions should become available ...
On the whole therefore (despite the childish hanker today for colour reproductions, no matter how crude) the black and white, made from a photo that preserved tones and values, gives the most satisfactory image of the original.[34]

Skira, on the other hand, believed that black and white falsified tones, and that 'a picture, for all its architecture, means primarily colour'.[35]

It was this latter view that predominated in the 1960s, an era characterized by the publication of geographically comprehensive, richly illustrated histories of art. *The Age of the Renaissance*, edited by Denys Hay and published by

Thames and Hudson in 1967, for instance, contained 600 reproductions of prints and drawings, and full-colour fold-out plates of easel-paintings, altarpieces, church interiors, and maps. Vasari needed no such images to illustrate his *Lives*, but 400 years later they had come to form the defining characteristic of the art book.

Representations of the Renaissance have not changed exclusively because of new technical knowledge or fresh critical approaches: the history of illustrated books, whether covering Renaissance civilization, architecture, painting, drawing, or sculpture, has been one increasingly affected by the production process; it is subject to a whole network of international economic transactions and to the intangible but vital interaction between publishers and their markets. In the 1920s books sold if they were illustrated, and in the post-War period if they were in colour. During the 1930s it was virtually impossible to publish and sell well-illustrated art books with any degree of financial success. This observation argues strongly for a revision of our habitual ways of seeing reproductions as illustrations to texts or as substitutes for original works: they are themselves artefacts and commodities. As such, these images can be bought and sold, cropped or enlarged, to fit within a predetermined layout. More significantly, they can insert an a-historical or even anti-historical element into the art book. Francis Haskell's *History and its Images: Art and the Interpretation of the Past*, published by Yale University Press in 1993, is a case in point: a chapter on the historical significance of style illustrates Ruskin's mid-nineteenth-century visit to Venice with an Alinari photograph of the Palazzo Ducale taken in the early twentieth century. That in the 1990s it was still acceptable to reproduce views of Venice showing women in Edwardian dress as an illustration of an event which had occurred some fifty years earlier demonstrates a persistent blind spot: it is assumed that readers look at the architecture represented and not at the photograph itself. Despite a vast literature on the complex meanings of photography, when art is reproduced in books the plate still tends to be seen as a transparent rendition of the original, rather than as an independent image. The history of illustrated art books over the last 150 years has not been a continuous evolution towards ever more faithful copies and objective representations. Instead, the simulacrum has usurped the place of the original, not just bringing an art work into visibility and dictating the way it is read and understood but replacing it with a type of image that is highly vulnerable to economic forces, political change, and the vagaries of taste. Whereas 'illustration' once meant the object as image, now 'image as object' is the only accurate way to characterize the tangible, three-dimensional existence of the reproduction, with its own distinct place in the material and visual culture of the modern world.

Acknowledgements

The author would like to thank the Secretary to the Delegates of Oxford University Press for their kind permission to quote from the archives.

Notes

1. A useful exploration of text/image relations and the history of layout in illustrated books can be found in A. Zali ed., *L'Aventure des écritures: la page*, exh. cat. Paris 1999.

2. L. Lanzi, *The History of Painting in Italy, from the Period of the Revival of the Fine Arts to the End of the Eighteenth Century*, transl. T. Roscoe, 6 vols, London: W. Simpkin and R. Marshall 1828; F. T. Kugler, *A Hand-Book of the History of Painting, from the Age of Constantine the Great to the Present Time*, transl. [Mrs Hutton], pt I, *The Italian Schools of Painting*, ed. C. L. Eastlake, London: John Murray 1842; and J. Burckhardt, *Die Kultur der Renaissance in Italien. Ein Versuch*, Basel: Schweighauser 1860.

3. A. Jameson, *Sacred and Legendary Art*, 2 vols, London: Longman, Brown, Green and Longmans 1848.

4. *Berenson and the Connoisseurship of Italian Painting*, ed. D. A. Brown, Washington: National Gallery of Art 1979, p. 33.

5. G. Morelli, *Italian Painters: Critical Studies of Their Works*, transl. J. Ffoulkes, London: John Murray 1892, pp. 77–8.

6. J. A. Crowe and G. B. Cavalcaselle, *A New History of Painting in Italy from the Second to the Sixteenth Century*, London: John Murray 1864, preface to volume I, p. [V].

7. J. A. Crowe and G. B. Cavalcaselle, *A New History of Painting in Italy*, 3 vols London: John Murray (1st edn 1864–86) 2nd edn 1903, I, pp. v–vi.

8. *Lives of Seventy of the Most Eminent Painters, Sculptors and Architects by Giorgio Vasari, Edited and Annotated in the Light of Recent Discoveries*, ed. E. H. and E. W. Blashfield and A. A. Hopkins, London: George Bell and Sons 1897, I, p. xxii.

9. Ibid.

10. P. Rubin, *Giorgio Vasari: Art and History*, New Haven and London: Yale University Press 1995, p. 233.

11. Blashfield, Blashfield and Hopkins (as in n. 8), p. xxiii.

12. R. Pavoni, *Reviving the Renaissance: The Use and Abuse of the Past in Nineteenth-Century Italian Art and Decoration*, Cambridge: Cambridge University Press 1997, p. 97.

13. M. Cozzi and L. Zangheri, 'Architecture, Ornament, the Neo-Renaissance and Photography', in Pavoni (as in n. 12), pp. 95–125, esp. p. 113.

14. H. Wölfflin, three articles first published in *Zeitschrift für bildende Kunst*, Leipzig, NF VII, 1896; NF VIII, 1897; and NF XXVI, 1914. They were subsequently translated by Vincent Barras and republished as 'Comment photographier les sculptures?', in *Pygmalion photographe*, Geneva 1985, pp. 127–36.

15. The debate has been greatly enriched by G. A. Johnson ed., *Sculpture and Photography: Envisioning the Third Dimension*, Cambridge: Cambridge University Press 1998.

16. J. White, *The Birth and Rebirth of Pictorial Space*, London and Boston: Faber and Faber (1st edn 1957) 3rd edn 1987, p. 151.

17. J. Pope-Hennessy, *An Introduction to Italian Sculpture*, vol. II: *Renaissance Sculpture*, London: Phaidon 1958, p. 271.

18. H. W. Janson, *The Sculpture of Donatello*, Princeton NJ: Princeton University Press 1957, p. ix.

19. L. Goldscheider, *Donatello*, London: Phaidon 1941. Information from Allen and Unwin Archives, University of Reading: Musarion Press, 65.20, expenses claim attached to letter from Phaidon Press to George Allen and Unwin Ltd, 10 December 1940.

20. It was eventually published in 1938.

21. OUP Archives (Oxford), CP 47. CP/ED/000851, C. F. Bell, note on file, 23.9.1924.

22. OUP Archives, ibid., Bernard [and Mary?] Berenson to C. F. Bell, 28.9.1924.

23. OUP Archives, ibid., 'J' (Johnson) to Bernard Berenson, 5.11.1924.

24. R. Van Marle, *The Development of the Italian Schools of Painting*, 18 vols, The Hague: Martinus Nijhoff 1923–38.

25. OUP Archives, CP 47. CP/ED/000851, C. F. Bell to ? Johnson, 8.11.1924.

26. OUP Archives, CP 47. CP/LD/000851, letter from Charles Bell to 'Thomas' [A. L. P. Norrington, Secretary to the Delegates], 12.8.1934.

27. OUP Archives, 817 106, P. J. Spicer to Anthony Blunt, 20.7.1955.

28. A. Malraux, *Psychologie de l'art*, 3 vols, vol. I: *Le Musée imaginaire*, Geneva: Albert Skira 1947, p. 32.

29. L. Venturi, *Italian Painting*, 3 vols, vol. I: *The Creators of the Renaissance*, Engl. transl., London: A. Zwemmer 1950, n.p.

30. M. Boujut, '40 Ans d'édition: Skira ou la perfection', *Combat*, 9 December 1967, n.p.

31. B. Berenson, 'Isochromatic Photography and Venetian Pictures', a letter to *The Nation*, 1893, quoted by E. Samuels in *Bernard Berenson: The Making of a Connoisseur*, Cambridge MA: The Belknap Press of Harvard University Press 1979, p. 173.

32. Quoted in Samuels (as in n. 31), p. 103.

33. OUP Archives (file on *Italian Painters of the Renaissance*), Bernard Berenson to A. L. P. Norrington, 25.4.1951.

34. B. Berenson, *Italian Painters of the Renaissance*, London: Phaidon 1952, preface, p. x.

35. A. Skira, 'Reflexions on the Art Book', in *Albert Skira, the Man and His Work*, New York: Hallmark Gallery 1966, n.p.

8.1a   Photograph of Donatello's *The Ascension with Christ giving the Keys to Saint Peter*, in Paul Schubring, *Donatello: des Meisters Werke*, 1922, p. 64

8.1b   Photograph of Donatello's *The Ascension with Christ giving the Keys to Saint Peter*, in Paul Williamson, ed., *European Sculpture at the Victoria and Albert Museum*, 1996, p. 76

8.2   Photograph of the head of the rider in Donatello's *Gattamelata*, in Ludwig
Goldscheider, *Donatello*, Phaidon edition, 1941, p. 121

8.3a   Photograph of Leonardo da Vinci's *Head of a man with sketch of a lion's head*, in Kenneth Clark, *A Catalogue of the Drawings of Leonardo da Vinci in the collection of H. M. the King at Windsor Castle*, Cambridge 1935 edition, vol. II, no. 12502

8.3b   Photograph of Leonardo da Vinci's *Head of a man with sketch of a lion's head*, in Kenneth Clark, *The Drawings of Leonardo da Vinci in the Collection of Her Majesty the Queen at Windsor Castle*, Phaidon 1969 edition, vol. II, no. 12502

Giotto took over the liberation broken off at Rheims, as Masaccio was to resume it a century later. True, he began in the Byzantine style, from which the eyes in his panels were never to be wholly emancipated. While the Nazareth sculptor had treated the Byzantine style as if it were a form of realism, Giotto at first does not use it so as to attain the transcendent, but merely to obtain effects of three-dimensional mass. This interest in technical research (which led him to give modelling to his early prophets) was to persist until its culmination in the figures of Joachim and of *The Presentation in the Temple*.

He seems to break away from Byzantium by the use of a preliminary lay-out, at once formal and hesitant, which, after it has been worked over, leaves us with only an inkling of its presence. Of this the noblemen in *Saint Francis Revered by a Simple Man* are an instance—whether or not Giotto was its sole painter. But, from his Prophets onwards to the bishop in *Saint Francis Renouncing his Riches*, mass is the means by which he makes his effects. In these works relative depth is not achieved by the use of perspective or tone values. Whereas in the works of Roman and Northern painters it was obtained by burrowing into the canvas; Giotto embosses his canvas. Compared with all earlier paintings—Romanesque frescos, miniatures, Byzantine panels—,his frescos look like bas-reliefs; we need only examine them upside-down, to see how similar they are to sculpture.

GIOTTO. RESURRECTION OF LAZARUS. [REPRODUCED UPSIDE-DOWN.]

93

8.4   Photograph (inverted) of Giotto's *The Raising of Lazarus* in vol. II of André Malraux, *The Psychology of Art*, New York 1949–50 edition

Index

Page references to illustrations are in italics